N L P

Also available from William Morrow and Nightingale-Conant

The New Dynamics of Winning by Denis Waitley
The Confident Decision Maker by Roger Dawson
Sales Magic by Kerry Johnson

The NLP Comprehensive Training Team

N L P

THE NEW TECHNOLOGY OF ACHIEVEMENT

Edited by Steve Andreas
and Charles Faulkner

CONTRIBUTING AUTHORS
Steve Andreas, M.A., Charles Faulkner, B.A.,
Kelly Gerling, Ph.D., Tim Hallbom, M.S.W.,
Robert McDonald, M.S., Gerry Schmidt, Ph.D.,
Suzi Smith, M.S.

WILLIAM MORROW AND COMPANY, INC.

New York

Copyright © 1994 by NLP Comprehensive

Permissions, constituting a continuation of the copyright page, appear on pages 348–349.

It is the policy of William Morrow and Company, Inc., and its imprints and affiliates, recognizing the importance of preserving what has been written, to print the books we publish on acid-free paper, and we exert our best efforts to that end.

Library of Congress Cataloging-in-Publication Data

NLP, the new technology of achievement / The NLP Comprehensive Training Team
    p.   cm.
  Includes bibliographical references.
  ISBN 0-688-12669-3
  1. Neurolinguistic programming.   I. NLP Comprehensive
(Organization)
BF637.N46N57   1994
158'.1—dc20

94-17712
CIP

Printed in the United States of America

First Edition

1   2   3   4   5   6   7   8   9   10

BOOK DESIGN BY BERNARD SCHLEIFER

Acknowledgments

It's popular to imagine the heroic author standing alone with his or her words. Today, we know the truth is that many hands and minds, acknowledged or not, contribute to completing anything. This book began as an offer to do a tape set with the Nightingale-Conant Corporation.[1] Along the way it's added six authors and editors and a host of others. There are many people to thank. In particular, we'd like to start by acknowledging NLP's original code-velopers Richard Bandler and John Grinder and their early collaborators Leslie Cameron-Bandler, Judith DeLozier, Robert Dilts, and David Gordon. The NLP Comprehensive Training Team would also like to thank Steve and Connirae Andreas, cofounders of NLP Comprehensive, whose work as editors, authors, and teachers led many of us to explore this new world in the first place. They have been our mentors and guides. We are honored to be collaborators with them. There are also members of the NLP Comprehensive Training Team who, while not direct contributors to this volume, have, by their instruction and example, offered us much inspiration and direction. They are Lara Ewing, Gary Faris, Tom Best, and Tamara Andreas. When you are reading this, you can forget that books do not just magically appear. We know differently. There are the individuals whose job it is to get things done and clear the way for the author's words. Foremost among them, we'd like to thank Lisa Jackson, general manager for NLP Comprehensive. Her efforts were instrumental in bringing this work to where it is today. On Nightingale-Conant's side, we'd like to thank Mike Willbond, senior vice president of publishing, our audio producer Georgene Cevasco, and our video producer Maitreyee Angelo for their efforts on collaborations with NLP Comprehensive. While this work already has listed two editors, our thanks are also due to Sue Telingator, our "inside editor" at Nightingale-Conant, to Will Schwalbe, editorial director at William Morrow and Company, and to Karen Cooper for her late-night, last-minute polishing. Finally and fully, we would like to acknowledge and thank the thousands of NLP practitioners we taught as we were developing this material. They were our strongest supporters, our toughest critics, and our ablest guides.

It is a common experience for many people, when first introduced to NLP, to be concerned about the possible uses and misuses of this technology. We recognize the incredible power of the information presented in this book and recommend you exercise caution as you learn and apply these techniques.

Contents

Any sufficiently advanced technology is indistinguishable from magic.

—ARTHUR C. CLARKE

CHAPTER ONE

Changing Your Mind

The greatest revolution of our generation is the discovery that human beings, by changing the inner attitudes of their minds, can change the outer aspects of their lives.
—WILLIAM JAMES, *eminent American psychologist*

Entering a World of Change

This book will change your life. We know. What you're about to read has already changed ours. We are the trainers and consultants of NLP Comprehensive, an organization of individuals dedicated to helping people reach their unlimited inner resources. The accounts of personal change you'll read in these chapters happened to actual individuals. In many cases, their changes took place in the same amount of time it will take you to read about them. These transformations, which include changing fear into confidence, despair into desire, and worry over the past into goal-oriented action, are the result of specific and learnable techniques. We've taught them to counselors, consultants, coaches, managers, engineers, athletes, entrepreneurs, executives, and parents—all kinds of people interested in effective personal and professional change. Collectively, we have edited or authored almost a dozen of the key books on this transformational technology, and produced more than three times that many audio and videotape programs.

Over the last ten years, through our books, tapes, and training sessions, we've introduced this new possibility for living to over a million people in situations ranging from corporate boardrooms to a one-room schoolhouse, from packed auditoriums to a cancer-treatment hospital room.

We didn't start here. We set out, probably very much like you, with little more than our sincere desire and hope that deliberate change was possible. We spent years searching across the fields of psychology and personal development for ways to implement change that works. From university educations to the school of hard knocks, and from expensive training seminars to silent self-examination, we measured what we found by the results it could produce.

A number of us spent more than a decade searching for the keys to real and lasting change before we found them. Our motives were personal as well as professional. We wanted to assist our clients in transcending their past difficulties and self-imposed limitations, so they could get on with the adventure of their lives. We wanted to affect the bottom lines of businesses and the people who work for them, to increase their productivity, profit, and professional satisfaction. And we wanted something for ourselves. As agents of change, we wanted skills that could enhance those who were already achieving and increase what was already excellent. For our own satisfaction, we wanted to be able to move beyond fixing problems to creating possibilities. We've always believed we could do, be, have, and become more, and that you can too.

Now, more than at any other time in human history, many approaches, old and new, are pointing toward improving human potential and increasing possibilities. Some of them are well known, with names like positive mental attitude, visualization, affirmations, inner child work, goal setting, and personal power. You may even have tried one or more of them at one time or another. If your experience was like ours, sometimes they worked and the results were truly marvelous. At other times, though, they didn't. And when they didn't, no matter how much we wanted or needed them to work, they wouldn't. It was these erratic results that kept us searching even further for the real roots of change. We knew we were already part of the way there. We wanted to produce results consistently. We wanted to know the difference that made the difference between an occasional or temporary relief and a deep, lasting change. We wanted to be able to deliberately facilitate transformational change and teach others to do it for themselves as well.

Creating Change

Before we guide you into creating new possibilities of thinking, feeling, and acting for yourself and those you love, we would like to take just a moment to introduce ourselves and let you know a little bit about what we do and how we work.

Steve Andreas, M.A., NLP Comprehensive cofounder, trainer, author, and NLP innovator, sits listening attentively to a woman as she describes how a shameful incident from her past resurfaces on occasion. She describes how this recurring memory has limited her feelings and life choices. Steve gently interrupts her story and asks how she would like things to be. She brightens and talks about a new career idea and a different kind of life. He asks some unusual questions about the first experience and then the second. At least she thinks they're unusual. No one has ever asked her if her memories were black and white or in color before. He then guides her through what seems to be a simple visualization, only at the end, tears have filled her eyes, not of sorrow, but of joy. She feels released from her past. Less than thirty minutes has passed. She remains free of the memory.

Charles Faulkner, trainer, author, and expert modeler, finishes his interview with the company's best financial decision maker. Here is a man whose thoughts and opinions affect the movement of millions of dollars a day. Charles points to the notes he has made on the board. In a language of pictures, words, and feelings, he describes the details of this decision maker's strategy in easy-to-understand terms. The members of the assembled team begin to realize that they can use these same steps to dramatically improve their own decision-making abilities. The rest of the morning is spent applying their new skills to a wide variety of problems and opportunities.

Kelly Gerling, Ph.D., corporate trainer and leadership catalyst, enters the conference room and takes in the scene. He can see the tension and despair on their faces. The company's direction is at stake, and the board has been deadlocked for weeks. He begins by asking for each executive's perception of the situation. As he acknowledges their concerns, he asks them to talk about their values. The feeling in the room begins to shift. No one has talked with them this way. They can sense some change is stirring. Two days later, they are designing their new strategic plan. A year later, the values expressed at those meetings have spread throughout the company, improving morale, and transforming them back into market leaders.

Tim Hallbom, M.S.W., trainer, author, and health-applications researcher, had just learned from NLP innovator Robert Dilts that allergic responses are comparable to a phobia of the immune system. While there's no real danger from the outside, the body's immune-system reaction is so strong that *it* becomes the danger. Tim mentions this to some seminar participants, and one of them announces he's allergic to everything. It turns out he has so many food allergies he's spending over two hundred dollars a week on a special diet. Applying Robert Dilts's procedure for reducing allergic responses, Tim guides him to neutralize the food triggers for his allergies. Following extremely cautious and conservative testing, the participant finds over the next few days that all his allergic responses have vanished. They never return. Several years and thousands of successful cases later, Tim is participating in formal clinical studies at a Vail, Colorado, medical facility to scientifically test this new approach.

Robert McDonald, M.S., trainer, author, and healer, believes that the deep connections of our lives are our relationships. The estranged couple before him wishes they did, too. Beginning with one and then the other, Robert draws them out. He helps them divide their disappointments from their dreams and rekindle what first brought them together. He then assists them in literally separating themselves from old co-dependent patterns and gaining a new sense of wholeness in and for themselves. Finally, he invites them to participate in a healing ritual in which they bring the fullness of each other together in a living, loving relationship. Tears come to Robert's eyes as well as to the couple before him. Their marriage not only survives, it thrives.

Gerry Schmidt, Ph.D., teacher, trainer, and psychotherapist, waits for the well-dressed executive to compose himself. It has been a year since he was blindsided in an automobile accident, yet he still finds himself panicking any time a car comes at him from that angle. He knows it's not rational, and he's only here on the recommendation of a friend. Gerry asks him where it happened, and how it might have looked from across the street, or the cab down the block, or from a traffic helicopter. Pretty soon the two are laughing about it, and without understanding why, the executive finds himself making up a joke about the incident. He drives home from the single one-hour session with ease. His fears never return.

Suzi Smith, M.S., trainer, author, and health-applications researcher, has thought of herself as a lot of things: wife, mother, teacher, corporate trainer. Somehow, though, the idea of being an international authority in a new field had never come up, and it didn't feel natural. As she traced her feelings back to their origin, she found a much earlier life experience. She realized her feelings belonged more appropriately to a student in her teens who was insecure in her knowledge. This was clearly not who she is now. Since this self-limiting belief would only hold her back from delivering the important discoveries that she and her colleagues have made, she decides to change it. Drawing to mind a memory of when she felt confident and competent, she literally uses those qualities to transform her old childhood memory into a resourceful one. She completes the process in less than ten minutes.

These accounts probably seem like overstated, and unlikely incidents, or barring that, miracles. When we first heard similar accounts, they seemed like nothing less than miracles to us, too. Now, after ten or more years as NLP practitioners, trainers, consultants, and counselors, we know from the thousands of personal experiences like them that rapid, deep, and lasting change is a reality. As the contributing authors to this book, we know that NLP defies the usual expectations of what's possible. It seems so grandiose and unlikely that some people will use that as an excuse to never examine it closely.

Yet if you were to look back over this century of change, you might be surprised to discover that the airplane and the automobile are both less than 100 years old. The idea of sending voices and music through space to distant places without wires was thought impossible and therefore unworthy of serious investigation. Then radio was invented. Modern medicine, with its surgery and wonder drugs, is less than 75 years old. Television, which has certainly transformed our age, is less than 50, while personal computers are not even 20 years old. What most people don't realize is that Sigmund Freud, the father of egos, ids, and oedipal complexes, began to publish his theories in 1900. While no one would want to drive a car made in 1900, at least not regularly, many people think psychology has changed little since Freud. They'd be surprised. There have been many psychological revolutions, which have revised our ideas of the brain and increased our possibilities for change.

Change or Pain

Every one of us has tried at one time or another to change our minds. When was the last time you tried to stop thinking a thought, or quit a habit, or change an uncomfortable feeling? Whether it was a lack of motivation, a short temper, a feeling of isolation, or simply a desire for more success, at one time or another, we've all wished we were different. We've all wanted to change.

You may even have made a conscious decision to change, backed it up with a written resolution, and told a few close friends about it. You picked up some books and tapes on the subject, maybe even joined a club. A few months later, the books were half read, the tapes were somewhere, and your friends, if they were really your friends, were kind enough not to bring it up. If your experience was anything like ours, despite your good intentions and real desire to be different, you found yourself still stuck in your old habits.

Or perhaps you succeeded brilliantly, even achieving your stated goals. Then you watched with a helpless horror as things slid inexorably back to the way they were before you began. When it comes to losing weight or changing life-styles, many people have had this experience. And as if to add insult to injury, if you redoubled your efforts and tried even harder, it seemed the more effort you devoted to your transformation, the more elusive and frustrating it became.

A part of us realizes this is completely at odds with the world we live in. After all, change is taking place around us at an incredible rate. We watch as new products make old ones obsolete at an ever-increasing pace. Our children play video games we barely understand. We find we have to take additional training just to do the jobs we already have. We hear that change is the only constant in life, that it's everywhere. We see it and we believe it, that is, until we try to change ourselves. We wonder what's going on here. Is it us? Is what we want to change really so difficult?

If you were to pause for a moment and look at your life from a slightly different perspective, you would see you've always been changing. After all, you started out as a baby, weighing only a few pounds. You grew into a child, and then a teenager and now an adult. Your physical appearance, in obvious or subtle ways, has been changing every year, with or without your appreciation. You used to like candy or peanut butter or dolls or motorcycles or something more than anything in the world, and even if you still like it, other things you never thought you'd like have become much more important. Through the years, from bicycles to Friday night bashes to T-bills or box seats, your interests have changed. Even recently, there are things you've changed easily. It was one of those times you weren't even thinking about it. It was almost as if you discovered that you were doing things differently. You just stopped eating a certain food, or wearing a certain style. Or maybe you developed a new interest or hobby. You didn't think anything of it. It took your friends to point out the change to you. "Oh, yeah," you said, "I changed my mind."

Any really effective method of change will have to explain both why we sometimes have an incredibly difficult time changing and make use of the absolute ease with which we sometimes do it.

Because if you think about it, change isn't something that takes a long time. It happens in an instant. Maybe you used to be nervous in front of groups, and then you got up one day and found you weren't. You sat in front of the TV for years and then decided to take a walk or take up a sport instead. You made the time to go back to school, or put extra effort into that new career move. You may have worried over it for weeks, or months, or even years. Then you noticed it had changed.

When you know how to do something, it ought to be easy. After all, you don't complain that your car starts easily when you turn the ignition key or that your remote control accurately selects the television channel you want to watch. In this light, it's almost human perversity that we're encouraged to measure the importance of a personal change by the amount of difficulty, suffering, or time it took us to get it. It's an example of "No pain, no gain." As if everything that has been painful in our lives has been a gain. If more pain were more gain, we'd be seeking it out, instead of avoiding it. If lengthy struggle and suffering were the royal road to success, we'd all be walking to work and still using pencils and pony express. Pain is a sign that it's time to change. If our hands feel a hot surface, we pull them away. Pain is a sign we're using a poor approach. It's telling us it's time to do something different. Lengthy struggle without success is a sign that what we're doing isn't working. It's time to do something else, anything else. It's time to realize that pain, struggle, suffering, and waiting are signs that it's time for another approach. They are optional additions to the change process, and easily dropped.

Software for the Brain

Recently the computer has captured the attention of scientists and psychologists alike as a model of our brain. If our brains are a kind of computer, then our thoughts and actions are like our software programs. If we could change our mental programs, just as we do when we change or upgrade software, we'd immediately get positive changes in our performance. We'd get immediate improvements in how we think, feel, act, and live.

The comparison with computers also explains why change is sometimes so difficult. No matter how much we want, wish, or hope, it won't upgrade our software. Neither will getting angry, or entering the same old instructions over and over again. What we need to do is add new instructions to our current programs in just where they belong. With a computer, the way to do this is laid out in the manual with the software. With human beings, it's been more of a challenge. As one NLP trainer put it, "Human beings are the only supercomputers that can be produced, or rather reproduced, with unskilled labor. . . . And they don't come with instruction manuals." That is, until now.

What we're about to offer you is the software manual for your brain. You may have a personal computer at home or at work. If you do, you probably have a number of different software packages on it, including a word processor, a spreadsheet, a drawing program, a page-layout program, utilities, and maybe a few games. If a computer salesperson told you you needed to get a separate machine for each program, you'd tell him, "No way."

Yet this is what most people inadvertently do to themselves. They learn to do something well—selling, managing, motivating, problem solving, designing, delegating, whatever it is—and after a while they think, "This is what I'm good at." They develop an area of expertise, and then they simply don't know how to change their mental programs to develop another one. If your personal computer didn't run a word-processing program and a spreadsheet, you'd get it checked out. But when people can't switch mental programs, they usually begin to make excuses. They may even explain to you that they have a lack of talent or the wrong body type or personality profile or even astrological sign for that kind of thing. Yet no one thinks that the shape, configuration, or date of manufacture of a computer automatically limits its performance to certain programs. The limitations are primarily in the software, not the hardware.

As Dr. Wilson van Dusen, Ph.D. and former chief psychologist at Mendocino State Hospital in California, put it, "I have observed the psychotherapy scene since the days when Freud was the main voice. Later brief psychotherapy took a mere six months. Now we have the thirty-minute and even five-minute cures of NLP. Speed is not the real issue. We must be closing in on the actual design of people." To change what we want, we need to change the way we're designed to change.

Consider what you could accomplish if you could get a hold of the instruction manual for your brain. In the chapters to come, you will learn how to:

- Run your supercomputer—your brain—the way it was designed
- Change your thoughts, actions, and feelings when and how you want to
- Change your habits, in less than an hour, even after you've struggled for years
- Be the way you've always wanted to be: confident in times of crisis, tenacious and motivated when it really counts, as well as sensitive and receptive to loved ones and to life's gifts

You've undoubtedly had times when you really clicked, when everything you did worked perfectly, when it just "flowed." And other times, when the pieces just didn't fit together, when nothing you did seemed to work out right. With NLP, you will learn to be able to turn those "pieces not fitting" into "flow"—on demand. You've certainly noticed there are people in the world who accomplish things with ease. You'll learn how you can study these expert achievers in order to make their successful mental programs more available to yourself and others. Our search for the essence of change has led us from hopeful dreams and good intentions to a specific and powerful transformational technology. It's an approach with a set of skills as precise as a program and as easy as an old friend. It will allow you to change what you want to change and keep that worth preserving. It is called Neuro-Linguistic Programming or NLP.

Putting NLP into Action

The bottom line is that NLP allows you to have the kinds of experiences you want. For years now, NLP trainers and practitioners have been teaching people how to relieve their traumas, create more positive feelings, change lifelong habits, resolve inner conflicts, and build new beliefs, often in less than an hour. In this book, you will learn for yourself some of the most popular methods NLP professionals use to accomplish these and other changes.

First, you'll learn the basic principles or presuppositions of NLP. You'll discover how your brain works and how you can make change more easily. Then you'll learn and practice specific NLP techniques, so you can create the changes you want and need throughout your life.

Practicing NLP will:

- Put you in charge of your own motivation
- Help you create a compelling future and a personal pathway to it
- Build closer relationships and enhance persuasion skills
- Clear up past negative experiences that may have held you back
- Enhance your self-appreciation and self-esteem
- Create a solid positive mental attitude
- Gain more access to your peak performance

At the same time you'll learn many of the characteristics of top achievers, the mental maps that make them so successful. You'll be guided step-by-step through specific programs for learning and using the characteristics of high achievers. You will discover how you can use NLP to accelerate your ability to learn any skill you want. This wider range of NLP applications is sometimes a difficult concept for some people to understand. They ask, "How can we apply the same methods to stage fright, negotiations, guilt, self-esteem, strategic planning, motivation, allergic responses, and human excellence?'' It works in the same way that electricity powers a variety of things like computers, telephones, and CD players. Electricity is basic to all of them. With any human accomplishment, your brain is basic to all of them. NLP is at the cutting edge of human development because it teaches the fundamentals of how your brain works. Regardless of the situation, NLP shows you how you can do more, have more, and be more.

To enhance and deepen your learning and change, in each chapter you will find mental exercises, what Albert Einstein called "thought experiments," that will help you to master specific NLP techniques. These exercises have worked for literally millions of people. They can work for you, too, provided you actually use them. We know better than anyone that we live in an age of information overload. Some people may be tempted to just read through the exercises to see if they are interesting. This is a good start, but you'll need to actually do them if you want the results. NLP is a kind of experience. It is how you do what you do that makes the difference. So when you do these exercises, be deliberate, attentive, and thorough. Select a time in your day when you know you will be able to devote the time you need and all your concentration. Actually imagine the specific situations we suggest and follow the directions carefully. Most of the time, these "mental exercises" will only take ten to twenty minutes. You may find it helpful to have a friend read an exercise to you in order to guide you through it, so you can achieve its maximum results. And remember, these are not one-time-only workouts. The more you want to benefit from this book, the more important it is to apply these techniques in the moments of your daily life.

CHAPTER TWO

What Is NLP?

At first, NLP seemed like a glittering starlet;
then I thought of it as a very mysterious, profound magician;
now it is like a loyal, trustworthy friend,
that I have no idea how I ever lived without.

—GERRY SCHMIDT
NLP Comprehensive Trainer

What Is NLP?

NLP is the study of human excellence.
NLP is the ability to be your best more often.
NLP is the powerful and practical approach to personal change.
NLP is the new technology of achievement.
NLP is the acronym for Neuro-Linguistic Programming. This high-tech–sounding name is purely descriptive, like cross-trainer shoes, a golden retriever, or a classic convertible coupe. Neuro refers to our nervous system, the mental pathways of our five senses by which we see, hear, feel, taste, and smell. Linguistic refers to our ability to use language and how specific words and phrases mirror our mental worlds. Linguistic also refers to our "silent language" of postures, gestures, and habits that reveal our thinking styles, beliefs, and more. Programming is borrowed from computer science, to suggest that our thoughts, feelings, and actions are simply habitual programs that can be changed by upgrading our "mental software."

Learning to Model Excellence

To get a better understanding of how NLP helps us model human excellence, let's look at the beginning of modern skiing. Until the 1950s, most people thought skiing was mostly a matter of natural talent. You strapped on your pair of skis, and were told not to allow them to cross over each other and to follow the more experienced skier down the slope, doing whatever he or she did. If you managed this without too many tumbles or broken bones and happened to like the experience, you were considered a good candidate for skiing, possibly even a natural.

Then something happened that completely changed this way of thinking. As professor Edward T. Hall, author of *The Silent Language,*[1] notes, 16-mm black-and-white films were made of several skilled skiers in the Alps. Researchers studied the films frame by frame and divided the smooth motions of skiing into what they called "isolates," or the smallest units of behavior. Looking at skiing that way, they found that even though the skiers had very different styles they were using the same isolates. When these isolates were taught to average and beginning skiers, they immediately improved. Everyone could improve their skiing by doing what good skiers did naturally. The key was to identify the essence of their skills, the isolate movements that made a great skier great, so that others could learn them, too. In NLP, that essence is called a model.

When this same principle is applied with NLP, it is extended to every part of a person's experience. You might want to improve your relationships, or eliminate an anxiety, or become more competitive in the marketplace. The key movements are not found in the muscles, but in your inner thoughts, like words, or pictures, or feelings, or even beliefs. In every area, NLP'ers are studying life's great achievers to discover their formulas for success, providing a unique way to teach you how to do the same thing—to actually follow the model of those who have succeeded in spite of the same problems and challenges you face every day. The following examples will show you how modeling with NLP can make a tremendous difference.

Imagine a parent who often yells at his or her child, trying to motivate him. By the time that child becomes an adult, he may have internalized this powerful and negative form of motivation and will have most likely learned to talk to himself using strong negative language. Although motivated, the price is all the bad feelings that those negative words stimulate. Through NLP, he learns to change this internal behavior and put in its place the same kind of positive motivations and good feelings that outstanding athletes and creative inventors use.

A business executive is deeply divided on an important decision, feeling conflicted and uncertain of his skills. Using NLP to assist him in changing the way he thinks to the same mental methods used by effective decision makers, he responds much more positively. Before he might have thought, "Should I do this? I'm not sure. Don't blow it; don't miss another opportunity." Now he asks himself useful information-gathering questions that lead to effective decision making and improved performance. Questions such as: "What do I need to know in order to make this decision?" or "What are the major benefits, and how can I quantify them?"

A successful athlete decides to compete in a new sport. While she played it a little as a college student, she hasn't practiced in years. To ready herself, she mentally reexperiences her moments of peak performance in her successful sport. As she feels the focus and energy of those moments, she imagines applying them in her new endeavor. She physically practices the new sport's routines and mentally rehearses all the fundamentals. At her first event, sports commentators are amazed and talk about her natural talent. She is glad she has worked hard and smart.

Everything each of these individuals did was the product of their mental habits. All the things you've learned to do are also the products of your mental habits. From how you wake up, to how you go to work, to how you work, to what kind of leisure you like, you are a creature of habits, a person with patterns. All of us are. What is your favorite food? What route do you usually take home? When you dress in the morning, do you put on the top half of your clothes before the bottom half or vice versa? In fact, university psychology studies have found that human behavior is almost completely habits. These habits or patterns are very useful. In addition to allowing us to do so many things without having to think about them, they also form the basis of creating new behaviors and recognizing unusual situations. The drawbacks become apparent when we want to change them. The man with a negative voice for a motivation strategy thought it was natural and appropriate because he was habituated to it. He didn't know anything else was even possible. The executive knew his strategy wasn't useful in certain situations, but didn't know how to go about changing it. The young athlete knew she needed to engage her previous habits to help her develop new ones. She knew if she vividly imaged having a new habit, her brain would naturally begin to make the mental and physical pathways.

With NLP, you can change your thoughts, feelings, and behaviors, and add new ones that will become just as systematic and regular as the old ones—and a lot more enjoyable.

Getting Started:
Some Quick and Simple Changes Using NLP

NLP exercises are like thought experiments, mental exercises, or a game. The laboratory or playing field is in your mind. Think of them as a chance to try out something new, to do things in a new way and have some fun. Here are some simple exercises to give you an idea of how this works.

Have you ever ridden on a roller coaster or some other amusement-park ride? Take a moment and remember a specific ride. Then imagine that you are seeing this ride from a considerable distance, perhaps sitting on a park bench. Watching from here, you can see yourself over there on the ride. Notice how you feel as you watch yourself from this distant point of view. Next, step into your seat on the ride, so that you can feel your hands on the guardrail in front of you. As you look down the track, see the scenery flashing by, feel the rattling motion of the ride, and hear the sounds of the screams around you. Notice how you feel as you reexperience the ride. Being *on* the amusement-park ride, feeling it moving you around, is a very different experience from imagining you're watching yourself on that same amusement-park ride in the distance.

These two very different perspectives have different mental structures. Being on the amusement-park ride is engaging and exciting, what NLP calls "associated." Watching the ride at a distance is calming and detached, what NLP calls "dissociated." You'll discover through this book that every experience we have has these and many other specific experiential structures. Discovering these differences and putting them to use is fundamental to NLP. If you want to get excited about something, you'll need to get involved, both physically and mentally, by stepping *into* the experience, associating into it. With NLP you can learn how to do this precisely where and when you want to. On the other hand, all of us also have experiences in our lives when some objectivity, some mental distance, would be calming and very helpful. By stepping *out* of these experiences, and out of the intense feelings they stir up, we can easily become more resourceful and creative in dealing with them. Being able to deliberately use these mental "structures of experience" is one of the goals of this book. Consider this for a moment. If you were able to choose to be associated inside all the wonderful experiences you've had in life, and you were also able to distance yourself, to dissociate and get outside of all the unpleasant experiences of your life, you would have the feelings of all your positive experiences and a perspective on your mistakes. Consider what a difference this would make in the quality of your life. If you realize how powerful and positive this could be, you're beginning to sense what NLP has to offer.

For this next thought experiment, start by taking a minute or two to clear your mind of your current concerns. Do this by simply scanning your body for relaxation. Notice any tense areas, and either relax them or first tense them even more, and then allow them to relax.

Now, think of a very pleasant experience, a specific and enjoyable time in your life—something you'd really enjoy thinking about right now. Once you get a specific and enjoyable memory in your mind's eye, notice how you feel. Then allow that experience to move closer to you, and become larger and brighter and more richly colorful. Now notice your feelings again. Have they changed in some way, perhaps getting stronger? Now allow that same experience to move farther away from you in your mind's eye, getting smaller, sketchier, and dimmer until it is some distance away, about the size of a postage stamp. Notice your feelings now. When you've completed this, allow your experience to return to its original characteristics.

What happens for most people is that their pleasant feelings become noticeably stronger as that experience comes closer, and become measurably weaker when it moves farther away. How and why this works is fundamental to NLP, and we'll explore it in detail in the chapters to come. Right now, we'd like to make a specific point. Most people have never imagined they could change the way they think and feel about things so easily, especially by such a simple process as changing the characteristics of their mental pictures. They can imagine changing their clothes, their cars, even their jobs and the cities they live in, but most have never even considered they could deliberately change their minds. If you want to feel your positive memories more intensely, you can simply move them closer to you in your mind's eye. If you want difficult memories to have less intensity, you can just move them farther away from you.

You can do the same thing with every aspect of your life. If you have an ongoing problem, you have the ability to mentally move it farther away from you. From a distance, you've got more mental "breathing room." You can relax and think about it with a clearer mind from this new perspective. Almost all of us can think of more and better solutions with neutral feelings than we can when we feel trapped and pressured. On the positive side, if you see something you want to gain in life, then you can bring the image closer to you to make it a more vivid and compelling part of your life. Almost all visualization techniques repeatedly stress the importance of keeping your dreams and goals in mind. With NLP, you will have the skills to do this quickly and easily. And these are only two examples. You've learned *just two ways* your brain ''codes'' your experiences, just a couple of the basic elements of NLP that can make a difference for you.

Some people pause at this point, saying, "I don't visualize all that well. Will I be able to use NLP?" The answer is yes. NLP uses all of our five senses: sight, hearing, feeling, taste, and smell. NLP research discovered more than a decade ago that most people have developed one of their five senses more than the others. For example, maybe you've always loved to draw or take photos or arrange beautiful things. If so, then making mental pictures and visualizing in your imagination probably comes easily to you. Or maybe you love books and words and conversation or music, and are more sensitive to what people say, and the tones of voice they use. If so, then hearing with your mind's ear, instead of eye, is probably more natural for you. Natural athletes are usually more finely aware of their movements and the feelings in their muscles as they move. Maybe you get strong feelings about people when you enter a room. These are indications that your emotional feeling sense is more developed than your other senses.

As you read this book, you may notice that different exercises emphasize different senses. This is deliberate on our part. First, because different people with differently developed senses are reading this book, and we want to offer something that "feels natural" for each style of thinking and understanding. Second, because it's important that you learn to appreciate and develop each of your senses, so that you have access to all of your "inner resources" even more.

So, let's zero in on language, a cornerstone of Neuro-*Linguistic* Programming and the one that uses your sense of hearing. In almost any conversation, you will hear people say things like, "Don't worry" or "Don't think about it." Stop and consider this a moment. If you were told, "Don't think about that big black bear," what immediately happens in your mind? Well, despite what you heard, you find yourself thinking about a big black bear. The same kind of thing happens when you are told, "Don't think about that problem." Our brains simply don't know how to put things into negative language. In order to know what *not* to think of, our brains have to first think of it.

All of us know managers and parents who, in trying to be helpful, tell us or others what *not* to do. What they are unknowingly doing is sending our attention in exactly the direction they *didn't* want us to go. Just a few examples include: "Don't worry about that client's temper," "Don't panic," "I don't think you're dumb," and "Don't even think about being laid off." Using negative language is also something most of us do to ourselves. We say, "I won't think about it," and we do. Other examples most of us are familiar with include: "I won't do that again," "Don't make me mad," and "Don't eat sweets before bedtime," just to name a few. We tend to think of what we don't want to do, and then often proceed to do it.

The programming part of Neuro-Linguistic *Programming* means that we can change our thoughts or programs from what they are to what we want them to be. In the case of negative language, we can take our negative thoughts and state them in the positive. Instead of saying what we *don't* want, we can say what we *do* want. Try it. Think of a negative statement you've been making to yourself, and experiment with turning it into a positive one, right now. Instead of telling yourself "not to worry," for instance, try telling yourself to "be alert to opportunities." Or "How can I best prepare for this challenge?" Or "How would I like to feel?" This not only feels better, it actually reorients your brain and prepares you to achieve more of what you want, by focusing on the positive things you want to happen.

If you just apply the three quick and simple NLP concepts in this section alone, you will know you can use NLP to bring more positive and successful behaviors into your life. First, make what you want to do and what you think about into a positive statement. Second, increase the mental vividness of what you want to do in order to increase its attractiveness for you. And third, associate into these successful behaviors and mentally rehearse them, so they feel natural. This step-by-step program approach is a hallmark of NLP. A practical approach to change, NLP is a how-to technology for personal transformation.

New Principles of Mind

By now, it's probably clear that NLP is based on principles that are very different from traditional psychology. While traditional clinical psychology is primarily concerned with describing difficulties, categorizing them, and searching for historical causes, NLP is interested in *how* our thoughts, actions, and feelings work together right now to produce our experience. Founded on the modern sciences of biology, linguistics, and information, NLP begins with new principles of how the mind/brain works. These principles or assumptions are called the NLP Presuppositions. If we could summarize all the NLP Presuppositions in one phrase, it would be: **People work perfectly.** Our specific thoughts, actions, and feelings consistently produce specific results. We may be happy or unhappy with these results, but if we repeat the same thoughts, actions, and feelings, we'll get the same results. The process works perfectly. If we want to change our results, then we need to change the thoughts, actions, and feelings that go into producing them. Once we understand specifically how we create and maintain our inner thoughts and feelings, it is a simple matter for us to change them to more useful ones or if we find better ones, to teach them to others. The NLP Presuppositions are the foundation for doing just that.

THE NLP PRESUPPOSITIONS

- **The map is not the territory.**
  Our mental maps of the world are not the world. We respond to our maps, rather than directly to the world. Mental maps, especially feelings and interpretations, can be updated more easily than the world can be changed.
- **Experience has a structure.**
  Our thoughts and memories have a pattern to them. When we change that pattern or structure, our experience will auto-

matically change. We can neutralize unpleasant memories and enrich memories that will serve us.

- **If one person can do something, anyone can learn to do it.** We can learn an achiever's mental map and make it our own. Too many people think certain things are impossible without ever going out and trying them. Pretend that everything is possible. When there is a physical or environmental limit, the world of experience will let you know about it.

- **The mind and body are parts of the same system.** Our thoughts instantly affect our muscle tension, breathing, feelings, and more, and these in turn affect our thoughts. When we learn to change either one, we have learned to change the other.

- **People already have all the resources they need.** Mental images, inner voices, sensations, and feelings are the basic building blocks of all our mental and physical resources. We can use them to build up any thought, feeling, or skill we want, and then place them in our lives where we want or need them most.

- **You cannot NOT communicate.** We are *always* communicating, at least nonverbally, and words are often the least important part. A sigh, a smile, and a look are all communications. Even our thoughts are communications with ourselves, and they are revealed to others through our eyes, voice tones, postures, and body movements.

- **The meaning of your communication is the response you get.** Others receive what we say and do through their mental map of the world. When someone hears something different from what we meant, it's a chance for us to notice that communication means what is received. Noticing *how* our communication is received allows us to adjust it, so that next time it can be clearer.

- **Underlying every behavior is a positive intention.** Every hurtful, harmful, and even thoughtless behavior had a

positive purpose in its original situation. Yelling in order to
be acknowledged. Hitting to fend off danger. Hiding to feel
safe. Rather than condoning or condemning these actions,
we can separate them from the person's positive intent, so
that new, updated, and more positive choices can be added
that meet the same intent.

- **People are always making the best choice(s) available to
them.**
Every one of us has his or her own unique personal history.
Within it, we learned what to do and how to do it, what to
want and how to want it, what to value and how to value it,
what to learn and how to learn it. This is our experience.
From it, we must make all of our choices; that is, until new
and better ones are added.

- **If what you are doing isn't working, do something else.
Do anything else.**
If you always do what you've always done, you'll always get
what you've always gotten. If you want something new, do
something new, especially when there are so many alternatives.

When people are learning something new, there is a strong
temptation to try to make it into something they already know. If
NLP were just a name for something else that you already knew, it
would be easy to explain, and there would be nothing new to know.
However, NLP *is* something new, a new way of looking at the
human brain and behavior. NLP asks new questions, which stimulate new answers. NLP starts with new assumptions, which create
new possibilities. To effectively study the patterns of human excellence, the NLP Presuppositions or principles are assumed to be
true—not because they have been proven, but because when they
are held in mind, they give their holder a much greater degree of
freedom of choice and opportunities. In the chapters to come, we
will look at each of them in more detail and more depth. Now, let's
look at how applying a few of them can lead to new and profound
ways of creating change.

Maps, Minds, Emotions, and Change

The first NLP Presupposition is: **The map is not the territory.** This phrase was coined by the Polish mathematician Alfred Korzybski. He never tired of pointing out that a road map or restaurant menu can help you find your way around the town or select a meal. However, they are both fundamentally different from the road you take or the entrée that's brought to your table. You can see this principle in action every day as people drive to work. Months or perhaps even many years ago, each driver looked over his or her street map, tried a few different routes, and settled on the best way to get from home to work and back. Since then, most of these drivers have been driving that same route every day. In the meantime, new connector and feeder roads have been added. Unless a driver has taken the time to update his or her ''mental'' map, there will necessarily be discrepancies between this map and the territory. This won't matter too much until the day workers begin road construction on that usual route to work. Traffic will back up as the drivers with older maps are startled out of their mental slumber to discover they have only a few routes, and are without a clue about the range of available alternatives. Meanwhile, drivers with a newer and more complete map, with many routes and alternatives, have already taken the previous exit and are on their way.

Another way to appreciate the importance of this Presupposition is to experience it directly. Take a few minutes to do the next exercise. Remember, the more complete attention you can devote to it, the more thorough the results.

We've all had disappointments in life that later turned out not to be the ''big deal'' we thought they were at the time. People often say they ''changed with time,'' but it wasn't the length of time that changed them. It was *how* they remembered the memory that changed. On completing the Movie Music exercise, the mental code, your map for that experience, is different because you changed it deliberately. Knowing how to do this means you don't have to wait for your feelings to change. You can do it now.

EXERCISE 1: MOVIE MUSIC[2]

In this exercise you will learn how to change an unpleasant memory. This technique works best with everyday problems of low to medium intensity.

1. Watch Movie of Problem Situation. Begin by thinking of an everyday difficulty. For example, recall a time that you were disappointed or embarrassed, a time when you didn't feel very good about things. Pick a specific and real event from your past. As you think of this specific event, notice what images and sounds come to mind and watch a movie of this event unfold before you. When you're done, notice how you're feeling.

2. Select Theme Music. Now select some "theme music" that *mis*matches the feelings you got from the movie you just watched. Your memory is probably serious and heavy. So select something light and bouncy, like circus or cartoon music. Some people prefer upbeat dance music, while others like overly dramatic classical or operatic music, like the *William Tell Overture*—better known as the theme music for the old *Lone Ranger* radio and television series.

3. Repeat Movie with Music. When you have selected music, have it playing nice and loud in your mind as you begin to watch your movie again. Have the music continue playing all the way through to the end.

4. Check Results. Now, rewind that movie back to the beginning. Play it without the music and notice your response to it this time. Have your feelings changed? For many, the incident has become ludicrous or humorous. For others, their unpleasant feelings have been greatly reduced or at least neutralized. If your feelings are not yet satisfactory for you, try using different kinds of theme music with your movie until you find one that works for you.

This kind of change is proof that **the map is not the territory.** You just changed one of your mental maps, updating it and offering yourself more alternative routes. This change is also a demonstration of the NLP Presupposition **Experience has a structure.** Before the exercise, the structure or pattern of your memory included a serious scene with heavy feelings. When you added the mismatching movie music, you changed the original structure so much that your feelings about it had to change, too.

Before you go on to the next exercise, do Exercise 1 with at least three more different kinds of unpleasant experiences. Experiment with different kinds of theme music to find out which ones work best for you with different kinds of experiences.

Now, take a moment to recall one of those changed memories. You'll find that it has a different and more resourceful feeling. Notice that with this new feeling you spontaneously begin to think of other things you could say or do that might be more useful if that kind of situation happened again. A new feeling is often a powerful way to unlock your creativity in a difficult situation. Here's another way to achieve more of them.

EXERCISE 2: THE PICTURE FRAME

1. Think of a Problem Situation. Think of another, somewhat troublesome experience, or everyday difficulty. The more you use situations and feelings that recur often, the more quickly the NLP changes will begin to radiate through your life. If your negative feelings from the first exercise haven't completely diminished or changed as much as you'd like, use that situation again here.

2. See Yourself in a Snapshot. Quickly go through your memory of this incident as if it's a movie, but this time pick out one moment, like a frame from a film, that best symbolizes the whole experience for you. As you look at that picture, notice if you are seeing yourself, that younger you, at that time, as if you were looking at a snapshot of yourself at the event. If not, simply begin, in your mind's eye, to pull back so you can see more and more of the scene until you see yourself, a younger you, wearing what you wore at that time. See it all as an observer looking on.

3. Add a Picture Frame. Holding that image in mind, consider what kind of picture frame you might want to put around this snapshot. Do you want a square or round frame, or perhaps an oval one? How wide should this frame be, and what color? Perhaps you'd like a modern steel frame, or maybe an old-fashioned gold one with swirled decorations and doves on it. When you've picked out a frame, add a museum light.

4. Make It into a Painting or Photograph. How could you transform that picture into something more artistic? You might even want to see it as an artistic photograph by Ansel Adams, or in the style of a famous painter, as if it were a Renoir or a Van Gogh. Now take your framed moment and place it between other pictures in the private gallery of your mind.

5. Check Results. Take a moment to clear your mind. . . . Breathe. Now, think of that incident that used to trouble you. Your feelings have probably changed. If not, repeat the exercise using a different frame and a different style of painting or photography until you find one that changes your feelings in a satisfactory way.

Some people immediately want to know how long these changes will last. Check it again now. Check it in an hour. Make a note in your appointment book or calendar to check it next week and next month. You will find that your thinking stays changed because you used the way your brain codes information to make the change. And you can decide to change it further any time you want.

Notice that you didn't force the change. You didn't repeat an affirmation for weeks. You didn't try to use willpower. Instead, you used your brain the way it's designed to be used. You're beginning to learn a few of the mental codes of NLP . . . the building blocks of thoughts, feelings, actions, and beliefs.

It was only a minor disappointment you changed, but a few minutes ago you might have thought of that incident and you would have felt bad. Now it's changed—permanently. In the future, every time you think of it, you'll naturally and automatically feel more resourceful. Now you have a rapid technique for taking any negative memory and changing it so that it no longer bothers you. As with the previous exercise, apply it to a variety of memories. Experiment with different kinds of frames and artistic perspectives.

We've always been able to change our internal images and sounds, to embellish them and combine them with other memories, but for most of us it always happened accidentally and unconsciously. Until NLP, no one had discovered how to **systematically** use this ability to improve our feelings, thinking, and the quality of our lives.

The next time an incident or old memory bothers you, you can give yourself a new perspective, not by wishing or hoping, but by consciously taking action to change the way you unconsciously think about it. By watching a memory like a movie with upbeat music, putting it in a picture frame, or making it into a painting or art photograph, you can cast it in a new and more positive light. With NLP, you can do the same thing with all of your difficulties, using your brain in creative ways to succeed at life's challenges.

Mentors and Models of Excellence

It should come as no surprise that many people in history have already used some of the NLP Presuppositions to propel themselves to great success. Academy Award–winner Anthony Hopkins credits his career to fellow Welshman Richard Burton, whom he met at the age of fifteen. "He had quite an influence on my life," Hopkins says, "because he got away and became an actor. And I thought, 'God, I'd like to do that.'[3] President Bill Clinton's story of meeting President Kennedy at sixteen is almost the same. In business, the practice of patterning oneself after a leader of industry has a name and illustrious history; it is called mentoring. Many junior executives go out and purchase the same brand of suit, tie, and beverage as their successful boss in an effort to gain some sense of what it is like to be that person. Some go further, telling the same jokes and even copying gestures and speech patterns. All of these are efforts to "get under the expert's skin," to discover what really makes him or her tick. The ''expert'' often joins in this, telling stories of trials endured and suggesting courses of action and study. With the first two fundamental NLP Presuppositions in mind— **The map is not the territory** and **Experience has a structure**— stepping into someone else's shoes takes on a new and profound meaning. Instead of just copying clothes or mimicking gestures, these efforts could be used to discover that achiever's inner mental map. Instead of simply studying what the achiever studied, it could be appreciated how the achiever appreciated it. Since experience has a structure, it will be that actual and specific achiever's mental map, something that can be discovered, copied, put to work, and passed on to others.

Think of the NLP Presupposition: **If one person can do something, anyone can learn to do it.** This is one of the most exciting things about NLP. It means that motivation, persuasion, confidence, self-esteem, decision making, creativity, and more are all skills you can learn, just as you've learned to drive a car, use a computer, ski, or play tennis. There is a structure to achievement. When you learn the elements of excellence that characterize the world's greatest achievers, you can learn to create the same kind of achievements for yourself.

People Have All the Resources They Need

You may think some people are smarter or naturally happier or more talented than others, that they have more natural resources to draw on, or that they have a head start in life. Perhaps. There is no doubt that some people have made a wonderful match between their inner resources and their opportunities in the world. Whether it's Roseanne Arnold's attitude and her television character, Michael Jordan and basketball, or Eric Clapton and a guitar, we see people excelling with their resources. And if we were to look at those resources in more detail, we would see that every one of them is made up of images, sounds, physical motor skills, and feelings.

Remember the two exercises you did earlier. In the first one, you had the sounds of the theme music stored in your mind. You just hadn't known that it could be useful in that problem situation, and you never thought of combining it in that way. Yet when you did, it became a powerful resource for change. In the second exercise, you had images of all sorts of picture frames and artistic styles of painting and photography. Again, you just didn't realize how they were powerful resources that could be usefully combined with an unpleasant memory. You had the resources already. NLP simply showed you how to make use of them.

Every image, sound, or feeling is a resource somewhere for something. Our brain endows us with the ability to see inner pictures. Whether they begin as fuzzy or clear, we can build these mental movies up into great motivating visions. Everyone has the ability to hear inner sounds. For example, we can listen in our mind's ear and hear our own inner voice and the voices of people we've known—a friend, a teacher, or a parent. While many people use this great skill to criticize themselves, a positive inner voice can keep us confident and on track. It can become an eloquent speaker and motivator to us. In the world of NLP, talent and inner resources are crucially different. What is called "talent" is simply a set of resources that have been combined, sequenced, and practiced until they become an automatic skill. Each of us has the opportunity to develop our inner resources into talents to excel at what we love in the world. NLP can show us how.

An inner picture or sound can truly be a resource. In this next exercise, entitled "Circle of Excellence," we're going to ask you to remember a time when you had a strong inner sense of confidence. Pick a strong, vibrant memory, one that you will enjoy reliving. By vividly remembering that time of confidence, you'll be drawing upon an inner resource from your past experiences. Then we'll show you how to create a special memory trigger, so that you can have that feeling whenever you want or need it.

At NLP Comprehensive, we are often trying out new techniques and possibilities for more comprehensive change. Because we have never done them before, we know the first time is going to be a lot less than perfect. We have a saying to remind ourselves of this: Anything worth doing, is worth doing badly . . . at first. If you were not successful or only partially successful in this exercise, try doing

EXERCISE 3: CIRCLE OF EXCELLENCE

What could you accomplish if you had more confidence when you wanted it? Which positive feelings from your past would you want to reexperience if you could transfer them from where they happened in your life to where you really want them? The Circle of Excellence will do just that.

1. Relive Confidence. Stand up and let yourself go back in your memory to a time when you were very confident, abundantly confident. Relive that moment, seeing what you saw and hearing what you heard.

2. Circle of Excellence. As you feel the confidence building in you, imagine a colored circle on the floor around your feet. What color would you like your circle to be? Would you like it also to have a sound like a soft hum that indicates how powerful it is? When that feeling of confidence is at its fullest, step out of that circle, leaving those confident feelings inside the circle. This is an unusual request, and you can do it.

3. Selecting Cues. Now think of a specific time in your future when you want to have that same feeling of confidence. See and hear what will be there just *before* you want to feel confident. The cue could be your boss's office door, your office phone, or hearing yourself being introduced before a speech.

4. Linking. As soon as those cues are clear in your mind, step back into the circle and feel those confident feelings again. Imagine that situation unfolding around you in the future with these confident feelings fully available to you.

5. Check Results. Now step out of the circle again, leaving those confident feelings there in the circle. Outside the circle, take a moment and think again of that upcoming event. You'll find you'll automatically recall those confident feelings. This means you've already preprogrammed yourself for that upcoming event. You're feeling better about it and it hasn't even happened yet. When it arrives, you'll find yourself naturally responding more confidently.

it over again, paying close attention to each step. The timing is quite important. So is giving your full attention to the exercise.

In Step 1, it's important to fully relive the experience, so that your feelings are strong. Pretend you are back in the situation. Stand or sit the way you did then and use the same gestures.

In Step 2, you need to take the time to create an image of your Circle of Excellence that is right for you, and then attach it to that confident feeling in Step 1. Sometimes it can help to step in and out of your Circle of Excellence several times to build up the feeling and to be sure the image of your circle has become a trigger for your positive feeling.

In Step 3, you want to be sure that the cues you choose are ones that you will notice just *before* you want to have your resource confident feeling available. If the cues are too late, you will already be on your way to feeling bad before your confident feeling has time to be triggered. This is easy to remedy. Simply find earlier cues and use them.

In Step 4, you want to step into your circle as soon as you become aware of the cues, so that the positive feeling is triggered before you actually need it. This way you are connecting your Circle of Excellence to the same cues that used to indicate a problem situation.

In Step 5, you are checking to see if you have made a solid connection. If you have, the cues will automatically result in the positive feelings of your Circle of Excellence. If not, back up and find the weak link so that you can strengthen it.

When you apply NLP, you're taking the initiative. You're deciding for yourself how you want to react to the events in your life. In this case, you took the feelings of confidence you've experienced in the past and attached them to a future situation that might have previously been intimidating. This is a process you can do for as many different future events as you want, with as many different feelings as you want. What's more, the Circle of Excellence is not just for problems. You can take something you already do well and improve it.

Let's say you are already able to make systematic and well-organized presentations, but you sometimes receive the comments that they are also a bit dry. You don't need more confidence, but you could add playfulness, or humor, or liveliness and make your presentations even better. You can use the Circle of Excellence to create more excellence in the same way as you did for eliminating problems.

If you've ever had a resource, even if it was only for a second, that means you have it forever. Using a Circle of Excellence, you can choose to use this resource the way you want, at the times when you want it. In any situation, you can choose how you want to feel and how you want to respond. You can choose to live your life on purpose. You really do have all the inner resources you could want or need.

If What You Are Doing Isn't Working, Do Something Else

How could we claim that **people have all the resources they need,** when so many are so miserable? When things don't work, most people continue to do what they've been doing that hasn't been working—usually harder and louder. But remember that our limitations are not in the territory, but in our maps. If you want to see the same scenery, continue to go down the same road. But if you *want* something different, *do* something different. Examining why you're not getting where you want to go, or for that matter, examining why you *are* getting where you want to go, won't help. No matter how many whys and becauses you come up with, you're still headed down the same old road. Instead, concentrate on *how* you are getting or not getting where you want and what you want in life. With NLP, you can improve and enrich your mental maps and discover what makes the difference between failure and success, between good and great, between accomplishment and fulfillment.

A Short History of NLP

The history of NLP is the story of an unlikely partnership that created an unexpected synergy that resulted in a world of change. In the early 1970s, future NLP cofounder Richard Bandler was an undergraduate mathematics student at the University of California at Santa Cruz. Initially, he spent most of his time studying computer science. Inspired by a family friend who knew many of the innovative therapists of the day, he decided to pursue psychology. After carefully studying some of these well-known therapists, Richard discovered that by completely repeating their personal behavior patterns he could get similar positive results with other people. This discovery became the basis for the groundbreaking approach in NLP known as Modeling Human Excellence. Then he met NLP's other cofounder Dr. John Grinder, an associate professor of linguistics. John Grinder's career path was as unique as Richard's. His ability to quickly assimilate languages, assume accents, and take on cultural behaviors had been refined while in the U.S. Army Special Forces in Europe in the 1960s and later when he was a member of intelligence services working in Europe. John's interests in psychology were in line with the fundamental goal of linguistics—to uncover the hidden grammar of thinking and action.

Discovering their similar interests, they decided to combine their respective skills of computer science and linguistics along with their ability to copy nonverbal behavior to develop a new "language of change."

In the beginning, on Tuesday evenings, Richard Bandler would lead a Gestalt Therapy group for assembled students and locals. He modeled himself after its iconoclastic founder, the German psychiatrist Fritz Perls. Richard went so far in copying Dr. Perls as to grow a beard, chain smoke, and speak English with a German accent. On Thursday evenings, Grinder would lead another group using the verbal and nonverbal patterns of Dr. Perls that he had heard and seen Richard use on Tuesday. They systematically began to omit what they thought were irrelevant pieces of behavior (the German accent, the smoking) until they found the essence of Perls's techniques—the difference that differentiated Perls from other, less effective therapists. They had begun the discipline of Modeling Human Excellence.

Encouraged by their success, they went on to study one of the great founders of Family Therapy, Virginia Satir, and the groundbreaking philosopher and systems thinker, Gregory Bateson. Richard assembled his original findings in his master's thesis, published later as the first volume of *The Structure of Magic*. Bandler and Grinder had become a team, and their research continued in earnest. What set them apart from the many schools of alternative psychological thought growing in California at that time was their search for the essence of change. As Bandler and Grinder began studying people with various difficulties, they noticed that every person who had a phobia thought of whatever they were afraid of as if it were happening to them at that very moment. When they studied people who had gotten over their phobias, they found that every one of these people now thought of their phobia experience as if they were watching it happen to someone else—similar to watching an amusement-park ride in the distance. With this simple and yet profound discovery, Bandler and Grinder decided to systematically teach the people with phobias to experience their fears as if they were watching them happen to someone else in the distance. Their phobic feelings disappeared instantly. A fundamental discovery of NLP had been made. *How* people think about something makes the crucial difference in how they will experience it.

As they sought out the essence of change from the best masters of change they could find, Bandler and Grinder questioned what to change first, what was the most important thing to change, and where was the most important place to begin. Their skills and growing reputations quickly earned them introductions to some of the finest examples of human excellence in the world, including Dr. Milton H. Erickson, M.D., the founder of the American Society of Clinical Hypnosis, and widely recognized as the world's foremost medical hypnotist.

Dr. Erickson was every bit as much an original as Bandler and Grinder. A strapping young Wisconsin farm boy in the 1920s, he was stricken with polio at the age of eighteen. Unable to breathe, he lay in an iron lung in his family's kitchen for more than a year. While this might have been a prison sentence for anyone else, Erickson was fascinated by human behavior and passed the time noticing how family and friends responded to each other, consciously and unconsciously. He constructed remarks that would produce a double take or delayed response in those around him, all the time honing his observation and language skills.

Recovering enough to leave the iron lung, he taught himself to walk by watching how his baby sister was learning to do it. Even though he still needed crutches, he took a cross-country canoe trip before heading off to college, where he eventually received degrees in medicine and then psychology. His early experiences and personal trials had made him very sensitive to the subtle influence of language and behavior. While studying medicine, he became very interested in hypnosis, carrying it far beyond watching pendulums swing and monotonous suggestions of sleepiness. He noticed that when thoughts and feelings passed through his patients' minds, they briefly entered natural trancelike states and that these could be used to induce hypnotic states. In his elder years, he became known as the master of indirect hypnosis, a man who could induce a profound trance just by telling stories.

By the 1970s, Dr. Erickson had become very well known among medical professionals and was even the subject of several books, but few of his students could reproduce his work or replicate his results. Dr. Erickson was often called the "wounded healer," since many of his colleagues thought his personal trials were responsible for making him become a skilled and world-renowned therapist.

When Richard Bandler called for an appointment, Dr. Erickson happened to answer the phone personally. Though Bandler and Grinder had an introduction from Gregory Bateson, Erickson replied that he was a very busy man. Bandler responded saying, "Some people, *Dr. Erickson,* know how to *make time,*" emphasizing "Dr. Erickson," and the last two words more strongly. Erickson's answer was, "Come over *any time,*" also emphasizing the last two words. Though Bandler and Grinder's lack of psychological certification was a strike against them in Dr. Erickson's mind, he was intrigued that these two young men might be able to discover what so many others had missed. After all, one of them had just spoken to him using one of his own hypnotic language discoveries, now known as an embedded command. By emphasizing the words *"Dr. Erickson, make time,"* he had created a separate sentence within the larger sentence that had the effect of a hypnotic command.

Bandler and Grinder arrived at Dr. Erickson's office/home in Phoenix, Arizona, to apply their newly developed modeling skills to the work of the talented hypnotist. The combination of Dr. Erickson's legendary hypnotic skills and Bandler and Grinder's modeling skills provided the basis for an explosion of new therapeutic techniques. Their work with Dr. Erickson confirmed they had found a way to understand and reproduce human excellence.

About this time, Grinder and Bandler's college classes and evenings groups were attracting an increasing number of students eager to learn this new technology of change. In the years to come, a number of them, including Leslie Cameron-Bandler, Judith De-Lozier, Robert Dilts, and David Gordon, would make considerable contributions of their own. By word of mouth, this new approach to communication and change began to spread across the country. Steve Andreas, at the time a well-known Gestalt therapist, set aside what he was doing to study their techniques. He quickly decided that NLP was such an important breakthrough that, with his wife and partner Connirae Andreas, they would record the seminars of Bandler and Grinder and transcribe them into books. Their very first one, *Frogs into Princes,* would become the first NLP best-seller. In 1979, an extensive article on NLP appeared in *Psychology Today* entitled "People Who Read People." NLP was on its way.

Today, NLP is at the heart of many approaches to communication and change. Popularized by Anthony Robbins, John Bradshaw, and others, bits of NLP have found their way into sales trainings, communications seminars, classrooms, and conversations. When anyone talks about Modeling Human Excellence, getting in state, building rapport, creating a compelling future, or how "visual" they are, they are using concepts from NLP. We're delighted that NLP is finally becoming better known. The thing is, a little knowledge may be a dangerous thing, or it may be nothing at all. Knowing *about* Modeling Human Excellence is different, and a lot less, than being able to do it. Knowing a little bit of NLP is different from having a chance to make it your own. That's why we wrote this book.

Reviewing What You've Learned

NLP is the study of human excellence. It's a process for modeling the mental patterns of thoughts, actions and feelings of real human achievers, like ourselves. The codevelopers of NLP learned how to rearrange internal experience so easily and elegantly because they started with some fundamental principles that are at the heart of Neuro-Linguistic Programming.

THE PRESUPPOSITONS OF NLP

- **The map is not the territory.**
- **Experience has a structure.**
- **If one person can do something, anyone can learn to do it.**
- **The mind and body are parts of the same system.**
- **People already have all the resources they need.**
- **You cannot NOT communicate.**
- **The meaning of your communication is the response you get.**
- **Underlying every behavior is a positive intention.**
- **People are always making the best choice(s) available to them.**
- **If what you are doing isn't working, do something else.**

Once we understand specifically how we create and maintain our inner thoughts and feelings, it is a simple matter for us to teach them to others, or if we find better ones, to change them to more useful ones. In this chapter, you've learned how to:

- Dissociate from your negative experiences and associate to your positive ones
- Increase or decrease the importance of an inner thought image
- Direct your thoughts where you want to go, not where you don't want them to go

- Neutralize negative feelings about past events with Movie Music and the Picture Frame technique
- Create more resources for yourself by using your Circle of Excellence to place them in your future when and where you will need or want them

Somewhere inside all of us are dreamers. We can't help but want and dream and desire. It comes naturally to us. It's a part of who we are, deep in our bones, and it has taken our species from living in caves and huts to exploring the moon. We dream and we want to fulfill our dreams. We want to unlock ways to realize our dreams.

T. E. Lawrence of Arabia wrote in his memoirs, "All people dream, but not all equally. Those who dream by night in the dusty recesses of their minds wake in the day to find it was vanity; but the dreamers of the day are dangerous, for they may act their dreams with open eyes, to make them possible."

You may not have thought of it, but your telephone, television, CD player, dishwasher, refrigerator, microwave, not to mention your toilet and shower, all started as someone's dreams. They have transformed our world, many of them in our lifetime. When you want to bring the simplest dream to realization, you change things, and you may be challenging the status quo, the state of mind that says, "Things are well enough the way they are." When you bring something new into your world, you may disrupt routines and shake expectations. You ask yourself and others to be different.

One way to help others to adjust to your dreams and change is to invite them along. Loved ones, coworkers, and family will see what you are doing and probably want to be included. They may be shy or reluctant to ask if they can join you. If they take this journey with you, they're more likely to want it to continue. When everyone has more choice in their lives, they accept more choice and flexibility in others. NLP is something to share and practice *with* other people, not *on* them.

NLP creates an environment for graceful personal change. It

works when you use it, and it will change your life. You can begin conquering the problems that brought you to NLP, and then you can turn your attention to creating new possibilities and new adventures. Far from becoming simply a means to an end, NLP allows you to live purposefully, to participate in creating the world you really want.

CHAPTER THREE

Getting Motivated

*What lies beyond us and what lies before us are tiny matters when
compared to what lies within us.*

—RALPH WALDO EMERSON

The Importance of Being Motivated

As motivational consultant and best-selling author Anthony Robbins put it, "There are two things that motivate people to success: inspiration and desperation." On the inspiration side is Dr. Edwin Land, inventor of instant photography and the founder of the Polaroid Corporation. His little daughter wanted to see a picture of herself right away, and asked her father why it took so long to develop pictures. This inspired Land to put the development process right in the film. In a similar vein, Bill Gates and Paul Allen, founders of Microsoft Corporation, saw an advertisement for a personal computer kit in *Popular Mechanics* magazine and saw the future of computing. Bill even called up his mother to tell her he might not call her for six months because he was writing a computer program that IBM was going to buy. We all know that program now as MS-DOS.

On the other side, as proof of desperation as a motivator, the list could begin with Anthony Robbins. A former vacuum cleaner salesman and health program seminar leader, Tony had tasted financial success and had it slip away from him. When he found his life reduced to a four-hundred-square-foot apartment in Venice Beach, California, washing his dishes in his bathtub, it wasn't the taste of success that pulled him forward, but the distaste of his current conditions that drove him to change them, that drove him to take

NLP training and turn his life around. Another example of desperation as a motivator is the Academy Award–winning actress Cher. When she turned forty, she surveyed her life accomplishments and, disturbed at the lack of them, set to changing her future. Whether they are scientists, actors, athletes, or business leaders, the motivation of positive inspiration and negative desperation makes a tremendous difference in people's lives.

So why do some people have such a tough time motivating themselves? You would think that success, achievement, and the fulfillment of one's greatest dreams would be so attractive, so irresistibly wonderful, that people would have no trouble getting motivated. Yet for many people, getting going is a major problem. High achievers say it takes motivation to reach their goals but how do they define motivation? The fact is motivation isn't some secret formula sold only to star athletes and motivational speakers. Instead, it's a simple mental strategy you can learn to use for yourself; something you can have whenever you need it.

There are specific times when we want to be motivated. And these are different from the times when we *don't* want to be motivated. This might not make sense until you remember that there are things you are very motivated toward that might not be such great ideas. How about when you want to eat more chocolate or that third piece of pizza, or to buy something else you don't really want or need? That's when what you really need is a procrastination strategy. Put another way, we need a motivation strategy when we don't feel like *doing* something, but we want it *done*. We want the results, but it's hard to get excited about the process. For example, if you think about doing your laundry, paying your bills, or taking out the garbage, you probably don't enjoy doing them, but you do want them done. When your boss wants a report on his desk by noon, and the subject puts you to sleep because it's so dull—you don't feel the desire to do it, you want it done. When we know we should exercise, but doing it is sweat, pain, drudgery, and time, we want it done. We don't always want to be involved in the process of doing something—we want what we'll get when it's finished. That's when we need a motivation strategy, and that's what NLP can give us.

How Does Motivation Work?

There are a couple of different personal styles of motivation. You can find yours in your everyday wake-up routine. When the alarm goes off in the morning do you mumble to yourself, "Oh no, let me sleep just a little more," and hit the snooze button? When the alarm goes off again, does an inner voice say, "It's time to get up?" Your brain might begin to show you pictures of yourself rushing to get dressed and missing breakfast. But the bed is so warm, the covers feel just right, and you think, "No big deal; I can wear what I wore yesterday. Who needs breakfast?" So you hit the snooze button again.

Then a few minutes later the alarm goes off again. And this time that inner voice says, "You've got to GET UP or you're going to be LATE and have *real* problems!" This time, your brain starts showing you pictures of getting to work late and having to explain it to your boss. But you think you can drive a little faster to work. So back to sleep you go.

But then that alarm goes off again, and now the voice loudly says, "IT'S TIME TO GET UP. YOU MUST GET UP!!!" Your brain starts showing you pictures of your clients impatiently waiting for you, threatening to leave. In your mind, your boss is yelling and screaming at you, threatening to fire you. And when this picture in your mind's eye has become big enough and bright enough and close enough and loud enough, then you say, "OK. OK. I'll get up." You're finally motivated. You got yourself going by making up scenarios of what you want to move *away from*.

Then there's another type of motivation. Have you ever awakened at a resort, fully aware you were on vacation? As you opened your eyes, you began to think of what you would get to do that day. The vivid scenes of the wonderful and delightful opportunities in your mind pulled you out of bed like a giant magnet. The question was only, "What shall I do first?" The question of getting up or not never even entered your mind!

Just like that, there have probably been times when you waken in the morning for work, thinking about the great things you get to do that day. You thought about how doing those things would take you *toward* what you really want with more enjoyment and feelings of accomplishment, competence, and confidence. You saw pictures of yourself doing things and moving *toward* the rewards for them. You saw how this day would connect to the next, leading *toward* the things you really wanted in life.

Discovering Your Motivation Direction

NLP has discovered that these two types of motivation work in very different ways with very different directions and results. These two key elements of motivation are what NLP calls the Motivation Direction. This direction can be either *toward* what we want or *away from* what we don't want. Motivation Direction is a mental program that affects our entire lives. At the biological or physical level, everyone has developed both *away from* and *toward* motivation; away from pain, discomfort, and stress; and toward pleasure, comfort, and relaxation. These are very different ways to get motivated, and both are useful in different situations. After all, there are dangerous places, hurtful actions, and negative thinking worth moving *away from,* just as there are wonderful places, supportive and encouraging people, and positive thinking worth moving *toward.* Everyone uses both directions to some degree, and it is fascinating that everyone tends to specialize in one direction of motivation more than the other. We become more motivated either *toward* images of success, pleasure, and gains, or *away from* failure, pain, and loss.

NLP research has found that people will tend to use the same mental program for motivation in widely different situations. For example, the person who wouldn't get up in the morning until he sees a mental image of his boss yelling at him and threatening to fire him—his Motivation Direction will be to get *away from* the pain, discomfort, and the negative consequences of his boss's threats. It is very likely he will move in this same direction in many other areas of his life. For example, he probably decides the time to take a break is when he's uncomfortable. When he picks his friends, he's likely to pick people who don't bother him. He probably won't make a career move until he can't stand his present job anymore. He moves *away from* what he doesn't want.

The alternative Motivation Direction is to move *toward* what you want: pleasure, rewards, and goals. For example, the person who wakes up in the morning raring to go can't wait to get out of bed to start achieving his or her dreams. This person might be asking, "What can I do today? What opportunities am I going to have today to get closer to the things I really want and desire in my life?" This person also uses the same kind of motivation to decide the best time to take a break—perhaps so that he can talk with a friend, or as a reward after completing something. When he picks his friends, he's likely to pick people that stimulate him. He probably makes that career move to go on to a bigger opportunity. He moves *toward* what he wants.

At first glance, a side-by-side comparison of the *toward* and *away from* motivation strategies make the *toward* motivation considerably more appealing. People with a *toward* motivation are likely to say, "There's a better way to live. Just imagine what you want and go toward it." But consider this. When the room temperature is uncomfortable, you do something to change it. When someone begins telling half-truths and making innuendos, you do something about it. These are examples of an *away from* motivation strategy in action. If you're a successful business person, perhaps one of the things that got you there was the memory of the poverty in which you grew up. If remembering those hard times in the past motivates you to keep driving for a better quality of life now, then you've made an appropriate and productive use of your *away from* motivation.

The benefits of *toward* motivation are more obvious. The people who move *toward* goals and rewards are greatly valued in our society. If you look in the "help wanted" ads of your local newspaper, you'll find ads seeking self-motivated, ambitious, forward-thinking self-starters—in other words, people who are motivated *toward*. This demand for *toward*-motivated individuals has many job applicants pretending to be something that they are not. This isn't of service to anyone. When we examine the advantages of both directions of motivation, we find that a *toward* orientation is more goal-directed and an *away from* orientation is more directed toward identifying and solving problems.

The Effects of Motivation Direction

Both types of motivation have advantages and disadvantages, moderations and extremes. For example, sometimes some people are so motivated *toward* their goals that they may not even consider what problems they might run into, or what difficulties to prepare for along the way. This "pedal-to-the-metal" kind of mentality is a common trait in young entrepreneurs. As a result, they have to go through the "school of hard knocks" and maneuver around several potholes before they realize the importance of avoiding difficulties and either do it themselves or hire someone to do it for them. At the other extreme, some people can become so *away from* motivated that they are too terrified to try anything. They can get so involved in the problem they are trying to solve that they forget why they were doing it.

By this time you've probably begun to wonder which type of motivation you use and hope that it's *toward*. Remember, it is possible to be very successful with either approach. While the *toward* motivation is the more commonly appreciated motivation of highly successful people, the less appreciated *away from* motivation can also make you very successful.

Martin Zweig, the famous and highly regarded stock forecaster, manages over a billion dollars in assets. His stock letters and books are known to investors worldwide. Dr. Zweig uses an *away from* motivation to minimize his losses. He will only take so much "pain" in the stock market and then he will get out. He has his limits and respects them, and this has made him very rich.

Dr. Zweig's very effective strategy points directly at three things everyone who uses an *away from* Motivation Direction needs to be aware of. First, when someone moves *away from* something, they're doing so because they're experiencing discomfort, even fear or pain.

These are strong incentives to action. But the farther they get from their problem or source of pain or discomfort, the less serious it seems. As a result of this, people with an *away from* motivation strategy will lose a lot of their motivation as the "threat" is experienced as farther and farther away—until the problem or threat arises again. *Away from* motivation is often cyclical; it will tend to run hot and cold—from high motivation to no motivation and then back again.

Second, because people with this direction of motivation are moving *away from* distress, discomfort, or pain, they don't pay much attention to where they're going to end up. Out of the frying pan and into the fire aptly describes what sometimes happens when too much attention is paid to problems. Their attention is on what they *don't* want, and not on what they *do* want. Or to put it another way, they won't see where they're going, because they keep looking where they've been—this is sometimes called "poverty consciousness."

Third, people who use an *away from* motivation need to pay attention to their level of anxiety or stress. People who are motivated *away from* things often experience a lot of pain and worry before they're motivated to act. If they let the stress or anxiety level get too high before they react, it could affect their health and well-being. In some businesses, it is a badge of honor to work well under pressure, yet the same decisions could be made with a lot less stress. High blood pressure and tension headaches are only two of the results of storing up stress in the body before finally taking action.

Instead, these same people could learn to react earlier and on slight levels of discomfort without so much stress, like Dr. Zweig and many other effective decision makers. After all, how loud does a telephone have to be to let you know it needs to be answered? How uncomfortable does a chair have to be before you will move? It all depends on your sensitivity. Achievers develop their sensitivity to people and environments so they can have the most flexibility of action, moving while they still have a choice, before pain or discomfort forces them to move. They know that the kind of motivation they use affects the quality of their lives. They know how to respond to discomforts while they are still small and become more motivated *toward* specifically what they want in life while being alert for problems and situations to avoid.

Fortunately, with NLP, we can learn how to use both *away from* and *toward* motivation. We know that pain, stress, and distress are optional. If you choose, you can get the most motivation with the least discomfort and with a great deal of pleasure.

How Managers Can Implement Motivation Direction

Since both *away from* and *toward* motivation are important, we can use them both to deliberately motivate ourselves. We can also use them to motivate others. This knowledge is especially useful to managers and supervisors. In their work, managers can quickly notice by words and reaction patterns of others that different people are motivated in different ways. For example, some people are more motivated by awards, bonuses, incentives, and praise. They'll work hard if they know they can gain a trip to the Bahamas, a new car, or the approval of a trusted superior. They talk about goals and targets, they tell you what they'd like to attain, gain, or achieve. With these people, an effective manager would use *toward* motivation incentives: targets, perks, rewards.

For those who use *away from* motivation, the same perks and rewards mean very little. As a manager, you might think to yourself, "I offer them all these rewards and they're still sitting on their duffs." You might get frustrated and yell at them, "If you don't produce, you're out of here!" Or you might prefer to express, in a soft, serious voice, concern with the imminent possibility of layoffs. Suddenly, they start working like crazy and producing like never before. As an observant manager, you can realize, "Ahhh. We have some people with *away from* motivation. These people are motivated by avoiding unpleasant or negative situations." In order not to be yelled at, to relieve their discomfort, they will produce.

Before this sounds like a pseudoscientific justification for "Spare the rod, spoil the child," or "No pain, no gain," allow us to quickly add that continually prodding people to move *away from* planned distresses or discomforts can dull their responses—just like the poor horses in a local carnival that have to walk around and around and around. There's also the danger of pushing too hard, in which case the person will just get *away from* the whole situation— physically if they can, and mentally if they can't.

A much more useful and productive way of thinking about *away from* Motivation Direction is as *away from* problems. Many of these people are excellent problem solvers. It's even in their language. They are the ones that come up to you and say, "Excuse me, we've got a problem here." They see a problem, and they have to solve it. When they've solved a particularly difficult problem, they experience an emotional relaxation, an inner "aha" or "eureka."

On the other hand, *toward* motivated people are going toward goals. You can hear it in their language as well as when they say things like, "My goal is wealth, or recognition, or to make a difference." As they get measurably closer to their goals, they experience an emotional peak, an inner "yes."

Utilizing Motivation Direction in Planning

If you are a manager, it's your job to understand both kinds of motivation and to motivate your people accordingly. Here's a strategic-planning model you can use with groups and teams where people with both types of motivation are present. Remember, their Motivation Directions are opposite, so they will tend to argue with each other if you don't provide guidance and direction.

Let's say you want your group or team to formulate their organization or group goal. As you begin to present what you want, look around the room for team members who are responding positively to your message. These *toward* motivated individuals are probably the ones nodding in agreement or who begin to eagerly join the discussion, adding to your lead, envisioning possibilities. Probably only a few moments will pass before an *away from* motivated team member will break in saying, "That'll never work," or words to that effect, and begin to list all the reasons why. It is very important that you listen respectfully, and then point out that problem-solving skills are crucially important later in the process, but that they are premature at this point.

Remember, the NLP Presuppositions state that **people are always making the best choice(s) available to them,** and **underlying every behavior is a positive intention.** As you look at that team member who raised the objection, you are seeing these Presuppositions in action. This person's personal history and natural Motivation Direction make it imperative that he tell you the error of your ways or the ways of the rest of the team before things get any more uncomfortable or painful. While you might experience his remarks as cold water on the spark of an idea just starting to burn, he sees a future blaze out of control that is best stopped right now. His intention is positive, just as are the intentions of all the other members of your team who also have objections. They *are* being team players, it's just that their timing is a bit early.

It is your role as manager to suggest to the group a better plan. First, let the dreamers dream fully. Allow the "goal setters" to envision their biggest visions, exploring the limits of possibility, so that the "problem solvers" have something to solve. You could even suggest that they begin by separating into two groups around their stronger interests or skills: goals and dreams on the one hand, and avoiding difficulties and problem solving on the other. With these two resource teams in different parts of the room or around the table, have the *toward* motivated team begin to develop the goal, dream, or target. Stress to the *away from* motivated team that they remain silent as they carefully note down all the negatives so no problem slips through.

When the *toward* motivated dreamers have completed their goal setting, thank them. For they, too, have made the best choices they can with the best of intentions. Then add that if there were any weaknesses in this goal or plan, we could wait for the marketplace or our competition to show us, or we can have the problem-solving team tell us now and develop a really solid plan that is ready for anything.

The goal-directed *toward* motivated team's job is to figure out where to go, and the problem-solving, *away from* motivated team's job is to discuss what might stop us from getting there—to identify the potential problems and help formulate solutions. By employing both Motivation Directions, you're using both upside planning and downside planning in sequence. Once your people have learned this pattern, communication between the two groups will be based on an appreciation of both types of motivation and thinking styles, and this will bring out the talents and resources of all the people on your team. Good companies and good managers balance these effectively, because both are crucial to success. Equally crucial is the sequence: *toward* first, and *away from* second.

Utilizing Motivation Direction in Communication

If you're giving a short instruction, however, it works better to reverse the sequence. Every day, each of us is called upon to give instructions to someone. It might be as simple as how to unlock the garage, or how we want a report prepared, or as important as the closing remarks of a client presentation. Years of observing ourselves and others have shown that very often people will first state what they do want and then state what they don't. For example, "Turn the garage handle all the way to the right, but don't jiggle it or pull on it." We've heard the same kind of thing in the office when a well-intended supervisor says, "Get me that report by tomorrow, and don't worry about making it perfect. This is not a client presentation." Remember the impact of negative statements that we discussed in the previous chapter. We tend to focus on, and even do, what is contained in the negative statement. When the negative is last, we tend to remember it more strongly, focusing our minds on what not to do, rather than what to do.

If it seems like we're making a big deal out of a little language, take a moment to listen to the following two statements. Read them as if someone you respect is saying them to you. Notice any difference in your feelings or attitude between them once you've completed both.

"This time, let's get this done on time and under budget. So no grandstanding, pet projects, or last minute changes, OK?"

"This time, no grandstanding, pet projects, or last minute changes. Let's get this done on time and under budget, OK?"

If you are like most people, the second statement is more appealing and positive than the first. The crucial difference is that in the first statement, you were first directed *toward* the goal and then left with the problems to avoid, and in the second, you were first offered the problems to avoid, and then pointed *toward* the goal. This crucial communication pattern gets played out at every level of our society. In the 1992 presidential debates, then-President George Bush first stated what he had done for the United States during his term in office, then added what he hadn't done or what mistakes he had made. While we're not suggesting this alone cost him reelection, consider what feelings this left in the minds of millions of television viewers and voters. This becomes even more significant when you contrast President Bush's language with that of independent candidate Ross Perot. As you may recall, Mr. Perot had no qualms about telling us how bad things were and how bad they could get. How could we stand to listen to him? Because he always left us with a positive action statement. He found ways to say, "America is in trouble, and we need to get down in the trenches and under the hood and fix this thing." What a different impression he left in the minds of voters.

While you may not be running for president of the United States, you are creating impressions every day with everyone you meet. You can get the maximum benefit of this insight into Motivation Direction simply by rephrasing your comments in the following order: first negative, then positive. First state what you *don't* want and then state what you *do* want. Some people insist they don't want to ever say or think a negative thought. This is admirable, but it is also unrealistic, because you'd never be able to give corrective feedback. Whenever you talk about something not being what you wanted, whether it was a meal, a meeting, a movie, a music CD, or a date—you're offering corrective negative feedback. Negative feedback is valuable in developing a clear contrast between what you *don't* want and what you *do* want. Sequencing them will lead you to have more of the experiences you want.

A majority of the people we have encountered use *away from* Motivation Direction more than *toward*. If you are one of these people, adding this new order to your self-communications will make a huge difference to you. Making your usual negative comment and then deliberately following it with a positive goal means you'll be ending each thought with a direction toward what you want, bringing you more into balance.

On the other hand, if you're one of those people that naturally gravitates to the *toward* end of the Motivation Direction, adding this communication pattern will greatly enhance your results with the majority of people you meet. Since a majority of people need to start by noticing what they don't want in order to get motivated, when you communicate with them, you can begin there and then assist them and yourself by offering them goals to go *toward*.

The Influence of Strong Values

By now, you have a good idea of what Motivation Direction is and how people use it to get motivated. There's another factor in all this that acts like a supercharger on people's motivation, and that is their values. Values are supremely important. They are the measuring sticks of life. What we value determines what life means to us, what actions we will take, what we will move *toward* or *away from*.

As we noted earlier, at the physical level, our Motivation Direction means moving *away from* pain and moving *toward* pleasure. At the levels of thoughts and feelings, it means moving *away from* or *toward* values. A crucial point here is that when people become disconnected from their values, they lose their motivation. All of us probably know people who are examples of this. They are so disconnected from their values that they sit for hours on end in front of the television, flipping the remote control from one channel to another, hoping to find something amusing or distracting. Too often we can find ourselves on automatic pilot and wonder afterward where the time went.

Some of the real authorities on the preciousness of life and the importance of lasting values are senior citizens. Ask some of these people who have lived out most of their lives what's really important to them, and none of them will say, "I wish I'd watched more television," or "I really should have spent more time worrying." Instead, they often reflect on the importance of connecting with family and friends. And they recount with relish the challenges, adventures, and triumphs of their lives. If they express any regrets, very few of them say they truly regretted anything they had done. What many of them regret was what they *hadn't* done. In a nutshell, they will tell you that they often let the time of their lives slip through their fingers. They hadn't identified their most important values and then done everything they could to fulfill them. Instead, they'd wasted their time on petty pursuits. Their wisdom can guide us to make other choices.

Can our connection with our values be a choice? Recall the NLP Presupposition: **If one person can do something, anyone can learn to do it.** Are there people in the world totally committed to fulfilling their values? Of course there are. It's simply a matter of discovering how these experts are already using their brains so that we can duplicate it. The NLP technique you're about to do will get your most important values right in front of you. It will also connect your values with your actions, so you'll spend more of your time on what you really want to achieve.

You may find it very useful to get a pen or pencil and some extra paper to note down the answers to these questions.

- What are my goals?
- What is important to me?

Your answers could be a career achievement, a style of life you want for yourself and your family, a vacation, a new job, an opportunity, or a relationship. Whatever it is, think of it now. Get it in mind; even get several goals in mind. Once you've done this, even if some parts of them aren't clear, ask yourself these three questions about each goal:

- What's important about this goal?
- What do I value or treasure about this goal?
- What meaning does this goal hold for me?

Sometimes one word will come to mind, like: freedom, challenge, acceptance, connection, or security. Sometimes it might take the form of a phrase, such as ''achieving what people thought was impossible,'' ''proving myself,'' ''creating something new,'' or ''making the world a better place.'' Whatever it is, these words signify your inner values. If we don't live up to our important values, if we don't fulfill them, we experience disappointment, emptiness, and worse—even when we are outwardly successful. Values measure the meaning life holds for us. All of our goals, dreams, and desires are simply the vehicles for fulfilling our values. If you are dreaming of a new home for your family, you probably have some values in mind. You will want the house to have so many rooms, and be in a certain neighborhood, and have a certain style. The values fulfilled by your criteria probably include: giving comfortable space to everyone, luxury, peacefulness, even an inner sense of success and achievement. These same important values will arise again when you think of purchasing a car or even changing jobs. They are what all of us use to measure our wants, our achievements, and success.

Our values influence our motivation. If we don't have strongly held values, we'll have little motivation. If our values are strong, our motivation will be equally strong. With NLP it is possible to influence this very directly. When you think of any experience, you use one or more of the sensory modalities: visual, auditory, kinesthetic, smell, and taste. For most people, thinking of an experience using all or most of these modalities will be much more motivating than using only an image, or only a word or sound. When you think of an experience using many modalities, it seems more real, and your response will be stronger.

For instance, just think of the word *lemon*, or get a quick image of a lemon and notice your response. Now see a richly yellow 3-D image of the same lemon, and imagine slicing it in half with a sharp knife. Listen to the sound the knife makes as it slices through, and watch some of the juice squirt out, and smell the lemon scent released. Now reach out to pick up one of the lemon halves and bring it slowly to your mouth to taste it. Listen to the sound that your teeth make as they bite into the juicy pulp, and feel the sour juice run into your mouth. Again, notice your response. Are you salivating a bit more than you did when you just had a word or a brief image of a lemon? More than likely. And now what happens if you imagine rich, red, flavorful strawberries? The way you think of an experience will determine whether you respond to it strongly or weakly. Now let's apply this realization to find out how you think of your highly valued experiences.

EXERCISE 4: IDENTIFYING WHAT MAKES AN EXPERIENCE COMPELLING

This exercise will help you find out how your brain "codes" images to increase your motivation by making them so strong you're naturally compelled to take the steps to achieve them. It's important to give your full attention to this exercise.

1. Strongly Motivated Experience. Think of a task that is really attractive and compelling to you. Think of something that isn't fun to do in itself, but whose rewards are so great that you really want to do it. When you think of it, you find it attractive and compelling. What's important is that *you* find it attractive and you actually *do* it. And when you're experiencing being attracted, look at the image in your mind the way a movie director might. Notice the cinematic qualities: the set, the lighting, the sound. See all this so clearly that you could make a movie of it, one with rich, vivid detail. Having done that, temporarily set aside this attractive experience.

2. Separator State. Take a breath, let it out, and look around.

3. Neutral Experience. Now think of something you don't care about, such as a paper cup, a pencil, or a piece of paper. When you've chosen something, look at it in your mind's eye. Experience the feeling of not caring about it. Again, be like a movie director and list the cinematic qualities of this inner image.

4. Separator State. When you've completed that, clear your mind again by taking a deep breath.

5. Compare Experiences. Notice the *differences* between what you found very attractive and what you didn't care about. Our

Continued

brains are designed to notice differences, and you need to compare things to appreciate the differences. Here are some of the kinds of differences that many people find:

The "very attractive" was brighter; the "don't care" was darker. The "very attractive" was in color; the "don't care" was in faded colors or black and white.

The "very attractive" was bigger and closer; the "don't care" was smaller and farther away.

The "very attractive" was located more in front; the "don't care" was located off to the side.

The "very attractive" had sounds or words, perhaps exciting ones; the "don't care" was silent.

Make a list of all the differences you find between these two experiences. These are the elements that your brain uses to indicate that something is valuable to you, and worth being motivated about. These are your keys to being motivated.

Discovering Submodalities

Now look again at your list of differences. Some of the items on your list may indicate modalities: an image, a sound, or word, a feeling, smell, or taste. However, many of the items are probably submodalities. Submodalities are the smaller elements within a modality.

For instance, in the visual modality, an image can be 3-D or flat, a movie or a still picture, framed or panoramic, clear or fuzzy, etc. A sound or word in the auditory modality can be high- or low-pitched, loud or soft, and have different tempo, rhythm, location, and tonality or timbre. A feeling can affect part of your body or your whole body, and can differ in intensity, location, temperature, texture, movement, direction, etc. Smells and tastes can also differ widely, though the English language is not as richly able to describe them. For most people, the submodalities for something very attractive are: big, close, panoramic, three-dimensional, rich in color, clear, etc. The image of what's most important or compelling is often leaning out toward them. The inner sounds are rich and harmonious, coming from all around. However, people differ somewhat in which submodalities make something attractive; what's important is to use what "very attractive" is like for *you*.

Review your two experiences of "very attractive" and "don't care" from the previous exercise, and look for any additional submodality distinctions between the two. Now that you have itemized the ways your brain uses to make an experience attractive, you have the keys to change your responses when your behavior doesn't match your values. Most of us have times when we consciously believe that it would be valuable to do something, but we can't seem to get motivated to do it. Here's what one NLP student did. She decided to look into her mind and find out how all the different foods she ate appeared. She was especially interested in those she felt very attracted to. Sure enough, chocolate cake was richly detailed, three-dimensional, and right in front of her mouth. On the other hand, asparagus and most other healthy vegetables and fruits languished in dreary black-and-white photographs down in a corner of her vision.

Since this woman wanted to eat better foods and meet her health and weight goals, she systematically changed the submodalities of her inner images for food. She made the chocolate cake and other sweets less attractive in her mind by changing their images in her mind's eye to black and white, flat, and farther away. Then she increased the attractiveness of asparagus and other vegetables and fruits, making them colorful, richly detailed, and three-dimensional. This had an immediate and automatic effect on her eating habits. She just found herself selecting healthier foods. By changing the submodalities of her images, she brought her behavior in line with her stronger value—to live a healthy life.

This technique can motivate us to bring into our lives the experiences we care about. We don't have to find ourselves in old age regretting that we didn't do the things that really mattered to us. The things we care about can become more focused, visible, and actual now.

You'd be surprised at the inner images many people try to use to motivate themselves. In their mind's eye, they see tiny, dark slides of their work being done, or a fuzzy, black-and-white picture of the reward for completing a project. No wonder they're not motivated. Now, you can make a rich and compelling picture of what you want and what you value. The bigger, richer, more colorful, more three-dimensional and clear, the better.

EXERCISE 5: INCREASING MOTIVATION

1. Valuable Task. Think of something that you know would be valuable for you to do, but you have a hard time getting around to doing it.

2. Check for Objections. Pause to ask all parts of yourself if any part of you has any objection to your actually carrying out this task. Be sensitive to any objections. If you can't easily satisfy any objections that do come up, think of something else that no part of you objects to.

3. Results and Consequences. Think about the end result of getting this task done—not the process of doing the work, but the positive benefits to you. How will you gain in many ways from getting this done? How do you think about these benefits now?

4. Change Submodalities. Now use the list of elements you discovered in Exercise 4 to change how you think about the results of getting this job done. Make these images bigger, closer, more colorful, etc. Add in the pleasant sound, encouraging voice, or whatever else makes an experience attractive and compellingly motivating for you. Keep doing this until you feel strongly attracted to this task, just as you did with the "very attractive" experiences in Exercise 4.

Create an Inner Life of Drama

NLP codeveloper Richard Bandler is fond of describing the average person's inner voices or dialogue as weak, weak, weak. Bandler says, "For most people, there are no inner voices spurring them on with encouragement. There are no backup singers." He puts NLP trainees through exercises to hear powerfully motivating internal music. He has them hear a rich, deep, powerful laughter inside at signs of difficulty or challenge.[1] When we do these things it makes our experience more vivid, and more alive, giving us a sense of excitement and anticipation for the things we do.

You can't expect life to be a drama on the outside if it isn't a drama on the inside. If you were about to take the stage to give a speech or make a presentation, you might want to hear a great rock-and-roll band or symphony in your mind, playing music that you find inspiring and exalting. As you stride toward the podium, the music becomes louder and faster, reaching a crescendo just as you reach the podium. The energy and inner excitement you feel will carry over to the group automatically because of the images and sounds you've amplified in your mind.

Exercises 4 and 5 assume that you have something in your life that you are attracted *toward* sufficiently that you're willing to do the work required to reach it. But what if your Motivation Direction is primarily *away from*? The same exercises will work for you, simply by changing "what you are compellingly attracted to" into "what you are compellingly motivated to avoid." Rather than making the positive consequences big and bright and close, etc., you need to make the unpleasant consequences of *not* doing the job big and bright and close. Many people think about such unpleasant consequences so that they linger days, weeks, months, even years, slowly increasing in intensity, causing much anxiety and stress. Many people have to experience too much internal pain before changing or taking action. Try this as an alternative. Think of what you want to avoid. Now have it rush toward you, getting bigger and more colorful and more real as it makes demands and an ominous, sinister laugh. If you are *away from* motivated and you experience it this way, you'll be motivated to take action immediately, saving you perhaps months or years of chronic stress. This is what NLP calls a *utilization* of an existing motivational strategy. Some of the best-known motivational speakers and coaches have built whole motivational systems around it. It is one choice, and NLP believes that choice is better than no choice, and more choices are better than a few.

Using Motivation Strategies for Your Health

Many NLP students want to utilize their *toward* and *away from* motivation strategies in the area of exercise and dieting. Most people think of this area of their lives as *losing* weight, which makes it an *away from* motivation. Obviously, some people will achieve better results by thinking of it as moving *toward* gaining fitness and health. Remember, either Motivation Direction will work, provided you have effective and compelling thoughts in your mind. The *toward* motivation of Demi Moore getting back in shape after her pregnancy, and winning a million-dollar movie role, is obvious. Some mothers simply want to be fit so that they are healthy role models for their children. Having important and compelling values in mind will make a huge difference. The values you choose are up to you.

Many busy executives plan to make time for their health, but it often doesn't become a priority until they have a heart attack. At that point, their inner images and voices of concern over disability on the *away from* side, or images of lost health on the *toward* side, become big enough and close enough and bright enough to displace business demands. Of course, they could avoid those big, scary, and expensive trips to their doctor's office or a brightly lit, antiseptic emergency room by changing their submodalities for those inner images now, increasing the importance of health or family or capability to continue to work. Remember to utilize an *away from* motivation strategy to begin to move *toward* what you want.

Many people have not developed sufficiently attractive images for health, fitness, and well-being to draw them forward. Remember, an effective motivation strategy requires a positive and rich image of the task *done*. Many people have difficulty getting themselves to exercise—they are almost always imagining themselves huffing and puffing in the middle of what seems like an endless exercise routine. There are only a few minutes to go, but it seems like the rest of time itself. Their internal dialogue is usually one of two variations: self-critical cajoling or flogging, or the futility of even trying to get in shape. No wonder they have difficulty motivating themselves. Contrast this with the inner world of a motivated athlete. Even as she's exercising, she concentrates on how good she will look and feel when she's done. Each workout machine or running track lap brings her one palpable step closer to that completed image and good feeling. Her internal voices help her focus and concentrate on getting the exercise done correctly, so as to obtain the most benefit for the time spent.

Does this seem like the impossible dream? Remember, with NLP, **if one person can do something, anyone can learn to do it.** The next NLP technique we are going to teach you is a way to have a greater *toward* motivation strategy.

EXERCISE 6: THE NEW BEHAVIOR GENERATOR

1. Preparation. Find a relaxed and quiet place to be guided through this technique. You don't have to close your eyes to do this process. Just make yourself comfortable and begin by looking off to your right. In your mind's eye, imagine seeing someone who looks just like you a short distance away. This "other you" will do all the learning in this exercise, as you observe. Only when you are completely satisfied with this process will the new skills be integrated into you. To ensure this, you might even want to experience yourself as being in a Plexiglas bubble, so that you are truly separated and detached from the activities going on with that "other you" out there.

2. Choose Task. Now, think of something you want to be able to motivate yourself to do. Pick something very simple. For example, it could be cleaning the kitchen sink, balancing your checkbook, or getting up in the morning. Something that you don't enjoy doing, but you want very much to have done, because of the benefits you'll gain as a result.

3. See Benefits. Watch that "other you," and see what it will look like when the task is completed, including the positive consequences of having it done, both the direct and immediate benefits, and the future benefits that will result.

4. Doing the Task. Now see that "other you" doing the task easily. As that "other you" does the task, that "other you" keeps

---

looking at that image of the task all finished and feels good in response to seeing it all completed. Notice that the internal voice of the "other you" is enticing and encouraging, reminding you of the future rewards and of how much you have already accomplished toward the goal. Finally, see that "other you" delighted with having it done and enjoying the reward when the task has been completed.

5. Review and Adjustment. If what you see isn't completely delightful, you can let a mist cover your inner vision while the wisdom of your unconscious mind makes the appropriate adjustments or changes. When the mist disappears again, you will see the adjustments that have been made in a way that's pleasing and good for you. Do you want to be that "other you" who has just used a new motivation strategy? Are you satisfied that that "other you" has mastered this new skill? Have that "other you" do the whole process again with another task to demonstrate it to your satisfaction.

6. Integration. When you are fully satisfied, let that Plexiglas bubble fall away, and draw into yourself that "other you" who has all these new learnings. Some people actually reach out their arms and imagine drawing that other self into themselves. Sometimes people feel a tingle or a release of energy when they do this.

7. Planning. Now take an extra moment to consider when is the next time you will have to perform the task you just motivated yourself to complete.

Reviewing What You've Learned

By now you've got a better sense of how you can use NLP techniques to increase motivation for yourself and others. In this chapter, you've learned how to:

- Determine your Motivation Direction—*away from* or *toward*
- Determine the Motivation Direction of others and use this information to improve their productivity

- Discover your important values and how they can influence your motivation
- Phrase *away from* and *toward* motivation for the best results with others
- Use submodalities of your thinking to change and increase your motivation
- Learn how to be more positively motivated *toward*

We could write a whole book on NLP and motivation. Each chapter would be filled with incredible challenges and outstanding success stories. If reading about the motivation and success stories of others has encouraged you to use this chapter to create your own motivation success story, then we've succeeded. If you read this material with interest, excitement, or even astonishment, and have not tried any of the exercises yet, you haven't even begun to tap the potential of NLP. NLP is an incredible set of ideas and insights into human thinking, feeling, behavior, and change, and in many ways this is the least it has to offer. NLP is about *experiencing* human excellence—stepping into new worlds and new possibilities, new motivations. This chapter sets the stage for an accelerating adventure in achievement that will unfold in the chapters to come. NLP only works when *you* do. Do the exercises in this chapter and you'll be ready for the next stage of the adventure: discovering your mission.

CHAPTER FOUR

Discovering Your Mission

If one advances confidently in the direction of his dreams . . . he
will meet with a success unexpected in common hours.

—HENRY DAVID THOREAU

An Important Mission

Can you recall seeing the first Apollo moon-landing? We've all seen the images they took in 1969: Neil Armstrong walking on the moon. What a magnificent accomplishment! How did we organize the resources of an entire nation to do what had never been done before? We did it with a grand vision of greatness—a mission. President Kennedy proposed to the country that we pursue the dream of putting a person on the moon by the end of the 1960s. He said, "We choose to go to the moon in this decade and do the other things not because they are easy but because they are hard. Because that goal will serve to organize and measure the best of our energies and skills."[1] The nation rallied around that mission, and we made it our own.

Once we had our mission, our imagination was engaged, and we had purpose. The space program was organized and focused, and then the dream, the vision, the mission, unfolded.

One of the consistent characteristics of living a mission is the unexpected. You can never predict all the benefits of pursuing your mission. In the case of the Kennedy-initiated space program, the most important thing we learned wasn't about the moon; it was what we experienced about the earth. We were awakened by images on TV of what our earth looked like from space, and we heard the voices of the astronauts behind those cameras.

On his space walk, Apollo 9 astronaut Russell "Rusty" Schweickart saw our planet as a whole. He said that he developed an extraordinarily personal knowledge of the interdependence of all life—an embracing of the planet that changed him forever.

> Frames and boundaries over which we fight are not real from the perspective of space. Individual responsibility comes out of that direct experience of seeing the planet as a whole. And the understanding that with the speed of communications today, and space exploration, travel, and satellites, that there is no longer room on the planet for a concept that is so fundamentally "them and us." And that we have to understand now that the real situation is we as life-forms on the planet are all interconnected, and that our behavior and our systems and our attitudes have to come to recognize and reflect that reality.[2]

He and the other space explorers gave humanity a view of the whole of life, the entire globe that sustains us. And what our space explorers did for humanity, your imagination can do for you. Using your imagination can help you to comprehend the whole of your life. Envisioning the big picture of your life will help you develop a plan, a mission, to live that life fully.

What Exactly Is a Mission?

A mission is a sense of purpose that lures you into your future. It unifies your beliefs, values, actions, and your sense of who you are. It's a fabric woven of the various threads of your interests, desires, and goals. Sometimes it's big, comprehensive, and even grandiose. Most of all, a mission is fun. When you are living your mission, you tend to behave like Steven Spielberg, who says, "I wake up so excited, I can't eat breakfast."[3]

NLP is the study of the thinking and behavior of individuals who demonstrate greatness in achievement. An obvious characteristic of individuals who achieve greatness is a sense of mission that gives their life purpose and direction. This is the main difference between those who achieve and those who don't.

Now that you've learned some of the basic principles of NLP and your motivation strategy, it is important for you to discover your mission. People with a mission focus on developing their skills. They relentlessly pursue achieving their mission "with every nerve" using "fierce desires" that create "so divine a power," in the words of Michelangelo.[4] They do it day after day, and they thoroughly enjoy it. You can, too.

The Difference Between a Job and a Mission

Most people lack a sense of mission. Rather, they have a job or career. They "attend" school. They "go" to work. In his classic study of Americans' perception of their work, Studs Terkel said:

For the many, there is a hardly concealed discontent. The blue-collar blues is no more bitterly sung than the white-collar moan. "I'm a machine," says the spot-welder. "I'm caged," says the bank teller, and echoes the hotel clerk. "I'm a mule," says the steelworker. "A monkey can do what I do," says the receptionist. "I'm less than a farm implement," says the migrant worker. "I'm an object," says the high-fashion model. Blue collar and white call upon the identical phrase: "I'm a robot."[5]

This discontent with their jobs by so many people leads to a split life. They divide their time between what they *have* to do to earn a living and what they *want* to do to have fun. The split life starts in grade school with class and recess. It continues throughout work life and ends only with retirement.

Yet great achievers transcend the work/play dichotomy entirely —they do what they love and love what they do. Nora Watson said it clearly to Studs Terkel: "I think most of us are looking for a calling, not a job. . . . Most of us have jobs that are too small for our spirit. Jobs are not big enough for people."[6] Call it a quest, a calling, a grand purpose, or a mission—it gives those who discover it for themselves a profoundly moving reason for being in the world. You must find a mission that pulls you with an attraction that arouses your passions and makes you tingle. If you do, it will get you fired up; you will wake up excited; you will strive to make every day a masterpiece. That is what characterized living a personal mission. How do you know if you have not discovered your mission? It is a matter of attitude and life-style. Ask yourself whether you have a job or whether you are creating your dream? Whether you go to work and then have fun on your time off, or whether you love your work so much that even on vacation, your thoughts turn to your work and your mission? Whatever you answer, the processes and ideas in this chapter will help. If you already enjoy a mission-oriented life, this chapter will make it even more clear, exciting, and passionate.

On the other hand, if you have been living an unpassionate life, split between the drudgery of working for money and occasional times to play, this chapter can help you discover your mission.

Some people don't even think about a mission because they don't even think they can get there. To erase any such nonsense, let's recall what a tremendous learner you are. To help you create an image of yourself as a great learner, use the next exercise.

Add your own enhancements to this exercise. Add spiritual, mental, and other unique capabilities you know you possess. You might want to do it daily for a while. With practice, the image you develop can turn into a sustained and immediately available belief system that will support you in all your activities.

The Importance of Belief

You will find your unique mission if you use the exercises in this chapter thoroughly. That's because you possess a unique combination of interests, desires, and developed skills, as well as a vast reservoir of undeveloped talents. Once you discover your mission and live it, it will unify your interests and your inherent talents as the learner in you flourishes!

You can use this ability to learn by knowing that, at any point in your life, you can choose a new direction, a new course of action,

EXERCISE 7: YOU ARE A LEARNER

1. Go Back in Time. Remember how, as a tiny child, you achieved fantastic learning accomplishments? Now, if you put yourself into an imaginary time machine, you can go back to that time of early childhood. Just pretend momentarily that you are in that time machine. Imagine you are going back to that happy time of accelerated learning as a child. Get a glimpse of what it's like. Notice that the people are very big—you look up at them. There is so much going on.

2. Notice Your Learning Capabilities. You are actively and passionately learning. You are learning a lot of things, especially the language. You are learning fifteen to thirty new words a day. Without even thinking about it, you are learning hundreds of rules of grammar. And that ability to learn remains in you.

3. Inventory Your Gifts. You have 15 billion brain cells that together are twinkling with the circuitry of a thousand cities. Your ears can hear 1,600 different frequencies, ranging from 20 to 20,000 cycles per second. Your eyes can detect a single photon of light. And the 800,000 fibers in each of your optic nerves transmit more information from 132 million rods and cones to your brain than the world's largest optical computer system. The more than 300 million tiny air sacs in your lungs provide oxygen to the 100 trillion cells throughout your body. Your 206 bones and 656 muscles form a more functionally diverse system of capabilities than any known creature. And these and other tremendous abilities to function and learn can be applied in many different ways. You can't count all your capabilities—there are too many.

4. Form a Single Image. Now, when you picture your ability to learn, you can see these kinds of capacities as a whole, bright image of your human nervous system—a system of functional capabilities unrivaled in the known universe. If you ever doubt your own capability to achieve your mission, this image can pop up as a factual account of your gifts, turning that doubt into confidence.

a new mission. You can discover and live your mission. If you believe you can, you will. Why? Because that belief activates in you the same phenomenal capabilities as those magnificent achievers you so admire. **If one person can do something, anyone can learn to do it.** In the mission-discovery process below, we will highlight several past and present achievers of greatness. You will learn to see the patterns that underlie their motivation. These patterns are a matter of attitude.

The Story of the Bricklayer

If a bricklayer who was building Saint Peter's Cathedral in the Vatican hundreds of years ago was asked, "What are you doing?" he might have said, "I'm laying bricks, building a wall, just doing my job." That's one kind of person—a person with a particular goal. Or he might have said, "I'm building one of the world's great cathedrals, a building that will stand for centuries as a monument to what human beings can achieve with the inspiration of God." That's a person with a mission. It's the kind of feeling you can aim for, in creating a mission for yourself.

A mission isn't something you force on yourself, or something you make out of current concerns. It is both larger and deeper than that. It is something you discover within. By discovering your mission, you can make sure the goals you pursue are yours; you can make sure that you'll be glad you achieved them when you do; and you can make sure that your journey through life unfolds with a passion that energizes every fiber of your being.

Learning How to Do What You Love

The fundamental lesson that all the great achievers teach us is this: Do what you love to do. That's simple enough. However, sometimes people just don't believe they could possibly be paid for doing what they love. Other times, they have forgotten what it is they love. Perhaps the most important thing that stops people from getting in touch with their mission is this: They just don't know how to do it. They don't know how to go from their day-to-day goals, values, and interests to that one unified direction of excitement and fulfillment—their mission. It is possible, however, to use a step-by-step series of exercises to assist you to determine your passion in life, what you were born to achieve in your lifetime.

When you think about yourself and your life, you can acknowledge right now that you have lived your whole life to this point and you have survived. And as we all know, there is a huge difference between merely surviving and fully living.

Being motivated to survive is something you've always done. If not, you wouldn't be reading this book right now. When you think back on your life, there probably have been times when you had to get a very strong sense of motivation for yourself in order to survive. Now you can redirect the energy of your survival instinct so that you can use it for going beyond surviving to living—to living the life that you choose.

We achieve the living of such a life by remembering that we have the capacity to learn. And it's learning—changing the way we think, the way we behave, the way we communicate—that will help us achieve our unfolding mission.

The Mission-Discovery Process

To find an exquisite example of passion for life, we need look no further than Susan Butcher, who races in the most grueling and difficult race in the world—the Iditarod dog-sled race. The Iditarod race stretches eleven hundred miles across the barren, cold wilderness in Alaska. It lasts ten days or more, and it's an amazing accomplishment to finish it at all. Susan Butcher has won this race four times.

How did Susan Butcher decide that she was going to be an excellent performer in this field? In 1975, she was living in the United States on the East Coast. She was twenty years old, and she didn't know what to do with her life. She asked herself, "How can I create a life that includes the two things that I love: wilderness and animals?" Her answer was to discover her personal passion. She said:

I just always loved dogs and all animals. And when my first dog died, I just wanted to replace him. And I ended up buying a husky, and he was six weeks old. And I thought, "Wouldn't it be neat to teach him how to pull a sled?" And so I did it as a hobby. But then four months later, I bought my second husky, and then two months after that, I moved in with a woman who had fifty huskies, and then I started mushing in earnest.[7]

So she decided on dog-sled racing. She kept moving west and north. She ended up in Alaska and built a log cabin to live in. She didn't have any security in going there and following her dream, but she did it anyway. And now she is the foremost achiever on the planet in her sport—a sport that, up to this time, has been dominated by men.

In the case of Susan Butcher, it is easy to understand the difference between a mission and a goal. Here's how she describes it.

We were in Fairbanks and talking to a friend of ours. And he said to us, "What do you see yourself doing in five or ten years?" We [she and husband David] tried to explain to him some of what it was. And when he kept questioning us on our goals, our goals didn't seem right to him. Our goals weren't to kind of make it somewhere [financially] and then say, "Aha, I've made it. I'm done with it."

And what we saw the difference was, and what we explained to him is the difference, is that we are content doing what we are doing now. And so yes, we're working extremely hard, and we're very, very busy, and perhaps, you know, one of our goals for the future would be to slow the pace down a little bit, but not to change it . . . not to reach a point in our career at doing dog mushing and then say I'm going to drop this dog mushing 'cause I've made the money off of dog mushing, and go off and do something else. We love what we do, and we are already living our dream. So we don't have to make enough money or reach a certain point in our career. WE MADE IT. I made it thirteen years ago—because I've been living in the bush, working with my dogs for all of those years.[8]

She says of her life: "A lot of people would look at my life and think it's a lot of hard work. But for me, it's a labor of love."[9] That's how you know when you are living your unfolding mission—when pursuing your goals is a labor of love. And it comes from finding your life's passions.

Another person of achievement who found and follows his passions in life is movie director Steven Spielberg. More people have seen Steven Spielberg's movies than those of any other director. He started making movies when he was a child, a mere eight years old. He decided that his mission in life was to be a storyteller through the medium of film. He is constantly creating, because to him, making movies is like playing. This is how Spielberg describes his work:

> In my films I celebrate the imagination as a tool of great creations. . . . I dream for a living. Once a month, the sky falls on my head, I come to, and I see another movie I want to make. Sometimes I think I've got ball bearings for brains; these ideas are slipping and sliding across each other all the time. My problem is that my imagination won't turn off. I wake up so excited, I can't eat breakfast. I've never run out of energy.[10]

So Steven Spielberg can be an example to us all of what can happen when you *do what you love to do*.

Ted Turner is another example of a person who is passionately living a mission. He is the founder of the Goodwill Games, founder of CNN, TNT, and Headline News, and creator of an incredible cable-television empire. In fact, he brought cable television news not only to the United States but to the world. Declared by *Time* magazine as the "Man of the Year" in 1991, Ted Turner is a person who is bringing Marshall McLuhan's "global village" into our daily reality through his organizations.

How did he start his mission? After he found out that his father Ed had initiated plans to sell out his business, Ted stood up to him at age twenty-four. In this verbal battle, he "threw back all of Ed Turner's own arguments against quitting in life." Soon after their argument, his father killed himself with a pistol. From that moment

---

EXERCISE 8: FINDING YOUR LIFE'S PASSION

1. Tap Your Inner Excitement. Like Steven Spielberg, Susan Butcher, and other great achievers, know your interests. Or as NLP cofounder John Grinder once asked: "What do you love to do so much that you'd pay to do it?"

2. Know Your Passions, Your Desires, Your Loves. Only you know what you truly love. It could be tinkering, teaching, inventing, or hundreds of other delightful possibilities. You might find hints in a hobby you enjoy. You might love people or love computers, or both. As you think of those interests, those desires, those loves, and those passions, feel your own inner signals of excitement and interest welling up from the depths of your psyche. Feel them. Take an inventory of the most fun events in your life. If you had ten million dollars, what would you pay to do?

3. Focus on Those You Admire. See and hear your favorite heroes and admired people, the men and women who you most want to be like, whom you've emulated and imitated throughout your life. These heroes may have similar interests, desires, and goals. Pay attention to them and enjoy them. See them in the screen of your mind's eye, in the inner theater, and feel the excitement you've tapped into.

4. Persist. Keep doing this over and over again until you have a rich collection of images of what you are passionate about doing.

---

on, Ted "sped forth on a quest from which he would never look back. . . ."[11]

His father's death prompted him to reexamine his deepest values. Up until then, Turner says, his father's idea of success permeated his thinking: "He was the one, really, that I had expected to be the judge of whether I was successful or not. . . ." This reexamination of what was important created some major shifts in his criteria for success. He said, "I spent a lot of time trying to figure out what it was that he did wrong. He put too much emphasis on material success. I can tell you, it's fool's gold. . . ."[12]

Our deepest tragedies can become a springboard for the next

phase of our life. In this case the torturous pain of death motivated him to reexamine his deepest values and principles, and in fact to develop some new ones.

Another person who deeply examined his values and principles was a coach. John Wooden's UCLA basketball team amassed the greatest winning streak (88 games) in any major sport. He is the only person enshrined in the Basketball Hall of Fame as both a player and coach. During his 27 years at UCLA, his teams never had a losing season. And in his last 12 years, they won 10 NCAA championships, including seven in a row. No team in college basketball has even come close to repeating these achievements.[13]

His relentless dedication is legendary. He still has records of every minute of every practice of his twenty-seven years at UCLA. And he never talked about winning. "To me, success isn't outscoring someone, it's the peace of mind that comes from self-satisfaction in knowing you did your best. That's something each individual must determine for himself."[14]

By combining his athletic skills, his father's creed of principles to live by, and a love of people, he became the most admired coach in the world. How did he formulate his mission?

This is the creed, given to him by his father, that made up a key part of living his mission:

1. Be true to yourself.
2. Make each day your masterpiece.
3. Help others.
4. Drink deeply from good books, especially the Bible.
5. Make friendship a fine art.
6. Build a shelter against a rainy day.
7. Pray for guidance, count and give thanks for your blessings every day.

Besides living his creed, what motivated him to choose his mission as a coach? In his own words he said:

As a matter of fact, I'm frequently asked why I chose coaching as a career and then stayed with it. Amos Alonzo Stagg, who coached football at Chicago when I used to make my annual "walk to Chicago," best sums up my feelings on the subject. Stagg, who worked with youth and coached well into his nineties, when asked why he coached once said, "It was because of a promise I made to God."

... I feel that my love for young people is the main reason I have stayed in coaching and have refused positions that would have been far more lucrative.[15]

He wasn't following someone else's values. He looked deeply into himself. He made the values and principles he was taught and those he formulated into his own. You can do the same thing that Ted Turner and John Wooden did. You can discover your deeply held values and principles and embrace them. Here is how.

EXERCISE 9: REEXAMINING YOUR DEEPEST VALUES AND PRINCIPLES

1. Think of Some of Your Interests, Loves, and Desires. Look at the goals that you are pursuing now. Next, look into the future and see those goals being achieved. You've thought about them a lot before. Pick the most important ones that come to mind—there may be two, three—even five of them. These goals are your specific desired future.

2. Determine Your Values and Principles. In whatever way you find most enjoyable, hold them in mind. Take each particular goal in turn; see it, hear it, experience that it is a goal you own. When you've done that, ask yourself: "What do I value about this goal?" If the goal is to travel, the answer might be "learning" or "fun" or something else. If the goal is a new job, the answer to what you value about it could be "excitement" or "challenge." The answer may be one value, or it may be several. For Ted Turner, his values might be harmony, solving problems, and excitement. Susan Butcher seems to value love, caring, and perseverance. Usually the answers are single words or phrases like the words in the following table of values and principles.

3. *List Your Values and Principles.* Now go through the goals you've been holding in mind and ask the question: "What do I value about this goal?" Make yourself a list.

4. *Find Your Deepest Values.* When you've finished, you will have a list of deep values and/or principles. Now ask yourself, "What is important to me about *all* these values?" The answer that comes to mind will be a value that is even more important. Knowing your important, deep values is a crucial aspect of self-understanding. Realize how your values have been motivating you, your achievements, your every action.

5. *Record the Name of Your Deepest Value or Principle.* Write down these values and principles for future reference.

VALUES AND PRINCIPLES

aliveness	justice
autonomy	learning
beauty	love
caring	making the world a better place
challenge	mastery
courage	order
creativity	perseverance
dignity	playfulness
elegance	revolution
excellence	safety
excitement	security
fairness	self-reliance
freedom	service
fulfillment	simplicity
fun	solving problems
grace	stimulating change
happiness	synergy
harmony	truth
helping	uniqueness
honesty	using my abilities
humor	vitality
innovation	wisdom
joy	zest

There are three ways that people become aware of their deep values. The most common way of becoming aware of your values occurs when they are violated. When something happens that makes you uncomfortable, upset, or incongruent in any way, there is a value present in your experience. If someone is disrespectful and you feel angry, the anger you feel comes from your value of respect—how you want to be treated respectfully in a relationship. If you feel anxious about an upcoming event because you are unsure how well you are going to perform, then the value of excellence is at the root of your anxiety. Often the most painful traumas in life determine what we value the most.

The second way to understand your values is through events that fulfill them. If someone is extremely respectful to you—they help you at risk to themselves at a time of great need for you—it feels great. Those feelings are the value of respect, coming forth from within you. While you watch your favorite sport or artistic event and get inspired by an excellent performance, the feelings you feel are indications of your deep values, whether you call them excellence, mastery, beauty, or whatever. The feeling is much more important than the name of the feeling. These words are not *the actual* values any more than items on the menu at your favorite restaurant are the actual meals they represent. Values are sets of feelings that let you know what is important to you.

The third way to experience our deep values is through conscious inner exploration. Through meditating deeply, anyone can discover and feel their deepest values.

The next thing to do with your values and principles is to connect them to a grand vision of the wholeness of what you can make of your life. Let's go back to Ted Turner. After he reexamined his values and principles, he began his mission in earnest. His newly discovered values and principles led the way to the grand vision of his mission.

Why, for example, did he create the Goodwill Games, which lost eighty million dollars in 1986 and 1990? "I did it to get the two countries on the playing fields again. I could just tell the Soviets were looking to be our friends," he said.

When asked why he lives his life the way he does, he responded:

I just wanted to see if we could do it—like Christopher Columbus. When you do something that's never been done before, sail on uncharted waters and don't know where you're going, you're not sure what you're going to find when you get there but at least you're going somewhere. . . .

We have a responsibility, because television news is so powerful, not to make a lot of money but to have an influence in our communities. And our community . . . is not just the local market or even our country, but the world in which we live. . . .

Why don't we aim, during the next ten years to have peace on earth? And in the Year 2000, turn the time back to zero? And let it be B.P. and A.P.—Before Peace and After Peace. That could be the greatest honor we could bestow upon our generation. So if we do that, then people will *be* here two thousand years from now. . . .[16]

Typical of the mission of a great achiever, he has a huge, nearly unachievable dream as a motivating vision. And he wants it that way. He believes that people should set goals they can never reach. "I'm not going to rest until all the world's problems have been solved. Homelessness, AIDS. I'm in great shape. I mean, the problems will survive me—no question about it."

While his mission is a very large one, it *is* also unfolding. He has gathered the resources in order to help pull it off. He put on the Goodwill Games to create a sense of communication and camaraderie among millions of people watching television during the years between the Olympics. And he provides a worldwide communication network through cable television. Ted Turner's mission is motivated by a grand vision of possibilities. That's one of the things that gives him excitement in life.

No account of achievement in the world today is complete without a description of Buckminster Fuller. The inventor of the geodesic dome, the namesake of the remarkable, newly discovered family of molecules, buckminsterfullerenes (*buckyballs* for short), the creator of the Dymaxion map, the Dymaxion car, and numerous other innovations, he is known all over the world as one of the premier thinkers and visionary inventors of the twentieth century.

By 1968, the number of original published items relating to Fuller's work had grown to over 2,100 per year. How did Buckminster Fuller achieve so much in his life? It started with his mission, which he discovered on one lonely night. After the death from illness of his four-year-old daughter, Alexandra, his double expulsion from Harvard, losing his company, financial ruin, and the birth of a second child, he found himself in a suicidal depression. Buckminster Fuller stood at the edge of a dark future.

Literally gazing into the darkness of Lake Michigan on a lonely night in 1927, he had come to a crisis. "Why am I an utter failure?" he asked himself. Either he would jump or think, and he chose to think. He began forming his mission in life. After an intensive reasoning process, he concluded that he alone didn't have the right to determine his worth in the universe and that it was necessary to surrender his fate to the ultimate wisdom of God. In this riveting account, he explains his discovery:

> I have faith in the integrity of the anticipatory intellectual wisdom which we may call "God." . . . "Do I know best or does God know best whether I may be of any value to the integrity of the universe?" The answer was, "You don't know and no man knows, but the faith you have just established out of experience imposes recognition of the *a priori* wisdom of the fact of your being." Apparently addressing myself, I said, "You do not have the right to eliminate yourself, you do not belong to you. You belong to the universe. The significance of you will forever remain obscure to you, but you may assume that you are fulfilling your significance if you apply yourself to converting all your experience to the highest advantage of others. You and all men are here for the sake of other men."[17]

While living this mission, his professional identity grew. He called himself "a comprehensive anticipatory design-science explorer."[18] As you can see from this account, he went through the first three steps in this mission-discovery process. And he completed

Step 3—he developed a grand vision of his purpose in life and his identity as a person.

EXERCISE 10: DEVELOPING A GRAND VISION

You may want to do this exercise alone, out in a natural setting somewhere.

1. See Your Interests, Values, and Abilities. The next step is to discover how your interests and your deep values connect into and form your mission. It can be accomplished by seeing a grand, whole, meaningful image of what purpose you could dedicate your life to. This will be formed from your interests, values, and present goals. Begin to play with the images that you see, which represent some kind of direction that you want to take. As you get a sense of what your mission can be, see various snapshots of yourself doing what you love to do, snapshots of your abilities.

2. Focus on Heroes and Heroines. Take a look at what your favorite heroes or heroines do. See yourself doing things that give you the same feeling you get when you think of them. See snapshots of the person you want to become. Any images you don't like can fade away.

3. Direct a Movie of Yourself. See yourself the way you want to be—doing the things you love to do. Whatever you choose to put on the screen, you're the Spielberg, you're the director. See the images that you feel passionate about. You can play with the images in front of you. Pretend that you're in the middle of an inner, three-dimensional movie theater. It's a place where you can see and hear and feel with great fidelity.

Notice how much you can see, letting the wisdom from within guide the visual display that you see in front of you. Visualize it, feel it, enjoy it. The images are often up close and in full, rich color. See yourself living out a scenario that gives you tingles in your spine. You can zoom in on that glorious, fun-filled, exciting future that you see. It allows you to do what you love to do and accomplish what you believe in.

Continued

4. Recall Your Deep Values. List your deep values as you watch your mission scenario. Notice how your values and your images can fit together with a remarkable consistency.

5. Ask for Help from Your Inner Wisdom. Ask for your inner wisdom, the higher powers, or God to guide your grand vision. This vision is going to be more of a discovery than a creation. Let it come to you. Ask and it will come. Take the time to see and hear those aspects of life that unify into a whole that you feel a powerful passion for. See some more images. See some time going by. See various bright, radiant, up-close, colorful images of what it is that you could create in your life. They can begin going in a certain direction, coalescing and representing many of your current goals, some of the things that you want. See them develop into a kind of grand visionary collection of images that represents your purpose and your mission.

6. Do What It Takes. Take whatever time you need—five minutes, an hour, a whole afternoon. This is your life, your future that you are creating. When you finish, write it down. Your images are so attractive, you have some glimpses of what your mission is. Now you can develop it more fully. Ask the visionary in you to give you the gift of this grand vision.

Now that you can see your grand vision of what you want to contribute to, you can make that vision into a cause to work for—a specific direction to channel your efforts to. Astronaut Rusty Schweickart felt the importance of a relationship between a grand vision of wholeness and a specific direction. His experience of the view from space helped him discover his mission. Here's how he describes it:

> There are fundamental limitations in our institutions serving that purpose [the needs of the whole planet] because the institutions themselves serve best those things below them in scale and worst those things above them in scale. They operate out of and upon fear, unfortunately.
> The intellectual capability that you and I have on occasion is to understand that our survival is dependent on others around us

rather than just being self-centered. I think the intellectual leap on the part of institutions to that understanding is not there. Basically, institutions of that kind, whether governments or corporations or whatever, are somewhat limited intellectually . . . and the only way they are going to change is for individuals to express themselves individually or collectively.[19]

Schweickart gave his mission direction by promoting the vision of the whole-earth view from space through cofounding the Association of Space Explorers. This group published the book *The Home Planet* and is engaging in numerous innovative projects.

The emotionally inspiring experience of seeing a grand vision needs to be channeled into a specific direction. That's what Rusty Schweickart did. It is the difference between being an idle dreamer and being a person with a mission.

EXERCISE 11: FINDING A SPECIFIC DIRECTION FOR YOUR GRAND VISION

1. Make a Proposal. Propose to your own inner wisdom that specific images, or a short video of images, develop in your mind's eye. In your own inner theater, experience those images that represent a direction your mission could take. Enjoy it. Watch what happens. It comes from your inner wisdom.

2. Add Special Effects. Add your own kind of stereo, surround-sound, high-fidelity music. You can see a pop-up menu of different kinds of music to help you choose your music. There are certain kinds of favorite music that convey to you a sense of importance, and a sense of the profound implications of embarking upon this mission in your life.

3. Formulate a Sentence. You may hear it faintly at first. Then, turn up the volume. As you see this image or images, hear the music; as you look at it, formulate a sentence or two in words—a brief mission statement that describes your mission.

Steven Spielberg may have said that, as he looked at what he

Continued

wanted to do in his life, "I am a planetary storyteller. I will tell stories that help people grow." Pretend to be him and get the feeling.

Susan Butcher may have said, "I am a person who lives in the wilderness, lives with animals and helps them grow. And I achieve greatness in what I do." Pretend to be her for a few moments.

Ted Turner may have looked at a panorama of images before him, bright and interesting, and he may have said, "I am a peace-maker. I bridge people together to achieve peace." Pretend you are Ted Turner. What do you feel?

4. Include Values or a Principle. Formulate your own words describing your mission. As you look and see the images before you representing your overall mission and your sense of purpose, you can see yourself out there living that purpose with a verbal principle that guides you.

5. Feel the Feeling. Along with those images, and the music, and the principle, and the words, a very, very profound feeling may be welling up from within you. It is a sense of the importance of this mission to you. These feelings flow from within you and they guide you.

6. Step into the Mission Direction. Now, as you look at those images, this mission direction in front of you, take the next step: Step into that mission. Step into it right now and enjoy being in various stages of its unfolding. Live this glorious future—imagining, living, pretending that you're really there in the richness and fullness of that moment in the future as though it were now. Enjoy it.

By jumping into the future, into the unfolding mission, you can sense how wonderfully it expresses your purpose and your inner-most values. You can keep doing this. You're exercising your mind in a delightful way.

7. Persist. Keep cycling through this kind of a mental process until you see your specific direction within your grand vision of your mission. The feeling you get by stepping into this mission is a deep value and resources to help you fulfill this mission. Record the specific direction for your mission for the next year in your journal so that you can keep it handy.

All of the notable achievers listed in this chapter—Susan Butcher, Ted Turner, Buckminster Fuller, John Wooden, Rusty Schweickart, and Steven Spielberg—aligned themselves with their mission. Any inner objections to achieving their particular missions were negotiated into support. The next exercise is a method to specifically create internal congruence for the pursuit of your mission.

EXERCISE 12: ALIGNING YOURSELF WITH YOUR MISSION

1. Begin Questioning Yourself. As you ask the following series of questions, sometimes you will get feelings and answers that support your mission. Other times, some part of you may object, "Egads! Why do you want to change your life around and do a mission like that?" Every objection contains important information about how to carry out your mission, as long as you listen to it and respect it.

Here are some questions to ask yourself:

- How does this mission relate to my responsibilities in my present job? Think about those responsibilities and activities.
- How does this mission relate to my family? Contemplate the others in your family and circle of friends.
- How does this mission relate to me and all the other activities I do? Begin pondering the implications of this mission for you.
- How does this mission relate to my own community and my future; how does it relate to my state, my country, to the life I am living?

2. Negotiate with the Parts of Yourself That Object. Any part of you that objects to this mission is a part to listen to, respect, and respond to respectfully. When an objection comes up, listen and respond. How you deal with these kinds of objections is crucial for creating congruence and alignment for your mission. Negoti-

Continued

ate with any part of you that objects to your mission. Negotiate just as you would with anyone you care deeply for. The steps are:

  a. Listen to the objection.
  b. Find the positive intention and deep value.
  c. Create alternative ways to achieve that value.
  d. Make an agreement to an alternative that works for all of you.

With an objection like, "I am not sure what my spouse will think of this," you might ask: "What is the positive value you seek by that concern?" If the answer is, "I would like his or her full participation in the mission," then you would develop alternatives for achieving that, such as honest discussions or detailed negotiations. Then you and the "part" would agree on a course of action from among those alternatives.

3. Understand the Reality of Physical Death. Realize that there will be a time when this physical body will be no more. Before that time, you can make your mark. Remember Buckminster Fuller standing at the edge of Lake Michigan. Create that intensity of desire to do what you are here to do in this life. The awareness of death can help you live a life that has incredible purpose.

4. Finding Reasons for Support. As you see your mission unfolding before you and hear the principle stated, ask yourself, "How is it good for me?" "How does it represent who I am, who I care about, and what is meaningful?" These questions can be your teachers and your guides. They can help you to reexamine and solidify and strengthen the sense of living this mission. Think about another question: "How does passionately living this unfolding mission provide a way for me to live the good life?"

While completing this set of questions, you'll know you have alignment with your mission by an increasing feeling for your mission—a feeling that says: "Yes, this mission is mine."

5. Persist. Keep cycling through these questions until you get that feeling. It comes from agreement with *all* the parts of you who would be affected by any change as major as a new or revised mission in life.

The basic method of self-alignment outlined here—asking for and welcoming internal objections, and respectfully negotiating a solution that will be satisfying to all parts of yourself—is one that can be extremely useful, as long as it is carried out with sincerity, respect, and humility. It is often a process that has no single satisfactory conclusion. Rather, it's one that you can usefully engage in over and over again.

Make sure you create full alignment of all parts of yourself with your mission. The natural consequence of such a unified commitment is bold, enthusiastic, and often outrageously effective action. And this inner commitment also creates an energy that makes others want to align with you and help you.

In order to nurture your commitment to the mission that you're on, and the specific actions that will lead to its unfolding, say your mission statement from Exercise 11 to yourself: "My mission in life reflects who I am. It defines how I use my inner abilities. And it guides how I act in the world." You may make up other statements to further your commitment to your mission.

In aligning your many inner parts to create a unified commitment, you set the stage for action. During the transition into your new mission, it is important to get support from those you care about. Make sure you preserve your relationships with them. Who knows, maybe some of them will want to help you with your mission. Because we are connected to so many other people, a commitment is not truly unified until we can get the support of others. It is important to align others with your mission as well.

When Buckminster Fuller rejected the basic premise of earning a living to pursue his mission, he knew this was not his decision alone. He had a wife and a baby daughter. He needed his wife's commitment, so he went back to his wife and told her of "his resolve to dedicate himself to serving humanity without regard to making a living,"[20] and she agreed.

Steven Spielberg got early support from his family for his moviemaking, and he sought out help from others. He developed such a unified commitment to making movies that he committed bold, outrageous acts in pursuit of his mission.

At age seventeen he took a tour of Universal Studios. There he met Chuck Silvers, head of the editorial department. Spielberg says, "Instead of calling the guards to throw me off the lot, he talked with me for about an hour. . . . He said he'd like to see some of my little films, and so he gave me a pass to get on the lot the next day. I showed him about four of my 8-mm films. He was very impressed."[21]

A few days after taking the tour of Universal Studios, he got his dad's briefcase and simply walked into the studio. He didn't ask permission. He didn't wait until he graduated from college and got an invitation. He just walked in. He said:

> There was nothing in it (the briefcase) but a sandwich and two candy bars. So every day that summer I went in my suit and hung out with directors and writers and editors and dubbers. I found an office that wasn't being used, and became a squatter. I went to a camera store, bought some plastic name titles and put my name in the building directory: Steven Spielberg, Room 23C.[22]

Enlisting Support for Your Mission

To enlist support for your mission, you might make a list of the key people in your life who would be affected by your new mission. Make an appointment with each of them specifically to discuss the implications of your mission on them and on your relationship. When talking to the important people in your life, describe your mission and the process you went through to discover it. Tell this person how important your relationship is with him/her. Convey that you want to do your mission and you want to preserve the good parts of the relationship with them. Ask them for support for your life's new direction. Find out about any synergies between your mission and that person's plans and goals.

Now you have set the stage for action. Not only will you get to enjoy pursuing your mission, you get something else, the satisfaction of helping others. There is something incredibly fulfilling in creating a legacy for others—both while you live and after you are gone.

A Mission: Creating for Others

Michelangelo, the famous Italian Renaissance artist, is a good example of someone whose mission left a legacy for millions. Michelangelo was commissioned by the pope to create the paintings on the ceiling of the Sistine Chapel, one of the greatest works of art. He was already well established in his mission of being a great artist and someone who would enrich people's lives through art. The Sistine Chapel, which is inside the Vatican's papal palace in Rome, is part of a building that was constructed hundreds of years ago. It will live on into the future.

Michelangelo saw himself primarily as a sculptor. His mission to create great art unfolded early. As an eighteen-year-old, he took the better part of a year dissecting corpses to learn the underlying structure of the human form. The following poem he wrote captures the essence of his mission:

THE ARTIST AND HIS WORK

How can that be, lady, which all men learn
by long experience? Shapes that seem alive,
wrought in hard mountain marble, will survive
their maker, whom the years to dust return!

Thus to effect cause yields. Art hath her turn,
and triumphs over Nature. I, who strive
with Sculpture, know this well; her wonders live
in spite of time and death, those tyrants stern.

So I can give long life to both of us
in either way, by color or by stone,
making the semblance of thy face and mine.[23]

Most of the examples of achievers in this chapter have been world-famous people. It is important to realize that you don't have to be world-famous to live a great mission.

The Story of a Magnificent Mission

Mary Jane Sheppard died on December 18, 1992. She was not world-famous, nor did she invent any paradigm-shifting technology or build any business organizations. And yet, she lived a magnificent mission. The mission Mary Jane Sheppard lived was as important as any lived by those more famous—raising a healthy, loving family. As wife of husband Harry Sheppard and mother to their four children in San Mateo, California, she was the light of love to their growing family and friends.

Yet Mary Jane's family was not limited to their immediate children and grandchildren. She made it a habit to "adopt" her children's friends and others she encountered. She radiated loving feelings. Her warmth and interest in others attracted friends like a magnet. While her husband Harry referred to her as a saint, her son Charlie describes her as a great mentor for helping him find compassion in his life.

In the kitchen they still openly display a series of cords hanging along one wall. On the cords are hundreds of painted clothespins. Each pin lists a person who stayed the night there, along with the date. Mary Jane's extended family became a community of people she brought together.

Jim Conlow, a member of Mary Jane's community, wrote a poem about her. It's called "The Maker." A section of it describes her this way:

A Maker is the greatest of Sorcerors or Saints
Life of love magic and connection
Making baked bread and gardens
Making children and children's children
Weaving the tapestry of compassion

Early in her life she followed all the steps of the mission-discovery process. She knew her primary passions—connecting emotionally with people. She discovered her deep values—love and compassion. She merged these passions and values into a grand vision of living a magnificent life of service to others. And she picked a richly detailed, specific direction or "cause" for her efforts—her community of friends and family. She deeply examined herself to align completely with her mission. Whatever internal obstacles to living her mission were set aside, jumped over, or, best of all, converted to resources. She developed a unified commitment, both within herself and with others that guided her every day. And her legacy, in the form of her village of friends and family, unfolded before her.

As cancer ended her life at age sixty-eight, through all of the pain, her love for others shone through and graced all of those who honored her presence in their lives. In the final moments of her life, she told her son Charlie, "I've done everything I came here to do." This is perhaps the ultimate reward for discovering your mission.

How do we know when we are living our mission in life? No one outside of us can tell us. It is something each one of us can only discover and know for ourselves.

Reviewing What You've Learned

Write your personal mission down before going on to the next chapter. You may change it at any time, and you probably will. It is important to summarize the results of using the process in this chapter so that you can make full use of the next chapter. Be sure to include reference to your life's passions and interests, your deepest values and principles, a grand vision, and a specific direction/action. Most important, make it fit into the essential paradox of a mission: something you can never finish, but that you can do every day.

A summary of the steps you need to reach your mission is:

- Finding Your Life's Passion
- Reexamining Your Deepest Values and Principles
- Developing a Grand Vision
- Finding a Specific Direction

• Aligning Yourself with Your Mission
• Getting Support from Others

Now it is time to set specific goals to achieve your mission and reevaluate your current goals in relation to it. Do you want to be the bricklayer who is just building a wall, who is just laying down a brick and putting some cement on it? Or do you want to be building a monument to what humanity can achieve? Goals without a mission lack passion and deep meaning. However, goals inside a mission turn visionary dreams to reality, energizing everything you do with meaning, enthusiasm, and fun.

CHAPTER FIVE

Achieving Your Goals

Whatever you can do or dream you can, begin it.
Boldness has genius, power, and magic in it.

—Goethe

Two Approaches to Achieving Goals

There are really two different ways to set and achieve goals. The traditional approach to achievement emphasizes outer-to-inner methods of goal setting. The message is: "If you achieve *x* great thing out in the world, then you will be a successful person and feel good." Goals set taking this approach are often not connected with what you really enjoy doing every day. And if they are not fun, they are better left undone, for they are not likely to lead to great achievement. Let's examine the four major pitfalls of this traditional approach to goal achievement.

Pitfall 1—The Vacation Life

People setting nonmission types of goals often pick some sort of vacationlike existence: "I want to retire within five years and live on a sailboat." "I want to relax by the lake and sleep every day until noon."

These kinds of goals only point to the painful, incongruent day-to-day life the person feels a need to escape. If pain creates a quest for nonaction, recognize that some rest and relaxation will help your actual mission come into focus. When the pain is healed, the quest of a mission actually leads us to challenges. Coach John Wooden said it this way: "There's no great fun, satisfaction or joy derived from doing something that's easy."[1]

Pitfall 2—Seduction by Status-Based Advertising

Many people initially pick goals for themselves that are canned, status-conscious images: "I'm going to have a house with ten thousand square feet that will be my castle, a luxury Mercedes, and a sailboat." These things can be very enjoyable. You might want to examine whose desires they are before you dedicate years of your life to achieving them. After all, your housekeeper and sailboat captain will enjoy your things even if you don't.

Recall Archie Bunker yelling at Edith to get him a beer when he saw a beer ad on TV. This was an automatic knee-jerk response to the ad, totally unconnected to his real goals in life. Likewise, these days many of our goal images come from advertising. After doing some inner searching, do you find that your images of the good life come from a class system that encourages "keeping up with the Joneses?" If so, you might enjoy exploring the nature of advertising in the American class system. Two good books on it are Paul Fussell's *Class* and Daniel Boorstin's *The Image*.

If you realize that media-induced consumption values are usually much shallower than the deeper values that support your mission, you can avoid the pitfall of seduction by status-based advertising.

Pitfall 3—If/Then Financial Goals

"*If* I can just save up enough money doing this job I don't like, *then* I'll be able to do what I really love." People who pursue money as an end in itself usually lack a mission supported by deep values. People in the last moments of life rarely lament not making enough money. They are usually concerned about deeper values than money, power, status, or fame.

We earn a living by the money we make, but we make a life by the service we provide. For money to serve your mission, a definition of money is needed. Here's a good one: "Money is something we choose to trade our life energy for."[2] Because we trade our life energy for money, it is an important and necessary aspect of anyone's mission. Money is to a mission what air is to your body— it is not an end in itself but a necessary means to achieve something important. Figuring out how to make as much money as possible is like sitting around hyperventilating—you'll probably get dizzy and your perceptions of reality will get cloudy, especially if you succeed.

The other problem with treating money as an end in itself is doing something you don't love. Besides the daily lack of congruence, with if/then financial goals, often the ultimate financial rewards come much later than people would like to think.

This is not to suggest that making lots of money in pursuit of your mission is bad. Many achievers of greatness use one part of their lives to generate money and another part to help a cause. Ewing Kauffman was a great example of a person with that kind of mission. As founder of Marion Merrell Dow, the pharmaceutical company, he accumulated over a billion dollars in personal wealth. He used nearly all of this money to fund a foundation, to help improve society, and to give the Kansas City area the Kansas City Royals professional baseball team.

Through his company and his foundation, Ewing Kauffman fulfilled his mission of having fun by helping others. For example, The Ewing Marion Kauffman Foundation funds college educations for hundreds of young people in the Kansas City area. He said: "You create a life by what you give. I'm having fun spending my money to help people now, while I'm alive."[3] Making a lot of money was never his primary goal. He wanted to improve society, and his legacy lives on in the form of the largest active foundation in the U.S.

Pitfall 4—Means Versus Ends

Let's suppose a salesperson sets a goal to make a certain sales quota by a certain time. What means to achieve this goal will the salesperson use? If this goal becomes that person's whole mission, disconnected from his or her deepest values, he or she may feel the need to use pressure tactics rather than honesty and integrity when dealing with a customer. That salesperson might be prompted to make false or doubtful statements about his or her product. If they are not true, the salesperson has fallen into the means-versus-ends pitfall.

While these kinds of tactics can help make sales quotas in the short run, the reputation of both the salesperson and the company will suffer. Most of all, without knowing it initially, the salesperson will suffer. When someone sets a goal that is not contained within the wholeness of a mission, pursuing such a goal by any means can create problems of self-deception. The salesperson will separate farther and farther from what is important, as heartfelt values are denied and discarded. "Our capacity for self-deception knows no bounds,"[4] says Thomas J. Savage, S.J., president of Rockhurst College in Kansas City. In contrast with that, when we act with the ethics defined by our deepest values, our goals fit within a well-thought-out mission, and we attract success, well-being, and others.

Mission-Oriented Goals Are Worth Achieving

So what goals are really worth achieving? Those goals that are what we call *mission-oriented* goals. If you have completed the previous chapter's exercises, your mission and the direction that represents its achievement have emerged from your deepest values. Furthermore, let's assume you have avoided the four pitfalls of traditional goal setting—that you know the meaningful, fun, and passionate direction your life is taking, *your mission*. It's time to focus on meaningful action goals actually worth achieving. Great missions are always lived by achieving specific goals.

Mission-oriented goals are attained by actions you take in the various roles your mission defines. What you do to fulfill the mission emerges from inside and shows up naturally in your mission.

Each role you play provides an identity for expressing your interests and passions, visions, values, and principles. In this way, mission-oriented goals are the reverse of the traditional outer-to-inner approach—they emerge from within.

The most difficult thing to do for great achievers is anything *but* what they love. World-class musher Susan Butcher describes it this way: "I wanted to move to a place where I could live in the wilderness and work with animals. And so, it's just a matter of, if you want to do something, you do it."[5]

A Mission Creates Meaningful Action

Great achievers, people whose lives are marked by significant achievements through a labor of love, can be models for us. We can learn, too, if we emulate those who know how. Recall, from Chapter Three, Steven Spielberg's mission to become a moviemaker. In his specific role as a movie director, he had to improve his skills at directing through collaborating with editors. If you'll remember, when he was just seventeen years old, he simply walked into Universal Studios and, without asking, occupied an empty room and put his name on the door. He started showing editors his 8-mm movies and got their input to help him improve his directing skills. Now that's bold action for goal achievement!

Because he had discovered his mission, this boldness-in-action pursuit of his specific goal emerged naturally from his already-established mental identity as a moviemaker. And the pursuit of these specific goals, backed by the deep, emotional, mission-based commitment to make great movies, sustained his efforts through time.

When deciding on a goal, it is essential to make sure that the goal you achieve is worth achieving. It needs to be a mission-based goal—that is, it's a necessary action in a role defined by your mission. What does a mission-based goal feel like? Here is an exercise to help bring out that feeling.

EXERCISE 13: UTILIZING YOUR FAVORITE HERO/HEROINE

1. Think of a Hero or Heroine. Choose a man or woman whom you greatly admire. Pick someone who excites and inspires you when you recall that person's accomplishments. Some choose a great person from history like Winston Churchill, Gandhi, Martin Luther King, Susan B. Anthony, or Eleanor Roosevelt. Others choose great religious leaders like Jesus, Moses, or Mohammed. You might want to choose someone you know personally, such as a family member, coworker, or friend. You can even choose from fiction or legend—Robin Hood or Wonder Woman. Let your feelings of inspiration guide you.

2. See a Particular Goal. Choose a goal that your hero achieved through living their mission. It might be Andrew Carnegie creating an industry and then endowing the public libraries of America. It might be Gandhi giving a speech, or participating in a protest. It might be Eleanor Roosevelt negotiating in a meeting to secure the passage of the Universal Declaration of Human Rights. It might be Maria Montessori paying full attention to a child. It might be Bill Gates, creating MS/DOS. Whatever you see, see a specific set of actions that represents the living of that person's mission—a goal. Make a short thirty-second movie of that goal. See the image close up in full, vibrant colors, and run the movie in your mind. Make it meaningful and inspiring. Then, run it back to the beginning and put it on pause.

3. Step into the Role. Become that hero/heroine in this particular role in this movie. Become aware of your values, purposes, principles, and your mission as this hero/heroine. Release the pause button of your mental VCR and run the movie, with you playing the role of the hero/heroine. Complete this scene from the inside. Get in touch with the feelings you have while pursuing this set of actions.

4. Question Yourself. Staying in this role, ask yourself these questions:

What are my motives?

Why did I do this action to achieve the end result—the goal?
How does this goal fit into my larger mission?
How does pursuing this goal *feel*?

5. Become Yourself Again. Reflect on what resources becoming your hero/heroine brings out in you for achieving *your* goals within your mission. The main lesson of this exercise is to bring out what your mission-based goals will feel like when you are pursuing them.

Using the Hero/Heroine Exercise While Reading

Many great achievers read plenty of biographies of their favorite achievers. Ewing Kauffman had read the biographies of all the U.S. presidents and major industrialists by the time he was twelve years old. He went on to live a fantastic life mission as a salesman, entrepreneur, pharmaceutical executive, community activist, baseball team owner, son, father, husband, and philanthropist.

You, too, can do the previous exercise while reading biographies. Using it routinely can help you bring out *your* inner resources for effectively functioning in *your* life roles. From the outside, it would look like you were simply reading about and pondering it. From the inside, this powerful technique makes a big difference in how you feel about your own roles. If you do this consistently, it will reenergize your capabilities to achieve greatness, helping you achieve your mission-oriented goals.

Why Roles Are Important

We've been talking a lot about roles. Why are they important? The more you learn about how to create your own roles, the more you can live the life you choose. Role identities are a key aspect of our belief system. They are structured in lots of different ways. With every new mission in life, you take on new role identities. Your mission determines your roles, and your roles determine your goals.

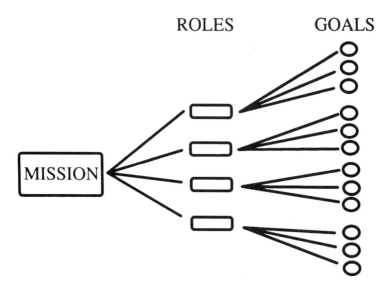

For example, a person may read a lot. However, if that person does not have an identity as a writer, he or she is not likely to learn how to write by reading. A person who strongly believes "I am a writer" reads in a very different way from someone who does not share that identity. A person with a writer role identity notices different things than a nonwriter. A writer reads not only to get the information, a writer reads to learn how to refine the skills of his or her own writing.

If a man's mission is to be the best auto mechanic he can be while expressing artistry in his craft, and love and kindness to family, friends, and his customers, his mission will require multiple roles. In this case the roles might be accountant, artist, brother, computer programmer, father, husband, investigator, problem solver, service provider, son, uncle, and worker. Each role has its own set of specific goals. And the way you think about each role makes a difference in how you live that role.

Roles for the Goal Achievement Process

Let's consider some of the roles in your complex life. In this chapter, we've organized life roles into four primary types: individual roles, work roles, personal and family roles, and citizen roles. While some of these roles overlap and there are many other ways to categorize them, what's important is that you determine the roles that matter the most for your mission.

Your Individual Roles

Your individual roles create the foundation for all of your other roles. There are many individual roles.[6] Here is a partial list with a few classic real life examples:

Individual Roles	Classic Examples
ARTIST	Picasso, Michelangelo
ATHLETE	Michael Jordan, Martina Navratilova
CREATOR	Thomas Jefferson, Amory Lovins
DISCOVERER	Nicolaus Copernicus, Isaac Newton
FOOL	Steve Martin, King Lear's fool
FRIEND TO SELF	Hugh Prather
HERO/HEROINE	Martin Luther King, Susan B. Anthony
HUNTER	Tom Brown, Jr.
LEADER	Mahatma Gandhi, Winston Churchill
LEARNER	Albert Einstein
MAGICIAN	Merlin
MEDITATOR	Pope John Paul II
SAGE	Jesus
SAINT	Mother Teresa
WARRIOR	Gen. Norman Schwarzkopf

Your mission will require many different roles. The list above refers to a few classic examples to make the idea of roles clearer in your mind. Bear in mind that the individuals used as examples also lived (or are still living) many other roles in their missions in life, just like you. Roles can be real, and they can be used metaphorically. For example, if you take on the role of the sage as part of your mission, that doesn't mean that you think you are Jesus or that you have to renounce all worldly activity and pray all day. Rather, the sage role can be used as a basic identity within yourself. You can say, ''I am a sage. As a sage, how can I live this role demonstrating love, compassion, and wisdom today?'' Taking on this identity as a sage may mean envisioning yourself thinking deeply before acting or reading spiritual texts on a regular basis. These actions and others become your goals for your individual role as a sage. Remember the basic NLP Presupposition that **if one person can do something, anyone can learn to do it.** In other words, as you believe, so you become.

To make these individual roles come to life for you and your mission, it is important to choose which ones pertain to your particular mission. If you are not yet sure what your mission is, go back to Chapter Three and use the processes described there to discover your mission. Remember: Discovering your mission is finding the purpose of your life. There is nothing more worth your time.

Let's start with the most basic individual role—being a great friend to yourself. Every person needs this role. What we mean by this role is how you communicate in this friendship with yourself. Your physical health, your emotional health, your spiritual well-being, all depend upon healthy, positive communication with yourself. Do you treat yourself as well as you do your best friend? Do you talk with yourself in a friendly, loving, and curious manner in the mirror on a regular basis? If your answers to these questions are not affirmative, you may want to consider becoming more of a friend to yourself.

Not only can we communicate with the image in the mirror, we can do more. Many people don't realize that they can communicate directly with the powerful and wise aspects of their mind. The emotional result of this kind of communication is a warm, loving, caring feeling about yourself. We'll elaborate more on this in Chapter Nine. The communication with your many different inner parts is an interesting and fascinating process. You have a part that wants security. You have a part that wants quality relationships. You have lots of different parts that represent different needs, wants, and priorities. Your relationship with yourself can improve through effective internal communication. Some people seem to love and understand themselves well. Others nag, criticize, and argue internally. If you do the second, think about choosing to make a difference in this area.

When you take this role through the Goal-Achievement Process, many possibilities will arise about performing effectively as a great friend to yourself. You will establish what values of your own relationship with yourself would be the most desirable, including changes you would like to make. Values such as respect, trust, love, inner harmony, inner cooperation, and total concentration are within your grasp. So it is with all of the other individual roles vital to your mission.

Now you can go through a selection process to choose the roles you will use for achieving your goals, using the next exercise.

EXERCISE 14: DISCOVERING THE INDIVIDUAL ROLES FOR YOUR MISSION

1. Look over the list of individual roles and ask the question: "Will being a great _____ be essential in living my mission?"

2. On a separate piece of paper, list roles you consider essential for the fulfillment of your mission.

3. If you have roles that you consider important to your life that are not really part of your mission as you have written it, then change your mission statement to *include* these roles in an important way. Include these roles on your list.

Your Work Roles: Service to Customers

Work roles are changing dramatically, and it's long overdue. Work is becoming more oriented to self-development than ever before. As you look at your career, your work life, and your financial resources, you may desire certain kinds of changes. Notice some of the images and words that develop in your mind; and realize their importance. Consider what career and financial achievements will further the unfolding of your special mission. And like Ewing Kauffman, recognize the fun that comes from giving.

Our professional, productive work roles normally require as much time, effort, and learning as any of our other roles in life. Often they require more. Having imagined how exciting certain changes in your work life could be, browse down the list of work's many roles below.

Work Roles

ARTIST	MOVER AND SHAKER
ASSOCIATE	PAWN
COACH	SERVICE PROVIDER
COLLEAGUE	STUDENT
COWORKER	SUBORDINATE
CUSTOMER	SUPERVISOR
DOCTOR	TEACHER
DRONE	VISIONARY
ENTREPRENEUR	WAGE SLAVE
LAWYER	WORKER
LEADER	WRITER

Think about *your* current work roles. If you are a lawyer, you could choose from a variety of possible roles including: hired gun, defender of the weak, mediator, educator, defender of justice, or accumulator of money. Every occupation is an opportunity for a wide variety of roles. What are *your* current work roles? Are you a wage slave, mover and shaker, leader, follower, hired hand, counselor, facilitator, machine operator, cash-cow milker, or entrepreneur?

List your current work roles on a piece of paper. Do you like them? Are they consistent with your mission? Remember that while working in a given job, you may have many different role identities to fulfill your mission.

If your current work roles fit into your mission, you may still want to refine and develop the actions that fulfill these roles. If you don't really like some of your current work roles, then change them—mentally at first. Imagine your work roles as your mission unfolds. Whether you can assume these work roles in your current organization or in a new one, create your desired role identities for your mission.

EXERCISE 15: DISCOVERING THE WORK ROLES FOR YOUR MISSION

1. Look over the list of work roles and ask the question: "Will being a great _____ be essential in living my mission?"

2. On a separate piece of paper, list the roles you consider essential for the fulfillment of your mission.

3. If you have work roles that you consider important to your life that are not part of your mission as you have written it, then change your mission statement to include these roles in an important way. Include these roles on your list.

Your Personal and Family Roles

What place is there for great family and personal relationships in your mission? Relationships with people create the richness of any life that is lived. Many high achievers look back on their lives and realize that their career efforts seriously interfered with intimacy in their personal relationships. Recognizing this, former IBM chairman Thomas J. Watson, Jr. said that an executive who doesn't have plenty of time for personal relationships is a bad executive.

Think about relationships with the important people in your family now and to come, your spouse and children, parents, brothers, and sisters. Who are the important people in your life? One way to determine this is the kidney test. If your life depended on a donated kidney, who would give you one of theirs?

AUNT	MOTHER-IN-LAW
BROTHER	NEPHEW
BROTHER-IN-LAW	NIECE
COUSIN	SISTER
DAUGHTER	SON
FATHER	STEPFATHER
FATHER-IN-LAW	STEPMOTHER
FRIEND	UNCLE
MOTHER	

Pick a role that is important, perhaps one that is performed less well than you would like. Think about how you want that relationship to be. How would you know you had a great relationship—one consistent with your mission, and with who that other person is?

EXERCISE 16: DISCOVERING THE PERSONAL AND FAMILY ROLES FOR YOUR MISSION

1. Look over the list of personal and family roles and ask the question: "Will being a great _____ be essential in living my mission?"

2. On a separate piece of paper, list the roles you consider essential for the fulfillment of your mission.

3. If you have personal and family roles that are important to your life that are not really part of your mission as you have written it, then change your mission statement to include these roles in an important way. Includes these roles on your list.

Citizen Roles: Relationships with the Larger Community and Nature

Take a look at the larger context of your life and work, the community, city, or nation in which you live. You may even consider the planet as a whole. There may be a community issue, improvement, or change that you would like to make in your role as a citizen. Do your favorite heroes and heroines live citizen roles? Does *your* mission include citizen roles?

People need to take responsibility as individuals to make the world work better. For some, this happens through their work roles and their roles as parents. Certainly the mother and father roles can be thought of as citizen roles. Others assume citizen roles in addition to their work and family roles. Still others make their work roles citizen roles. Dr. Martin Luther King blended his role as a minister with his citizen role as a social activist. In this role, he brought nonviolent action as a means to challenge the injustice of racism and segregation in the 1950s and 1960s. We all need some way to feel a connection between what happens outside of ourselves and what happens to us individually. Visionary cultural historian Morris Berman has described the need for this in a delightful way:

> The flesh of my body is also the flesh of the earth. . . . To know your own flesh, to know both the pain and joy it contains, is to come to know something much larger than this. . . . Something obvious keeps eluding our civilization, something that involves a reciprocal relationship between nature and psyche, and that we are going to have to grasp if we are to survive as a species.[7]

If you like the outdoors, if you are a nature-loving person, you might assume roles relating to the environment. Perhaps you want your city to have cleaner air, a mass-transit system, bicycle paths, and better traffic flow. You can even pick a large, very long-term issue such as the relationship between your species and the rest of the planet. That type of scope and grandeur is often part of many people's mission—remember, you can make a difference in the world. Individuals and small groups of people have always been the source of improvement in the world. As the great anthropologist Margaret Mead put it: "Never doubt that a small group of committed people can change the world, indeed it's the only thing that ever has.'' And changing the world starts with changing our own community. That happens person by person, business by business, family by family, issue by issue, goal by goal.

Here are a few examples to help you select the citizen roles you will use in the Goal-Achievement Process.

Citizen Roles

ADVOCATE   NATURE LOVER
BEAUTIFIER   NEIGHBOR
COACH   OFFICEHOLDER
CHANGE AGENT   ORGANIZER
COMMUNITY ACTIVIST   PHILANTHROPIST
COUNCIL MEMBER   REVOLUTIONARY
CRIME FIGHTER   VOLUNTEER
ELDER   VOTER
LETTER WRITER

**EXERCISE 17: DISCOVERING THE CITIZEN ROLES
FOR YOUR MISSION**

1. Look over the list of citizen roles and ask the question: ''Will being a great _____ be essential in living my mission?''

2. On a separate piece of paper, list the roles you consider essential for the fulfillment of your mission.

3. If you have citizen roles that you consider important to your life that are not really part of your mission as you have written it, then change your mission statement to include these roles in an important way. Include these roles on your list.

Listing Your Roles for Living Your Mission

Here is a summary list of roles people take on to fulfill their missions. As you look over the list, make note of those that are essential for your mission. Add any roles that are missing from your list.

R O L E S   S U M M A R Y

Individual Roles	*Personal/Family Roles*
ARTIST	AUNT
ATHLETE	BROTHER
CREATOR	BROTHER-IN-LAW
DISCOVERER	COUSIN
FOOL	DAUGHTER
FRIEND TO SELF	FATHER
HERO/HEROINE	FATHER-IN-LAW
HUNTER	FRIEND
LEADER	MOTHER
LEARNER	MOTHER-IN-LAW
MAGICIAN	NEPHEW
MEDITATOR	NIECE
SAGE	SISTER
SAINT	SON
WARRIOR	STEPFATHER
	STEPMOTHER
Work Roles	UNCLE
ARTIST	
ASSOCIATE	*Citizen Roles*
COACH	
COLLEAGUE	ADVOCATE
COWORKER	BEAUTIFIER
CUSTOMER	CHANGE AGENT
DOCTOR	COACH
DRONE	COMMUNITY ACTIVIST
ENTREPRENEUR	COUNCIL MEMBER
LAWYER	CRIME FIGHTER
LEADER	ELDER
MOVER AND SHAKER	LETTER WRITER
PAWN	NATURE LOVER
SERVICE PROVIDER	NEIGHBOR
STUDENT	OFFICEHOLDER
SUBORDINATE	ORGANIZER
SUPERVISOR	PHILANTHROPIST
TEACHER	REVOLUTIONARY
VISIONARY	VOLUNTEER
WAGE SLAVE	VOTER
WORKER	
WRITER	

Roles and Values

Each role in your life is a realm for achieving particular goals. These goals are the actions in the world that make a difference. They are the way you manifest your values. The unfolding of your mission depends upon achieving the goals in each of these many roles in your life.

Consider the roles that your mission defines, such as brother, sister, doctor, worker, revolutionary, intellectual, friend, learner, etc. For each role, you can ask the following question: "What is the evidence that I am a great _____?" Of course, your answer to this question will reflect your values. It is important to realize that your mission, to be fulfilled each day, needs to emerge from your deepest values. In Exercise 10, you made a list of your deepest values. Use it with the Sample Role Assessment Chart to be sure your roles are congruent with your values.

Once you know your constellation of values and have names for them to help you bring them to mind, you can use them as a set of standards for evaluating your performance in each of your roles.

Assessing Your Effectiveness in Your Life Roles

Let's say that you have ten main roles for your mission. They are father, brother, uncle, friend, coworker, supervisor, revolutionary, creator, friend to self, and local activist. Furthermore, let's assume that your four deepest values are fulfillment, fun, love, and courage. The chart below provides a way to examine how well your roles actually reflect your values. Use this chart to rate your roles according to how you demonstrate your values in each one, using an A–F grading system. Here is an example:

Sample Role Assessment Chart

DEEPEST VALUES

	Fulfillment	Fun	Love	Courage
BROTHER	B	B	A	B
COWORKER	C	C	C	C
CREATOR	B	B	B	C
FATHER	A	C	A	A
FRIEND	B	C	B	D
FRIEND TO SELF	D	D	D	C
LOCAL ACTIVIST	A	A	A	A
REVOLUTIONARY	A	B	C	B
SUPERVISOR	C	C	C	A
UNCLE	B	B	A	B

How to Use the Chart

The chart is really a way of organizing a set of assessment questions. The question is, "How well do I demonstrate the value _____ in my role as _____?" Starting in the upper left, the questions can be asked this way: "How well do I demonstrate fulfillment in my role as a brother?" As you look at the Sample Role Assessment Chart, you can see patterns where the activities of a role do not live up to the values. The most deficient role in this sample chart is "friend to self." When this person asks, "How well do I demonstrate fulfillment, fun, love, and courage in my role as a friend to myself?" the answer is not too well. Copy the blank chart below for doing your own role assessment.

When you can give yourself an A grade in a given role, then you focus on other roles. If you get A's on all of your roles, then add more values or more roles. The idea here is to develop a never-ending process of improvement. Any such quest will have peaks and plateaus. Your mastery of each role in your mission will contribute to an ever-improving mission, and when you choose well, to a fun, challenging, and meaningful life.

Your Role Assessment Chart

Values

Roles

Focus Your Efforts on a Specific Goal

In order to live your mission, it's important to pick specific goals. When you go to a new restaurant, you usually look at the menu with interest. You look at each item and think about it, imagine it, taste it. You can use this idea of going through a menu for the main roles in your life. And then you can choose from a particular area of your life, a particular role, and take that role through the four steps of the Goal Achievement Process. It would be like browsing through a menu of delicious entrées and, after browsing, choosing a particular role in your life for goal development.

Now take the time to pick one role, the role where you have the strongest feelings of wanting to create changes, or wanting to achieve new goals. If the Sample Role Assessment Chart were yours, the obvious choice would be "friend to self," because this role does not demonstrate your values well. Choose one role in your life at a time in which you can work on your particular goals. Each time you read this chapter, you can choose a different role needed for fulfilling your mission. The reason for this is the said: "Nothing ever happens in general, everything always happens specifically." This process will help you become specific and detailed in pursuit of examining your life and making changes in how you live it—changes that represent the fulfillment of your unique mission.

Because you have a developing passion for your mission, it's time to act. As you see your mission more clearly, the roles you will live become more obvious and natural. By using the following Goal Achievement Process, your roles will take on new life. The roles you have been living will improve extraordinarily, and your new roles will blossom each day. Now take that role you want to improve and go through the process. Roles are not just areas for goal setting—collectively your roles and how you live them are *who you are* in your life.

The Goal Achievement Process

Knowing what you want is fundamental to NLP. Just as important is being sure that what you want is really worth having, so that you will be satisfied when you actually achieve it. You will find it very useful to go through the series of questions below to assist yourself in developing your goals so that they are worth having, and so that they will fit with the person you want to become. These are known in NLP as the Well-Formed Goal Conditions.

Selecting a Specific Goal

First, what do you want? Pick one goal or desire from all of the work you have done in this chapter. If you immediately think of several goals, are they alike in some way? For example, if you want to get your projects done on time, finish some task, and begin exercising, these all relate to being motivated. If you think of several goals that aren't alike, pick one of them to begin.

NLP has discovered that the way you think about your goal makes a big difference. You can think of the same goal in a way that makes it easy to achieve, or in a way that makes it almost impossible. The next questions will make sure you are thinking of your goal in ways that will make achieving it easier.

Make sure your goal is stated in terms of what you *do* want, not what you don't want. For example, if your goal is "I want my coworkers to quit whining," or "I want to stop feeling bad when my proposals aren't accepted," or "I don't want to talk so fast during my presentations," you are thinking of what you don't want. You can easily turn this into what you do want instead. "I want my coworkers to take responsibility for their own tasks." "I want to accept feedback as an opportunity to improve my proposals and my communication skills." "I want to be aware of my voice as I speak and have the flexibility to adjust it, when I want."

When people think about what they don't want, or what they want to avoid, they often produce that in their lives, because that is where their minds are focused. These are additional examples of the effects of phrasing things in negative language. Changing your language from what you don't want to do to what you do want is a simple shift that can make a tremendous difference.

Make sure your goal is stated in a way that you can get it yourself, no matter what other people do. If your goals require other people to make changes, even if those changes would be a good idea, it places you in a more vulnerable and helpless position. It means you won't be able to get what you want unless you can get other people to change. While we all want things from and for other people, it's important that we formulate our goals in a way that we'll be able to reach them, no matter what other people do.

This may sound impossible or self-centered at first, so let's go through several examples. It can make a tremendous difference when we experience our own abilities and strengths. Say your goal is: "I want my boss to quit criticizing me." Since this requires your boss to change, it is not something that is within your control. This goal puts you in a vulnerable position, dependent on your boss changing.

If you reformulate it as: "What can I do, or experience, that will allow me to remain resourceful, no matter what my boss thinks?" this puts you in charge of your goal. This gives you a sense of your own worth and ability to act even when your boss criticizes you. Perhaps you want to feel confident when you're criticized, and to be able to sort out what parts of the criticism you agree with and what parts you disagree with. This puts you in a much more powerful position, because you can get what you want, and stay confident and resourceful, even if your boss continues in his criticism.

Let's take another example. Say your difficulty is: "My best employee has quit and I want her back." Since you don't ultimately have any control over whether she will come back or not, you can ask yourself, "What would having her back do for me?" Perhaps your working relationship was the best you've ever had. Maybe she was efficient and let you know when your instructions were unclear. Maybe you felt comfortable delegating to her, which allowed you to feel satisfaction with what was accomplished.

Now you have a list of the goals that are under your control. You can find other ways to bring efficiency into your life and improve your communication skills. You can find other ways of feeling comfortable and learning to delegate to other efficient people. You can do all of these things whether that employee comes back or not.

Now, do this same kind of reformulation with your goal, if necessary. Make sure it's truly stated in the positive and that it is something you can do something about.

Knowing the Evidence for Your Goal Fulfillment

How will you know when you have achieved your goal? Some people have no way of knowing whether they have reached their goals or not. That's because they have no way to measure whether their day-to-day behavior is taking them closer or farther away from their goals. They never get to feel the satisfaction of achieving something. For example, one of your goals might be to be more successful. If you don't have sensory specific evidence—what you'll see, hear, and feel—for what "successful" means to you, you may work at being successful all your life and even achieve a great deal, without ever feeling "successful." You can define success as getting someone to smile, getting a certain job, achieving a particular salary, or anything else specific, but if you don't define it, you won't get it. Recall the goal you selected in the previous section. Does the evidence for that goal relate closely to the goal? Make sure your evidence provides you with good, realistic feedback about whether you are reaching your goal or not. Say your goal is to be an effective manager, and your evidence for your effectiveness is that you feel good at the end of the day. Feeling good at the end of the day is wonderful, but doesn't necessarily have anything to do with being an effective manager. Better evidence would be that you observed your employees doing better at a variety of tasks than they did when they started.

Say your goal is to be an effective supervisor, and you feel that you are a good supervisor when your workers tell you that you are doing a good job. Again, this is far from the best evidence. If you want your workers to tell you, ''You're great,'' you are likely to be too lenient and miss opportunities for improving their performance. Again, better evidence would be to watch and listen for increased productivity, job performance, and job satisfaction.

Another typical difficulty with formulating goal evidence is to place it too far in the future. Too many would-be executives make their happiness and satisfaction contingent on having the right house, the right spouse, and the right salary. These are wonderful, but are they really so important you have to hold off happiness until they arrive? Most people find it much more motivating to have some rewards along the way. This can take the form of smaller-step goals and by making the evidence for a goal's fulfillment a bit easier to come by. After all, if you have to complete the report, to make the proposal, to close the deal, to gain the new account, to break your old record, to qualify for the raise, you might as well reward yourself for completing the report. There will be a lot more reports than raises, and the better you feel about them, the more of them you'll do and the sooner the raise will appear.

Now, check your own goal for how soon you get to be happy about its completion and make any adjustments so that it's motivating for you. Consider the possibility of taking a smaller-step goal on the way to your larger achievements.

Selecting Where, When, and with Whom You Want to Achieve Your Goal

It's very important to think about when you do and when you don't want your goal. For example, if your goal is "to feel confident," do you want to feel confident all the time? Do you want to feel confident about flying an airplane when you've had no flight training or walking a tightrope a hundred feet above the ground? People often want a certain feeling all the time when they don't believe they can have it at all. Feeling confident when you have the skills and training makes that confidence solid and appropriate. Then you can explore the countless other feeling possibilities in life, including: curiosity, desire, competitiveness, compassion, sensitivity, trust, tenacity, love, and so many more.

It's so much easier for you to achieve a goal when you are careful about where, when, and with whom it's appropriate. If you want a goal to spread across the fabric of your life, consider where in your life it would make the most difference and begin there. What will you see, hear, or feel that will let you know it's time to achieve your goal? For example, "When I see *x* opportunity, I want to feel motivated."

Now place your goal in your life where, when, and with whom you want it to happen so it really does.

Checking the Ecology of Your Goal

Sometimes in our rush to attain our goals, we can lose track of the rest of our lives. This could be summarized in the phrase "whatever it takes." Those who have done "whatever it takes" have a different story to tell. Their past is often a trail of broken marriages, failed friendships, and estranged children. When success finally comes to them, they find they have little ability to enjoy it because their lives have been so singularly dedicated to work. The mission exercises in Chapter Three were designed to give you a much wider view of your life and your place in the world so you can enjoy the journey and the reward. Now it's time to consider the others in your life as well. How will the achievement of your goals affect them. Consider both the positive and the negative. Will it take time away from other things? Will it change how you relate to coworkers, colleagues, friends, or family? Discover the difficulties that are produced by the fulfillment of your dreams, not to dissuade you from them, but to allow you, in advance, to prepare for them. How can you enrich, refine, or adjust your goal so that what might have been a negative consequence becomes a positive opportunity. Very often, it's as simple as including others in your success. Most everyone wants to belong, especially with success. Make these goal adjustments now so that when you get there, you'll be glad you did.

There are four exercises that will take you through the Goal Achievement Process. The first one, Exercise 18, concerns the goals you will make the rest of your life.

EXERCISE 18: CREATING A COMPELLING FUTURE

1. Set the Stage. Think of where you'll be tomorrow—picture it. Notice what it looks like, notice the colors, picture it in full detail. This image of the future occurs in a particular location in your inner theater.

Notice the inner three-dimensional theater that you've set up—it has sounds and images. You can even put yourself over there on the stage.

2. See Yourself in the Future in Your Chosen Role. Now, in this inner, mental theater, see yourself vividly in the future, achieving this goal. It's like the future is *right over there*—close, bright, and colorful, too. Over across a gap or line of time, you see yourself achieving that particular goal. Watch and listen to all the details as you see it unfolding in a very pleasant way.

3. Make Your Goal Well Formed. As you see yourself performing in that role in an extraordinary way, go through this checklist of six goal conditions to make sure your goal is well formed.

  · The goal you see is positive—it is what to *do,* not what to avoid doing.

- You *want* to do the goal. It's a "want," not a "should."
- *You* are the one doing it, not someone else.
- You *can* do it—it's not impossible.
- The goal is *specific,* not general.
- The goal is *ecological:* You can anticipate the effects of the goal and make sure they are positive for those affected by its achievement.

4. Make Your Image Compelling. Now use various kinds of visual special effects in your imagery as you look at yourself having achieved that goal over there in the future. You may use X-ray vision in order to see the inner workings of your mind and body. You may use certain colors, in order to illustrate emotional states you're enjoying there. You can use multiple screens to see different things happening, and different situations or different times that relate to that specific goal. See the goal in bright vividness, and notice its three dimensions. As you make the achievement of your goal big and close, vibrant and compelling, also sense your body and your feelings. Take your time and enjoy this vision—this masterpiece that you are creating, directing, and becoming.

5. Notice the Pathway. Pay attention to what is achieved and how attractive it is—drawing you to it. Now notice that there is a pathway from the present moment to that particular future. It's a kind of pathway through time.

Now you can see, hear, and feel this compelling future—your goal for a given role. This attractive goal fits into your mission. And there is a pathway to it.

Knowing when you are going to perform well in a particular role is not enough. You need a way to get there, and you need to know how to walk that path. The development of a realistic, doable plan is the major difference between idle dreamers and visionary achievers. You can take the step to be a visionary achiever by using the next exercise.

EXERCISE 19: DEVELOPING A PLAN

1. Visit Your Goal. Return to the time when you have just achieved your goal in that particular role in your life. Be in that future, and enjoy your achievement. Notice your feelings as you look around. Listen to your own thoughts, too. Because the goal is achieved, you're celebrating. Sense the date and time. Realize how much you enjoy having reached this stage of your mission. Taste the sweetness of having reached this goal.

2. See the Future. Now turn and look farther into your future from this point of having achieved the goal. Look and see how your mission continues to unfold out into your future.

3. See the Past. Now turn around and look into your past. Notice the pathway that got you here. See in your past that ''earlier you'' reading this material back there, back then. See that person and notice the path from back there to where you are now.

4. Walk Back Along the Side of the Pathway. Now examine the way you achieved your goal. Stay alongside the pathway and begin walking back in time, looking at the pathway. Your wise and unconscious mind can show you parts of what you did along the way—you can see and hear what led up to the achievement of the goal. Maybe certain people helped. Certain particular learnings and realizations took place. Watch, hear, and enjoy what actions made it possible to achieve this goal. There are certain steps and actions that you carried out. Maybe a few show up very clearly. Maybe you can see almost all of them. If some of it is fuzzy, then you may need more information.

5. Notice Specific Steps on the Pathway. As you look at the pathway, you'll notice many specific steps. Ask yourself, ''How did I bring about my abilities and act in the world to get to the place of this goal's full achievement?''

See and hear the resources, the abilities, the actions, and the contacts with people, all those different elements that led, step-by-step, toward your goal. Take your time. Delight in seeing what you did to achieve your goal. Notice what happened after that one action. See the many actions, the new resources, the new abilities, as they happen. As you see those steps, see how it is part of your unfolding mission. Having walked alongside that pathway, and having observed the many specific actions and abilities that-got you there, make note of the sequence of events and the time it might take to do those steps.

6. Go Back to the Present. Return to the present moment in time with a new appreciation for the steps on the path to your goal.

7. Appreciate the Goal. As you look ahead to your goal, pay attention to how wonderfully attractive that goal is. If you want to take more time to make that goal even more compelling and attractive, then go ahead.

The first time you do this process, there may be gaps. Usually a gap shows where you need to gather more information from some outside source—books, friends, consultants—to enable you to accomplish that particular step. If so, go through it again. The important thing is that these sequences become your automatic mental-software programs through repetition. These first two exercises need to be like a NASA project-management software program in your brain. They can be performed every morning or any other time you want to use them.

By traveling back along the pathway to achieving that goal, your wise and unconscious mind has revealed important aspects of how you will achieve your goal. To further refine your understanding of the sequence of steps along your pathway to achieve your goal for that role, it is important to walk *forward* on the path to mentally rehearse these activities in the sequence in which you will perform them.

EXERCISE 20: RAPID REHEARSAL

1. Assume the Role. Say, "In my role as a great _____, I want to fulfill my deepest values in action." Look out in time at your goal for this role, see the goal.

2. Walk the Path. See the path you'll take to make your goal happen. Walk ahead in time at a rate of speed just fast enough to rapidly rehearse the sequence of events on your path.

3. "Beam" Yourself Back. When you reach your goal, notice when it's completed. Then return to your current time.

At this point, you have created your compelling future for an essential role, you have traveled in time to visit that goal, you've seen the path you need to get there, and you've rehearsed that plan forward. The imagination is an amazing power! Now it's time to act—to "make it so," as Captain Jean-Luc Picard of *Star Trek* says. Action needs to spring from that imagination of yours. If you are to be a visionary achiever rather than an idle dreamer, there is one more step to take.

EXERCISE 21: TAKING ACTION

1. Assign a Realistic Completion Date. Browse through your calendar and write down an estimated celebration date on which the goal will be achieved.

2. Schedule Your Steps. Find some really great times in your schedule to do each of the action steps on your pathway that leads to your goal. Write down the times in your calendar.

3. Keep an Eye on Your Mission. Notice now that your mission is always in the background of your mind's eye. It has a strong and compelling feeling of purpose that energizes you, drawing you forward. Enjoy holding this vision of your role and your goal and how you are going to achieve them. You can appreciate your vision from many points of view. You can see it from the present and the future, and the steps you're taking. You can go to the future and look back and see how you got there. And you can also move alongside that pathway and see what you did from an observer's point of view.

4. Do It. Now, when that moment arrives on your calendar, do each step you've planned, knowing that you are on your pathway to your sparkling future while at the same time enjoying a fulfilling and fun present. It's time to act, with the full commitment of the resources of the most intelligent, resourceful creature in the known universe—a human being: YOU.

Reviewing What You've Learned

The difference between just having a dream and being a disciplined achiever is this: Not all dreamers achieve, but all achievers are dreamers. They energize their dreams with *action*. Happiness comes to those who dream dreams and *do* precisely what it takes to make their dreams come true. Some important concepts we've explored and experienced in this chapter include:

Mission—discovering the purpose for your life
Roles—the multiple identities you assume to fulfill your mission
Values—what is important to you, and shown by your emotional reaction to how you perform your role
Goals—the specific results you want in order to live your roles in an extraordinary way, consistent with your mission and your values

Remember that using the steps of the Goal Achievement Process helps you fulfill your mission:

- Designing a Well-Formed Goal
- Creating a Compelling Future
- Developing a Plan
- Rapid Rehearsal
- Taking Action

As you use these procedures over and over again, your mission and the particular goals necessary to achieve it will develop at a highly accelerated rate.

As who you are unfolds in this set of role identities, your deep feelings of purpose will intensify. Internally, you can hear the sounds and know the principles that guide you on this mission. You can feel those inner signals of purpose and importance, your deep values, as they well up inside of you.

When your goals are illuminated by the greater purpose of your life's mission, they take on special meaning; you have energy for them because they are *both* fun and important. Mission-based goals come from who you are. They are not a list of things to do. They emerge naturally as you pursue your values and your mission. Like your heroes and heroines, you feel a special feeling of congruence when actively pursuing the milestones on your mission, the landmarks on your journey through life.

CHAPTER SIX

Creating Rapport and Strong Relationships

The Importance of Good Relationships

Most successful professionals intuitively know the importance that other people play in their lives and careers. It would be no exaggeration to say that people are the most valuable resource that we ever have. Since relationships are so central and since the most successful professionals in any field build strong and lasting relationships, it is important to know how they accomplish this.

Many self-development training programs attempt to address this issue by describing successful individuals. Some of the better ones go so far as to tell you what to do. Anyone who has tried to learn a new physical activity—a sport, for example—knows the problem with this. It is one thing to know *what* to do; it is quite another to know *how* to do it. Others tell you what *not* to do. If you've tried to hit a golf ball, someone might have instructed you to avoid pushing with your following hand. That's what not to do. Everyone who has ever played golf can probably tell you that. What to *do* is more useful: "Lead with the forward hand." However, very few people can tell you *how* to actually do that seemingly simple instruction. If you want to fully integrate any set of skills into your life, you need to know both *what* to do and *how* to do it. You are about to learn some of the specifics, the "how tos" that can make you the most successful person you can be.

Research has demonstrated that 83 percent of all sales are based upon the customer liking the salesperson. Studies show that people are more apt to stay in jobs where they feel liked and appreciated than in work where they might be paid more. Famous achievers like Lee Iacocca and Mary Kay know the importance of relationships. Iacocca is often described as open and immediate. He makes personal contact, and he is liked and trusted. People feel good being around him. Mary Kay's tremendous success is directly attributable to her primary business concern—people. Ask her about management and you'll hear about her people. She says: "Treat others the way you want to be treated—on and off the job. Listen closely to others' concerns and show that you value them." NLP research has shown that many high achievers develop liking and appreciation very rapidly. They naturally make people feel comfortable around them and demonstrate a concern for others' values. Those who are marginally successful or unsuccessful typically lack these abilities.

Many approaches to sales and management communication training recognize the importance of rapport. They often suggest that the way to establish rapport is matching the clothes or the life experience of the other person. So, if the other person likes baseball, you try to like baseball, too. This approach will work some of the time. But some people can build strong relationships even where there isn't any mutual interest such as baseball.

We use the word *relationships* instead of rapport for a reason. Rapport is only one important aspect of every relationship. Because establishing and maintaining rapport is so valuable, you need to learn several ways for you to do that successfully. Right now it's popular to teach techniques for rapport—in fact "instant rapport" is the promise of some. However, most relationships last considerably longer than that. Unless you plan to manage or sell to new and different people all the time, unless your business doesn't want and value referrals, then you need to consider what happens in your relationships over time. Successful people have the ability to develop relationships that last.

How to Build Relationships

As a business professional it's useful to ask the question: "What business am I in?" Some people think that if they sell things, they are in the business of selling. They aren't. They *are* in the business of building relationships—because that's how you sell things. Those in management are also in the business of building relationships, because that's how you get things done.

The most successful corporations (as well as the individuals in them) know the importance of making this distinction. McDonald's sells fast food. However, their business is developing relationships through the value of their product and the entertainment value of eating at their restaurants. IBM sells computers, but their domination of the market for decades was due to the quality of their service relationships with customers. In business management, many popular and useful books focus on customer relationships. As this new focus has created success for organizations, successful individuals have learned the value of relationships in whatever they do.

There are three steps in what the most successful professionals do to build relationships:

1. Determine mutually satisfying goals.
2. Establish and maintain nonverbal rapport.
3. Produce positive feelings in others.

Step 1: Determining Mutually Satisfying Goals

The first step in building successful relationships of any kind: your goal for the relationship. What kind of relationship do you want? Too often, people have no idea what they want in a relationship, which leaves it vulnerable to vital misunderstandings and missed opportunities.

Think of your first job interview. You were probably totally concerned about the job. You thought that the only goal of that meeting was to get the job. Your primary goal in that meeting was actually to get the interviewer to like you . . . or at the very least for him or her to identify how you would be an asset for that company. By achieving that goal, you would have had a much better chance of getting the job.

One successful commercial real estate developer understands this principle well. Whenever she meets with someone for the first time to determine if they might work together on a project, she has a very definite goal in mind. She goes into the meeting planning to build rapport to help the person have a positive experience of her and so agree to another meeting.

Building relationships that contribute to your success means becoming aware of your goals for the various relationships in your life. You may already have highly developed goals for your life. When you think of those goals, do you include the people necessary to achieve them? It's great to have certain sales goals in your mind, for example. However, when you think about these goals, if you see only the products or services you will sell, you are leaving out something much more important. When some people think of their goals, they are right in front of them in their mind's eye while the people whose help they need to accomplish their goals are much farther away, as if they didn't matter very much. That's not useful.

If masters of relationships like Lee Iacocca or Mary Kay consciously understood their own thinking, they would tell you their secret. They would tell you to make people closer and more vivid in your mind's eye, because your relationships with the people in your world make achieving your goals possible.

Harvey Mackay, author of the best-selling book *Swim with the Sharks Without Being Eaten Alive* and successful leader of a large corporation, knows the value of relationships with customers. He became legendary in the field of sales for his commitment to building relationships with potential buyers of his company's office products. He trains all of his salespeople to find out about their customers in detail. They are instructed to learn about sixty-six aspects of their customers' personal and professional lives: such things as where they vacation, what they do for fun, what matters to them personally, what they value in good relations with outside salespeople, etc. They are trained to send cards, thank-you notes, and information that might interest or educate them. Mackay knows that not all of

EXERCISE 22: MAKING PEOPLE PART OF YOUR GOALS

1. Choose a Goal. Pick some specific goal that you want to achieve. You can pick one that you are already familiar with or take the time to think of a new one. In either case, remember to use the Goal Achievement Process that you learned about in Chapter Four.

2. Identify the Goal Image. Notice how you represent this goal in your mind's eye. What pictures are you becoming aware of as you think of this goal? What sounds do you hear and what do you say to yourself as you think about this goal? What feelings do you have when you think of this goal?

3. Decide on the People Involved. Now think of the people who will play a necessary part in achieving this goal. Have you included them as part of the pictures and sounds and feelings in your mind? If they are not included in your representation of the goal, put them there. With whom do you want and need relationships to achieve this goal? Make sure that you have appropriate images and voices of these people in your representation, illustrating the part that they will play in helping you achieve your goal.

4. Define How the People Relate to the Goal. Now notice the relationship between these people and the goal. Are the people in the foreground of your image, or are they in the background? Are the people in color or black and white? What is their size compared to what's around them? You probably want the people to be clearly and vividly in the foreground as part of your goal, because it is through your relationship to these people that you and they will be able to achieve your respective goals. Make adjustments in the way you represent your goal so that your relationship to the people is obviously indispensable in order for you to succeed with your goal.

5. Future Planning. Think of a time in the future when you will be actually working on this particular goal. As you rehearse that situation, intentionally think of the goal the way you just created it, emphasizing the importance of the people and your relationships with them.

his people will do all of this with every prospect. However, by gathering lots of data, his sales force has more opportunities to build significant relationships. Harvey Mackay made his business a success by knowing that relationships make you successful.

Set Goals That Involve Others

Once you've learned an effective way to achieve goals, you might become overly focused on *your* goals. We all know how it feels to help someone else get *their* goal at *our* expense, and we know it doesn't feel good. But on the contrary, our research found a very selfish reason to consider the other person's goals—it makes *you* more successful.

Successful large organizations apply the Golden Rule to their customers. The highly respected Strategic Planning Institute has created a data base called PIMS, which documents the profit impact of market strategy from over three thousand business units in all sectors of the economy. This is a tremendous source of data for business managers, and is referred to by Peters and Waterman in their books on excellent business practices. The PIMS data tells us that those companies rated in the top third in perceived product quality (which means they think of their customers' goals as their own) average a return on investment of 30 percent, compared to those companies rated in the lowest third, which had a 5 percent return! The moral of the story is that in business and in relationships, success goes to those who think of their customers' goals as if they were their own.

A huge amount of data shows the importance of long-term thinking in business. The salesperson who thinks only of the next sale will be much less successful in the long run than the one who looks into his or her future, thinking not about this one sale, but of the type of relationships that will naturally lead to many other sales, referrals, and additional business in the future.

When goals involve other people, you must consider the other person's point of view. We've all learned the Golden Rule (and not the version heard in a recent sales meeting: ''He who has the most gold makes the rules''), and hope that we will use it when we think about our goals for relationships. ''Is what *I* want as good for the *other* person as it is for me?'' If it isn't, then you need to change your goal to include what will be beneficial to the other person. Individuals who do not consider the interests of their friends, associates, clients, or customers are less successful than those who do. Think of when and where this will be useful. In what specific contexts do you want the goal? A very successful residential real estate salesman knew what he wanted for his customers and himself. Of course, he wanted them to be happy with their purchases; but he also wanted them to think of him when they happily showed their friends their new homes, in case their friends were also interested in buying or selling a home. He was very deliberate in his communication with his clients to let them know that he wanted referrals. One thing he did was take photographs of his clients with large smiles on their faces, standing in front of their new homes, as he handed them the keys. He sent them a couple of large, framed copies of these photographs, which often sat on their desks in their homes for years to come.

EXERCISE 23: SETTING RELATIONSHIP GOALS

1. Define Your Relationship. First, think of a specific person with whom you already have a relationship, or pick one you are just getting to know. What do you want in your relationship with this person? Continue to focus on this person, because your goals with other people may be quite different from your goals with yourself.

2. Use the Goal Achievement Process. Next, run this goal through the Goal Achievement Process you learned at the end of Chapter Four. Notice how this sequence repeats the important elements that you already learned. If you want specific success, you need to meet the five conditions below for a well-formed goal.

3. Determine Your Conditions.

A. Wants. What do you want for this relationship? What is its goal? Think about what you want in positive terms. Remember to make your goal a *do* want, rather than a *don't* want: ''I want a

Continued

source of referrals" or "I want a special friend" (not "I don't want to have to cold call," or "I don't want to be alone").

B. Actions. What can you do to make this goal happen? If what you want in a relationship is something that you can't control, then you can easily become very frustrated. For example, in a conflict, since you can't control the other person, there's no point hoping that he or she will behave in a way that you like better. Instead, a useful goal might be for you to stay resourceful and calm so that you can ask good questions, hoping to find out what the other person really wants. This is something you can control.

C. Evidence. What evidence will let you know when you have reached this goal? What will you see, hear, and feel that will let you know that you are achieving your goal? Be as specific and realistic as possible.

D. Context. Think of when and where this will be useful. In what specific contexts do you want the goal?

E. Consequences. If you successfully achieve this goal in this relationship, what effect or impact will it create for you? Of at least equal importance, what impact will it create for the other person? As you consider the effects of getting your goal for this relationship, what do you expect the impact to be immediately? What results will you continue to want in six months or a year? What about even longer than that? Make any adjustments that may be necessary.

Now let's consider a simple and effective way for you to develop relationships that can make you even more successful.

Whenever you think about any relationship that could be important to you, answer these questions. First: What do I want in this relationship that is positive? Second: What can I do to make this happen? Third: What will I see or hear or feel that will let me know that I have achieved this goal? Fourth: When, where, with whom, in what context do I want this goal? Fifth: What is the expected impact of getting this goal, both for me and for the other people involved— short-term, long-term, and even longer?

Whenever you think about relationships, create goals that meet these five conditions. Then, as the relationship develops, remember to keep these goals in the forefront of your mind to help you and the other person get what both of you want.

Step 2: Establishing and Maintaining Nonverbal Rapport

Try a brief experiment to demonstrate the importance of rapport for yourself. Think of a communication situation in your life where you were unsuccessful at getting what you wanted with another person—whether it was characterized by conflict or just frustration. Now think of another communication situation where you did get what you wanted—both you and the other person were satisfied with the result of the interaction. Now compare the two for the presence or absence of rapport. When people make this comparison repeatedly, they find that their communication successes are characterized by rapport and their failures by a lack of rapport. Rapport is a fundamental prerequisite for all effective communication. If you don't have rapport, you simply will not be effective with other people.

Rapport is a natural human ability. We naturally build rapport in a variety of ways. When a couple has been together for a long time they often are described as being a lot alike, and they actually begin to look alike. When you observe someone who has a mentor, he or she may adopt the mentor's brand of clothing and use the same phrases and tone of voice. Business people dress to belong to their corporate culture. Fitting in is a powerful human need. We all have many examples of these behaviors, because we do them already. They all are based on some form of being similar, familiar, or alike. Finding ways to be alike reduces our differences, and so we find the common ground upon which to base a relationship.

You have been in rapport without thinking about it hundreds of times every day. And yet there were also times when you were out of rapport. It's important to be able to recognize when you have rapport and when you don't. If you don't notice when you're out of rapport, you won't be able to do anything about it.

How do you know the difference? To find out, try this experiment the next time you get a chance. Pick a situation with a friend or associate where you already have rapport and the situation is casual, there isn't something really important going on—you are just visiting, for example. After you are both talking and the conversation is moving along smoothly and you're naturally in rapport, try the following. Sit in a posture that is very different from that of the person you are with. You could also try moving in different ways, or speaking at a very different rate or volume. Notice how this changes the interaction. It will probably become choppy. Your friend may even ask you what's wrong. Notice what happens to your feelings. That uncomfortable feeling is a signal that you are not in rapport. The word *uncomfortable* is the word a lot of people use to describe how they know when they're out of rapport. Just take the time to note what you experience when you don't have rapport. In the future, you can use that feeling as a signal to let you know when you need to do something to get rapport. That feeling can be your "loss-of-rapport detection alarm." The goal is to train yourself to recognize when the alarm goes off, and then do something to regain rapport. Assuming that you successfully broke rapport with your friend during the experiment, please take the time to rebuild it quickly with one of the techniques that follow.

There are two different ways to think about rapport. The first way is to intentionally build rapport whenever you begin an interaction with someone and you want to communicate successfully. The second approach is to assume you have rapport with someone and make sure that you have your loss-of-rapport detection alarm turned up to a high level of sensitivity so that you'll notice if rapport is lost. It can be helpful to use both approaches, especially as you first become adept at rapport skills.

Whichever approach you fully master first, be aware of the value of the loss-of-rapport alarm. For example, in the sale of an expensive item, like a home, the relationship between the salesperson and the buyer often lasts for many weeks or even months. Although the relationship may start with high levels of rapport, it is common for rapport to be lost before the closing, particularly when unexpected difficulties come up. When this happens, it is crucial for the salesperson to be able to detect that rapport is lost and know how to rebuild it quickly. If you don't, the customer often goes someplace else. While an example from sales is so obvious, the same concern is just as true in any business or personal relationship. As anyone who has been married for a while recognizes, that relationship started with—and, of course, hopefully still has—lots of rapport. Most of the time we all prefer the comfortable, smooth flow of communication that is based on rapport. Even in the best relationship, however, there are times when rapport is lost and must be regained. Use rapport skills to get back that common ground for a relationship—that foundation for you to do good business or to have a good marriage or to be good friends.

How to Achieve Rapport

When you don't have rapport with someone, you are acting differently than they are. The way to regain rapport is to become more similar. The most effective communication professionals gain rapport by matching nonverbal behavior, sometimes called matching, mirroring, or pacing.[1] For example, if you are in someone else's office and they have you sitting directly opposite them, you can still build rapport. One way to help both of you feel more comfortable is to match the other person's posture. As you sit with the person, notice how he or she is sitting and slowly begin to adjust your body to match his or her posture. Notice the angle of this person's spine—is it very upright? Slightly leaning to one side or to the front? Notice if the person's head is tilted to one side or very upright. If you suddenly sit just like the other person, you might be thought to be mimicking him or her, and that will break rapport. The goal is to slowly and unobtrusively approximate the posture. This is not a new technique. You have undoubtedly noticed that when things are going along really well in some interaction with a friend, that you are likely to sit or stand just like one another.

Matching occurs naturally when two people already are in rapport. However, matching can also be used consciously to establish and increase rapport. You can match literally *any* behavior you can observe. Posture, facial expression, rate of breathing, voice tone, tempo, and pitch—all are powerful ways to match someone else. By taking these steps to match the other person you will more nearly enter their world, because all these nonverbal behaviors are expressions of their state of mind. Matching isn't a gimmick to control others; it is a specific way for you to adjust your own behavior in order to get "in sync" with that person. It will help you feel and understand what it is like to be them at this moment, and that will not only gain rapport, it will facilitate all your communication. Doing things deliberately for rapport helps you back to the relationship that you would have naturally if people weren't distressed, preoccupied by thinking about something else, or simply not paying attention.

Matching Voice Tone and Rhythm

Sometimes you are not able to match postures and facial expressions with someone. Certainly, if you are on the phone, you can't do either of these. Whether in person or on the phone, one of the most powerful ways to establish rapport is to match the tone, tempo, and rhythm of the other person's voice. As you respond to the other person, simply use the same tone of voice and the same speed or tempo. When you do, you will be matching the pitch and cadence of the other person's thoughts. If you have ever been really excited about something and you were rolling along the tracks of your thoughts at about ninety miles an hour and the other person hadn't even gotten to the train, you know that you didn't have much in common with that person at that time.

One of the easiest ways to remember to build rapport is to notice some aspect of the other person's rhythm. Notice if their language is generally pretty fast and continuous or slow and continuous. Some people pause more often and then speak again. Others go on and on, without even seeming to pause to take a breath. As you notice a pattern, you can adjust your own speech to approximate the other's pattern. When someone says, "This technique doesn't work," nine times out of ten it is because they did not actually change their own speech pattern to match the other person's—they just *thought* they did. It's important to take the time to really notice the subtleties of speech and practice matching them.

A very dramatic example of the effect of speech tempo occurred in a national telephone company in Denver, Colorado. A customer service employee, Mary, had to transfer service for a new phone customer from his old location, New Orleans, to his new location in Denver. In the process of the transfer, Mary called another employee, Jane, to discuss the records being transferred. While Mary and Jane had never talked before and therefore did not know each other, as they talked on the phone, it was apparent that they were getting along cordially and getting the job done. It was also apparent to anyone listening to both sides of the conversation that they were speaking in a very similar tone of voice at about the same rate of speech, which was moderately fast.

A few moments after talking to Jane, Mary placed another call to New Orleans to get service records transferred. Lucille, in New Orleans, spoke in a considerably slower tempo with lower and softer tones than Mary, who was still speaking rapidly, with a higher tone. While Mary and Lucille didn't know each other either, and were not discussing anything except business, there was obvious tension between them within a few minutes after the conversation began. The frustration between them was apparent in their voice quality, and the conversation ended with both people clearly upset. The only possible cause was a large difference in voice tempo and tone.

Another example of the impact of matching voices involved the Bell System when it consisted of regional operating companies. One regional company had the lowest rating for customer satisfaction. People in that region normally spoke in a high-pitched, nasal monotone. After a consultant taught them the power of voice matching, they trained all the operators in this company to match their tempo and tone to the customer. Within nine months of the training, this regional company had improved its rating in customer satisfaction from lowest to second best. The only major difference was the voice training.

Although we want you to be sensitive to the nonverbal signals that indicate loss of rapport, you can also ask the other person to report how they felt during the different steps of this exercise. Usually they will be able to tell you when the conversation flowed easily and when it didn't—without knowing exactly why.

EXERCISE 24: DEVELOPING VOICE MATCHING

1. Choose an Unimportant Situation. Pick a context where there is nothing at stake, like a casual meeting with an associate or a stranger in a public place. As an alternative, you could get a friend to do this exercise with you by sitting back to back. The effect of this exercise is most obvious if the other person does not initially know what you are going to do.

2. Try Matching. As you talk to the other person, notice the tempo and tone of his or her voice. As you talk to him, subtly adjust your voice until the tone and tempo of your voice are as close to the other person's as possible. Notice the quality of the communication: Is the flow of information smooth or difficult? Is there a feeling of rapport or not?

3. Try Mismatching. After a few minutes of smooth, flowing conversation, alter your voice to be very different from the other person's in terms of tone and tempo. Notice what impact this change has on the quality of the communication.

4. Now Go Back to Matching. Change back to matching the other person's voice quality and notice how you are able to regain the rapport that enables a smooth flow of communication.

You can also match another person's rhythm of movement. Like speech, a person's physical movements have a pattern. Some people move a lot, others little. Some move with large and smooth gestures and some with small and abrupt ones. By subtly adjusting your movement rhythms to approximate the person you're interacting with, you will greatly enhance the basis for your growing relationship. You can use an exercise similar to the one above to become adept at matching the rhythm of someone else's movement patterns.

As you practice these skills, you will develop your ability to build rapport quickly, in the moment, and to regain it quickly and easily when you lose it. The next step is to think about keeping rapport through time. Creating consistent feelings of rapport is what makes the difference between ''instant'' rapport and the highest quality relationships.

Learning to Align Yourself Physically

One of the things that people do when they are in rapport is to align themselves with the other person. A simple experiment will demonstrate this to you. When you are in a group of people that begins to gather, notice what happens in the first few minutes as people are beginning or regaining relationships with each other. You will notice that as people get into rapport with each other, they naturally align with each other's posture and movement. Alignment can occur on several levels, as when two people share common interests, they become closer. If, for example, you are casually talking to someone on a plane and discover that they are from your hometown, you may have enough in common to keep you talking at least part of your flight.

A more powerful way in which people align with others is with their physical use of space. When you are sitting with someone in your living room and want to show them a photo album or a book, you usually sit next to them. This position naturally leads to a sense of togetherness and sharing. When some business people meet at a table with a colleague, they consistently sit opposite them. Others sit at the side of the table nearest the other person. You'll notice how verbal expressions reflect the impact of these different choices.

Would you rather "square off" with someone? We all know what happened in the Old West when you did that! Or would you rather "share space"? By aligning your body so that you are literally pointed in a similar direction, you are more likely to see things the same way, get in tune with each other, and feel in sync. Whether you sit or stand in alignment, it's as if you share the same space, and are headed in the same direction. You and the person you are talking with will naturally make hand gestures toward this common space. If you are in agreement and sharing common interests, it's easy to feel aligned. When you have conflict or are in the process of building common interests, your physical alignment can help accelerate cooperation.

A very effective manager of a small service company used these principles well. She had her desk set up in the standard fashion with her chair behind the desk and a couple of chairs in front of it. When she wanted to keep someone at a distance or needed to "level" with someone by delivering difficult news or feedback, she would have them sit across the desk from her. However, when she wanted to build rapport or deepen an existing relationship, she would walk from behind her desk and arrange the seats in front of her desk so that they were at about a right angle. That way, as she and the other person talked, they were sharing the space between them and felt more aligned.

Another example of the powerful effect that alignment can produce was first reported by some Japanese companies. In many companies, employees gather before the workday begins and do calisthenics or some form of exercise in unison. These companies have seen productivity increase, and workers who are more satisfied with their work. A recent and intriguing finding is that there also may be a reduction in on-the-job injuries. These benefits come from the rapport level among the workers as they begin their work with such an aligning activity.

Aligning yourself with someone is a great metaphor to help you remember what to do literally when you want to build the common ground upon which relationships develop. You can align with common interests, body orientation, or emotional state.

Developing Emotional Rapport

You can build rapport with people who are upset by aligning with their emotional state of mind. Some psychology training teaches just the opposite, claiming that when someone is upset and especially angry, you should remain calm. So when someone is yelling, "I'm mad as hell at you, and I don't know why you did that!" you might respond calmly and slowly, "So what seems to be the problem?" Is this likely to calm the person? Would it make them feel better if someone else were calm when they were angry? Not usually . . . in fact, it usually makes them even angrier.

When someone is emotionally stressed, it's a lot more effective to align with the emotion that is said or demonstrated. This doesn't mean you agree with what someone is saying, but that you acknowledge what they are unquestionably feeling. By acknowledging the emotion, both verbally and nonverbally, you can align with it, even without knowing anything about how they got into that feeling state.

So when someone says, "I'm mad as hell at you!" you might respond with: "You're really upset with me. I'm really concerned about that." Of course, it's vital to be sincere about your concern, so that your voice tone carries the same message as your words. By noticing and responding to their emotional state, both verbally and nonverbally, you're letting them know that you are receiving them, just as they are. This uncritical acceptance is perhaps the greatest gift you can give any human being.

The next step is to check that the other person really heard your acknowledgment. Usually the other person will spontaneously relax a bit, and become visibly less upset. Since most people get upset when they feel unheard or uncared for, acknowledgment reduces their upset feelings.

After you are sure that the other person is responding to your having acknowledged them, you can begin to move toward problem solving. "Could we sit down for a moment and talk about what upset you, since I'm sure the reason you want to talk to me is to resolve this issue and to maintain our relationship. Isn't that true?" That's going to be hard to disagree with, and likely to help the other person feel that you really heard and understood them.

This response presupposes that the person yelling has a positive intention behind the yelling—the real reason that person wants to talk to you is to resolve the issue and to maintain your relationship. Adding this to your response helps you and the other person remember that everyone's intention is always positive, although it may not seem that way at times. A great deal of the NLP technology is based upon this idea. Whether or not it is true that people's intentions are always positive, if you behave as if that were true, it will certainly improve the quality of your communication and your life! Acting and speaking as if it were true can defuse even intense conflict situations.

Producing Positive Feelings in Others

The third consideration in building relationships is recognizing that each of us represents something to others in their lives. The question is, What do you want to represent? You might as well decide what you want your presence to be associated with, since it will be associated with something. You probably want people to have a positive association to you, although the specific response you want may depend upon the context for your relationship. It's useful to test how others respond to you presently. When you walk into a room or encounter someone you know, especially when it's unexpected, notice the person's response. When he or she sees you, how does that person respond? Do you see eyes light up with enthusiasm and delight? Do you see a quick smile or a frown and look of stress or concern? This test is a good measure of what you represent to that person even before you start communicating.

One midlevel manager, Bob, well trained to MBWA—or "manage by walking around"—was transferred to another division of his company. He understood the value of being available to those who reported to him and in learning from them what they did and how he could be useful. Part of his purpose in walking around his first day on the job was to build rapport. What Bob didn't know was that employees were not used to a manager walking around, and found Bob's presence intimidating—even though his manner was warm and friendly. As you can probably guess, the manager who preceded Bob was a potent source of intimidating feelings. Bob recognized what was happening because he had paid close attention to the responses of the people he supervised. The next day as he walked around, Bob offered warm doughnuts, fresh from the baker. As people were eating their doughnuts, he got a chance to talk to them about what they were doing, what their concerns were, and so on. After walking around with doughnuts for a few days, he noticed he was getting a very different response than he had before. Bob had changed the way he was perceived.

The strategy for becoming a source of good feelings for others is simple. Identify what feelings or emotional states you want to have associated to yourself. Then, be a great example of that state of mind and do things that encourage that state of mind in others. When you do this, sincerity is crucial, because when a person is insecure, the nonverbal behavior tends to signal the opposite of the verbal behavior. A great deal of recent research indicates the importance of having your nonverbal behavior consistent with your verbal behavior. Employees who were surveyed expressed confusion by the mismatch between the verbal and nonverbal messages of their managers. They reported that when they were confronted with a mismatch between verbal and nonverbal messages, they almost always responded to the nonverbal portion of the message—the voice quality and the facial expressions—rather than the words. Even a small child can learn to lie with words, but since their nonverbal behavior is much harder for them to control, it almost always gives them away. This is why most of us tend to trust the nonverbal message much more than the verbal one when the two don't match. If you want to be powerful with your messages, let your face and voice reflect and support your verbal messages. The easiest way to accomplish this is to be sincere, because then all your behavior will naturally be congruent—all delivering the same message.

To ensure that people associate good feelings to you, just one more element is required, and that is your competence. By setting clear and well-formed goals, by aligning or matching another person's behavior (especially nonverbally), and by associating good feelings to your presence, you will have the basis for high quality and strong connections with other people. With the tools of rapport alone, you can create responsiveness in another person in a matter of seconds. However, to have relationships that last over time, you need to be able to "deliver the goods"; you need to be competent. No amount of doughnuts and coffee will make up for inability to get the job done.

A president of a small high-tech company initially had the admiration of his staff because of his exceptional rapport skills. However, when his poor management skills became apparent in the bottom line and the company was forced into bankruptcy, his staff felt equally strong feelings of anger and betrayal.

In business relationships, competency is the currency of long-term rapport—and this is also true in personal relationships as it enables you to deliver on whatever agreements or promises you make. Customers, peers, supervisors, colleagues, and friends come to us with their goals, whether they are conscious of it or not. Our integrity, capabilities, and skills in providing what they want will ultimately determine their satisfaction from the relationship. If your rapport skills only make people feel good but you do not provide the value that they want, then they will leave feeling confused about the interaction, and eventually about you. Relationship skills are a great addition to being competent, but they are no replacement for it.

Reviewing What You've Learned

This chapter discusses the techniques and value of establishing rapport in all your relationships. Having personal interactions that make both parties feel appreciated and heard makes every relationship move much smoother. The three aspects of this are:

- Learn to see the interaction from the other person's viewpoint. Determine mutually satisfying goals. Notice the other person's feelings and responses and acknowledge them. Be sure you have been heard. Attribute positive intention to their behavior. Begin to move toward problem solving. Use the Goal Achievement Process from Chapter Four to clarify your goals for this relationship.

- Establish and maintain nonverbal rapport by matching the positions of others. This allows you to literally see the world from their perspective. Matching another's voice tone and pacing creates rapport, where the perceived distance between two people is diminished. Matching another's emotional state does this as well.

- Produce positive feelings in others by being a great example of the state of mind you'd like others to feel about you and encouraging it with your actions.

These three techniques can be a part of your natural repertoire and can help you have much greater success, achievement, freedom, happiness, and satisfaction in your life. Practice creating relationships that will enhance you and the lives of the people with whom you will be doing business. Every day, think of someone with whom either you are unsure of the relationship or with whom you want to establish a new relationship, and use your new skills to establish rapport.

CHAPTER SEVEN

Powerful Persuasion Strategies

The Myths of Persuasion

One myth about great persuaders is that they are born that way. Well, think about it truthfully: None of us is born talking . . . much less persuading anyone of anything. It is a set of skills we learn, like all the other things we learn. Each of us has a predisposition to a particular set of skills, but no one has them all mastered without training. The top communicators will tell you that they made a commitment to themselves to seek, study, and learn, because they knew that's what it takes to become a master. There's a direct relationship between learning and profit. The more you learn, the more you earn . . . in terms of personal satisfaction, as well as financially.

The second myth about great persuaders is that they are smooth talkers. Some are. However, of much greater importance is the fact that they are great listeners, a secret that many high-powered consultants and motivational speakers have already discovered. Listening is vitally important for at least two reasons. First, people feel good when they know they are truly being heard. In most sales transactions and even in our daily interactions, other people usually don't really listen to us. Most of us only feel really listened to in the best parts of our really special relationships. Being heard is a special experience that people like and want more of.

Second, listening is a fine way to find out what's important to a particular person. This is the information that tells us whether they need or could want what we have to offer. When you know what a person wants and needs, there are two possibilities: Either your product or service fits these needs, or it doesn't.

If there is a fit, then you have the information to demonstrate compellingly to this person that what you offer does, in fact, fit his requirements. And if there isn't a fit, then you can simply state it directly, and gracefully move on to the next prospect, saving you both a lot of frustration and wasted time. One very successful real estate broker very often says the following when she can't find a fit between what the buyer wants and what is available on the market:

> You have told me the kind of house you're looking for, and I've shown you three houses that are the closest fit to what you want at this time. There simply isn't anything on the market right now that meets your needs. I don't want to waste your time and mine trying to sell you something that won't satisfy you. I'll keep your card in my active file, and I'll let you know the moment anything comes on the market that might satisfy you.

Many sales training and communication programs talk as if you should want to motivate others to do what you want them to do, when they don't really want to do it. There are two great disadvantages in trying to make someone do what doesn't fit: First, it will take a lot of work and time to try to persuade someone of what doesn't actually fit for them. Second, if they don't feel manipulated, they will ultimately be dissatisfied. Since repeat business and personal referrals are the major source of most sales, a dissatisfied customer is far worse than a customer who is treated well, and who is respectfully told that your product is not appropriate for his or her needs. By the way, the real estate broker mentioned above gets most of her referrals from people she *didn't* sell a house to.

The benefits of this approach are beautifully illustrated by the old movie *Miracle on 34th Street*. A department-store Santa Claus suggests to many customers that they go to other stores for certain purchases because they can get better quality or lower prices there. When the store manager finds out about this, he is horrified and is about to fire the Santa when he is deluged by people thanking him for having a Santa who is so helpful and honest, and pledging to come to his store first for all future purchases.

Persuasion is the ability to offer compelling value to *others*. The key to this definition is that the values are not yours, but *theirs*. Their values are what they are going to respond to. Persuasive people are those who can see and hear how others express their values—and who can ask key questions to discover values. Then they can demonstrate how what they are offering will actually satisfy that person's values and provide benefits to them.

You can also think of persuasion as motivating others. Applying the same ways of thinking about motivation for yourself that you learned in Chapter Two, you can keep in mind the important point that you are motivating others to do what *they* want; what is in *their* best interests; what will satisfy *their* values.

Many of the best communicators have learned this lesson. They are eager to find out what their customers, colleagues, and friends want. They are motivated and happy to serve their clients if they have what the others want. Remembering this principle will make it much easier to qualify and then persuade potential buyers to do what is in their best interests. In order to use this principle, you need to be able to quickly find out what customers, clients, associates, or friends do want. This means learning what they value.

Discovering the Values of Others

Several simple methods can help you to find out the values of others. People give many clues in their dress, the things they own, their habits, and the way they treat people. Characteristics such as neatness, attention to detail, sloppiness, warm concern for coworkers, and needs for privacy all express values. It can be natural for you to notice these.

You may want to discover the values that others use to make decisions in purchasing, work quality, management style, personal relationships, or any other relevant situation. Finding these values is easy. Simply ask, "What's important to you about a phone system?'' or, "What do you value in an employee?" or "What does a motivated staff mean for your company?" or "Think of your best manager. What are the characteristics that make her a good manager and set her apart from the ordinary managers?"

All these questions ask for values, the standards of performance that the person you want to influence will use to make decisions. These are the same questions you asked yourself to find your motivation strategy and get yourself motivated.

Many successful salespeople use the following approach:

I believe that our product (service) is excellent. However, I also know that it is only appropriate for those who want, need, and value what this product (service) has to offer. Some people think of me as a salesperson, but I think of myself as a consultant whose job it is to find out whether there is a good match between your needs and our product (service). In order to do this, I need to know what you want in a _____.

Let your prospect tell you what she wants to buy. If you have it, he'll buy it.

The Relationship Between Persuasion and Value

You'll also begin to discover that desires and values come in several varieties. For your purposes, it's important to distinguish two types. One might best be called "material specifications." When you ask what's important in a product or a service, you may get a very specific answer. The answer might be that it has to operate at a specific temperature, have a certain output, fit within a certain space, be a certain color, etc.

Once the product or service meets or exceeds the material specifications put forth, you want to examine the second type of values, called "criteria." A criterion is a way of specifying a more general value. For example, a part might have to be a certain size to meet material specifications. And because of its size, it will last longer (that's a criterion), need less repair (that's another criterion), and reduce inventories (still another criterion). All of these criteria will help increase profits, which is an even more important criterion. This is similar to what you did earlier in formulating your mission and passion in Chapter Three. The more important the criterion you appeal to, the more all-encompassing and valuable it is. If you have the right-sized widget, that's usually less important than having widgets that last longer, which is less important than having widgets that increase profits.

When you buy tires for your car, they have to be the correct size, which is a material specification. You would also naturally prefer tires that last longer and cost less, and here your criteria tend to be more general and less specific. However, your personal safety is probably even more important. Most people will pay more for a tire that doesn't last quite as long if they know that it truly is safer. When the Michelin tire company says, "Because so much is riding on your tires," they are appealing to a criterion that is very important to many people—the safety of their families.

When you know a person's most important criterion, such as safety, it is usually much easier to make a sale, for two very different reasons. First if your product or service truly satisfies their higher criterion, the prospect will be *very motivated* to buy. And second, when you're selling safety, there are *many different ways* to provide it that the buyer hasn't thought of.

For instance, let's say a customer asks for a specific size and type of tire. If you know that his greatest concern is safety, you probably know exactly which type of tire in that size is the safest, and you also know that this will be compellingly motivating to him. However, you could also go even farther in satisfying his needs. It may be that using a different size wheel would permit mounting a tire that is even safer, and you may be able to sell him wheels as well as tires. You could go even further to point out that no matter how good the tire is, an antilock braking system will do even more to ensure the safety of his family. A new car would satisfy his need for safety far better than what he originally asked for. When you have many different opportunities to make a sale, you'll make more sales.

The point here is simple and incredibly important. The higher and more important the criterion you can identify in someone else, the more options you will have to satisfy it. And the more options you have, the more likely you will be able to provide value through offering your product or service. Remember: The higher the value you satisfy, the more persuasive you will be.

In order to find more important values, you simply ask, "What's important to you about having _____?" (Insert the last value he or she said in the blank.) Each time you ask this question, you will get a more important value. An interaction (selling retirement investments, in this example) might look something like this:

"I want to invest some money."	*Criteria*
Q: "What do you want in a retirement investment?"	
A: "I want a government bond or a treasury note."	Bond or note
Q: "What would having a government bond do for you?"	
A. "They have a track record and are insured."	Track record & insured
Q: "What's important to you about the track record and insurance?"	
A: "So my retirement is secure."	Security
Q: "So what's really important to you about this investment is that it's secure."	
A: "Well, I'd also like a good return, but that's not as important as security. I don't want to take a chance and lose what I have."	

By knowing that this customer's most important criterion is security, the financial advisor can now better help the client get what he needs. He has many more options, and some of them may be much better for the customer than the bond or note he originally asked for.

With experience in your particular field, you will learn the types of highly valued criteria that customers typically have. With that information, you can more easily tailor your presentation and selection of products and services to meet their needs.

Exploring Motivation Strategy

Even more information can be found by exploring how people think about their values. Remember Chapter Two, discussing *toward* and *away from* motivation? Now we're going to find out what those strategies are for those around you, those whom you want to influence. When you ask someone, "What will getting that do for you?" he or she will either answer with more value words or will answer with words that indicate the direction of his or her motivation strategy.

For example, many clients looking for a home want lots of space. When the broker asks, "What will having lots of space do for you?" one client might say: "It will *allow me* to have the freedom to move around," while another might answer, "The space will *keep me* from feeling cluttered."

These two clients are examples of the two opposite types of Motivation Direction. People who are motivated *toward* use words like: "attain," "gain," "achieve," "rewards." Those who go *away from* use words like: "avoid," "ease," "relax," "get away from."

This is one of the linguistic parts of Neuro-Linguistic Programming. You can actually hear these distinctions in a person's language. Some value words obviously show you the Motivation Direction. For example, fun is a value with a *toward* Motivation Direction; challenge is also *toward*. Security is a value with an *away from* direction. Freedom could go either way, so it's important to follow up this value with the question: "What does having freedom do for you?" If she says "to get *away from* constraints," you know it's an *away from* value. If he says "to allow me to experience more," it is a *toward* value.

Many people say, "I want success." When you ask, "What will having success do for you?" some will say what success will allow them to move *toward:* "So I can travel," or "So I can get married," or "Then I can have a ranch and raise horses." Others will describe what they can move *away from:* "So I can quit my job," or "So I can get out of debt," or "Then I can get divorced." Similarly, money can be used as either a *toward* or *away from* value. As you learn information about the Motivation Direction of others, make a mental note or actually write it down. Knowing this information will allow you to adjust your communication to be much more persuasive.

When trying to motivate or persuade someone, be sure that you are using their preferred Motivation Direction in combination with their criteria word. If she tends to use *away from* in a certain situation, then if you want to motivate her you would point out what *won't* happen if she buys your product. "If you buy this car, you will *avoid* (an *away from* word) further expense in repairs and maintenance" (her criterion word = expense). However if he tends to be more motivated by *toward* words in a specific situation, describe the positive outcome to increase his motivation. Buying this car will earn you the admiration and respect of people who appreciate a high-performance car (his criteria = admiration, respect, performance).

Determining Thinking Strategies

Using a person's thinking strategy is another way to motivate and persuade. How do you know which thinking strategy to appeal to? The eye movements and the language of sensory thinking modes are probably the most widely known parts of NLP. Cofounders Richard Bandler and John Grinder, along with then-student Robert Dilts, discovered that the unconscious movements of a person's eyes reflected internal thinking strategies. A basic knowledge of eye movement and body movement can greatly increase presentation persuasiveness because people sometimes stay in a certain mode of thinking for a while. As you'll recall from Chapter Two, we have five sensory systems, but we primarily use three of them for thinking: the visual, the auditory, and the feeling. You can tell when someone is processing information *visually* when they are unconsciously looking up. That is, not looking at anything on the outside, but at something obviously internal. Additional cues include: when they are pointing at a place in space like a screen, when they talk at a rapid rate, sometimes with thoughts apparently disjoined, or when they use words referring to seeing *pictures, images,* or *movies.* When these behaviors are continued for several seconds, a person is primarily processing his or her experience visually.

Distinct from people using visual processing are those who keep looking down and to their left, when they list points, possibly on their fingers, when they mumble to themselves, when they talk out loud in a monotone, often touching or stroking their face or when they use words referring to what people *said, heard,* or *read.* When they continue to do this for several seconds, they are primarily processing their experience with sounds and words; that is, *auditorily.*

The third category is when people keep looking down to their right, sighing, touching their heart area or smoothing their hands on an arm or a thigh. Sometimes when they talk slowly, they use words referring to how they *feel* or *grasp* or *touch* the world in concrete ways. When they do this for several seconds, they are primarily processing their experience using *feelings.*

All people can and often do use all of these different sensory modalities for thinking. Usually, we are moving quickly from one to another and back as our experience changes. When you notice someone is using one of these modalities for a few moments, you can match his or her thinking style and increase rapport.

With the visually specialized thinking style, offer a picture or movie: "The way I *see* how you're *viewing* this purchase . . ." With the auditorily specialized thinking style, offer words, especially in a list: "From what you're *telling* me, I *hear* you saying that . . ." With the feeling thinking style, offer something with feeling: "If I *grasp* what you've *given* me so far, your sense of the situation is that . . ." When your client smiles with recognition that someone understands her, you can be sure that what you are presenting is being easily understood and responded to.

Adding Submodalities to Motivation Direction

In previous chapters, you have learned how to make something more compelling, and more motivating to you by increasing the vividness of the submodalities in your mind's eye. You can make what you're attracted toward or compelled to avoid much more intense by making them closer, bigger, more colorful, and three-dimensional. Professional persuaders naturally add this powerful dimension to their proposals and presentations to others. You can learn to do it consciously. For example, you might say to a prospect who is motivated *away from*, "There are certain difficulties you've told me that you want to avoid—down time, lost productivity, and cost overruns—before they get *too close,* like they're breathing down your neck. Let me explain how what I offer can provide relief."

With a prospect who is motivated *toward*, you might say, "I don't know how *colorful* and *action-filled* a future you want this company to move toward. Let's talk about how *big* your plans are and how my contribution can make them even *bigger* and add *dimensions* to them now."

When you use words in this way, adding submodality richness and vividness to the values and images that your prospects, clients, or employees are already responding to, this is very persuasive. It is a way to make your product or service more compelling, attractive, and influential.

The easiest way to do this is to make your own internal images and sounds more intense and compelling by adjusting your own internal submodalities. If it's big, compelling, and dramatic for you in your own mind, this will be expressed naturally in your actions, words, expressions, gestures, and voice tone. Think drama, think bigger than life. You're like a storyteller of old, bringing to life your ideas and vision. After all, that's what all the color slides, computer-generated graphics, and fancy presentations are really about. They are to capture the attention of the audience, and help them experience that their highest values will be fulfilled with what you are presenting with movies, graphics, lasers, or music. Now you can do that with your prospects in a way that is more personal, more exact, more on-target than any computer yet imagined. When we hear something, even from another conversation, we can't help but make images and sounds of it in our head. The professional persuader knows this intuitively. In NLP we know it explicitly. **You cannot *NOT* communicate.** We are communicating all the time. The only question is: "How elegantly?" or "How intentionally?"

Do you want to just let your proposal be seen, or do you want people to experience how it will light up important goals and realize larger and more impactful benefits? You can add this influencing pattern by practicing using submodality words, adding sparkle and color to your speech.

With a little practice, you will find it easy to combine these simple persuasion patterns into every qualifying interview, every new business contact, every routine occasion. This will make enormous changes in your personal effectiveness. Soon, the ability to influence others will become second nature for you.

Remember: Listening makes the prospective client feel good and provides you an opportunity to learn about the client's needs and values. Values include both specific material specifications (such as size, color, and output) and more general criteria (such as durability, profitability, safety). To determine values, ask, "What do you value in a _____?" Determine which of these criteria are *most* important to the client, as these are the most compelling and motivating and will provide you with the greatest freedom to satisfy the client's needs. To find more important criteria, ask, "What's important to you about _____?" When you know the client's needs and values, you can easily determine if there is a match between them and the product or service you provide. Knowing the client's direction of motivation, *toward* or *away from,* lets you describe your product in a way that is parallel with how the client already thinks. *Toward:* "This product will provide x benefits." *Away from:* "With this product, you won't ever have y problems." Determining how the client primarily processes information allows you to match the way they experience events most powerfully, using "I *see* what

you mean'' with the visual person, "I *hear* what you're *saying*,''
with the auditory person, and "I've got a *grasp* on what you've *laid*
out,'' with the feeling person. Using submodality language to describe your products' qualities and the benefits it offers will make it
big, bright, colorful, and compellingly attractive in the mind of the
buyer.

Establishing Personal Congruence

There is one more influential pattern that you must learn at this
point, one that underlies all the other patterns we've described. Like
a solid foundation, it supports them all. It is not a technique; rather
it supercharges all of the above. It comes under many names: excitement, enthusiasm, charisma, personal power. In NLP we call it
personal congruence. Congruence means that all parts of you are in
total alignment with what you're doing at the moment. It means to
have such rapport with yourself that what you say comes powerfully
from within and can attract and influence others before a word is
spoken.

Perhaps the best way to illustrate congruence is to describe
*in*congruence. If you've ever made a presentation while part of you
was worrying about bills, or the kids' school, you know what it's
like to have your attention divided between what you're actually
doing now and other concerns that need to be taken care of later.
You have also probably noticed that your presentation suffers when
your attention is divided in this way.

Congruence is total attention to what you're doing now. In Robert A. Heinlein's science-fiction classic, *Stranger in a Strange Land,*
a woman describes Michael Valentine Smith's total attention in this
way: "When he's kissing you, he isn't doing *anything* else!''

When we're incongruent, the parts of us that are not focused on
the task at hand typically express themselves in nonverbal behavior
like foot tapping, glancing out the window, a high-pitched, strained
voice tone, etc. At best, these will only distract and confuse your
client. At worst, he or she will interpret these signals to mean that

you are incompetent or dishonest. Study after study indicates that approximately 80 percent of communication is *non*verbal. These studies also find that when people are faced with a verbal message that has an incongruent nonverbal component (such as the words "I respect you," spoken in a snickering voice tone) they will usually *respond* to the nonverbal message—even when they don't consciously recognize it! Since people respond so powerfully to incongruence, it can undermine or destroy your communication, even when everything else you do is appropriate.

In the previous chapter, you learned many specific ways to build strong relationships with others. Since you've decided that the people with whom you do business and those with whom you have other kinds of relationships deserve this kind of consideration, there's one more person you should consider deserving of it—*you,* including all the different parts of you. A wise person once said: "You're the only person you have to wake up with every morning . . . and since you're going to do it the rest of your life, it might as well be something you feel great about and enjoy." In life we often push ourselves along because we need a shove to get going. Certainly there are times when we do need to plow through our resistance or suppress some feeling. But you can quickly get tired of doing that. There are probably times when you just want to attend to yourself. Consider the possibility that you might want to pay attention to yourself even more than you do now.

When it comes to ourselves, some of us have more experience at breaking rapport than building it. Think of just a few of the times when you've ignored what you intuitively knew was right for you— times you didn't do something that you valued highly. Perhaps when you've done that in the past, things didn't turn out well. Sometimes you might even have felt out of rapport with yourself— where one aspect of you wanted one thing and another part of you wanted something else. Often people only notice these feelings *after* something goes wrong. "You know, I had a funny feeling about that situation at the time." The first step in dealing within congruence is to notice it clearly as it is happening, so that you can do something about it before it's too late.

EXERCISE 25: FINDING YOUR SIGNALS FOR CONGRUENCE AND INCONGRUENCE

1. Incongruence. The first step in getting back into relationship with yourself is to know when you're not. Think of a memory of being out of rapport with yourself. You were incongruent. Pick a time when you were strongly conflicted and were *not* "all systems go." When you remember what it is like to be in that situation, notice what you see; who is there; what is going on; what are your choices; what are you saying to yourself out loud and inside your head; and what the other person is saying and doing.

2. Incongruence Signal. Now, notice how you feel. Literally scan your body with your awareness and notice that there is some way you know that you are not in complete agreement with yourself. While you may not be able to put into words exactly how you know when you are in conflict in this way, it is important that you can notice the feeling or sensation that alerts you to being incongruent. Often the signal for incongruence is an unpleasant part-body sensation of "wrongness" felt somewhere in the chest or belly area. Sometimes people notice that the left half of this area has one feeling, and the right half has a very different feeling. At the midline, where these two different feelings meet, there is a sensation of mismatching, which is usually felt as uncomfortable. Where exactly do you feel your feeling of incongruence in your body, and what is the quality of this feeling? Now remember this feeling. By remembering this feeling in detail, you can use it in the future to signal you whenever you become incongruent. Now relax a moment.

3. Congruence. The next step is to pick a memory of total congruence, and re-create it in your mind. In this situation, what do you see? What do you hear? What is happening?

4. Congruence Signal. How do you feel? What is the feeling that serves as a signal to you that you are "all systems go"? Usually the signal for congruence is a pleasant whole-body feeling of excitement or readiness. People have many ways to describe this feeling of congruence. Some will say, "I can't describe it, it's

Continued

just that I *know*. It's an intuition." Some people hear a strong voice say, "OK, let's go!" Almost everyone reports some physical sensation that accompanies their sense of "go for it." Often there is a sense of overall symmetry and alignment in the body. Often there is a feeling of openness, frequently in the chest. Another feeling is of being drawn forward, again primarily in the chest.

Notice where in your body you feel your signal for congruence. Find some words for the quality of this feeling, and remember both the feeling and the words. This can serve you in the future as a signal of powerful congruence, when all parts of you are aligned.

5. Compare Feelings. Now compare the feeling of congruence that you just experienced with the previous feeling of incongruence, and notice how different they are. Comparing the two will make each of them clearer to you. If these feelings are in different parts of your body, you may be able to compare them by feeling them at the same time. However, most people usually find it easier to compare the two feelings sequentially, by switching from one to the other fairly quickly.

By comparing these two feelings in detail, and remembering these differences, you can always know in the future when you're incongruent or congruent, and use this as ongoing feedback at the time. If you had any difficulty telling the difference between congruence and incongruence, you probably didn't take enough time to really remember what it was like to be in each experience. You need to really go back to the two experiences to recapture all the sensations and feelings, and then compare them.

Regaining Your Own Rapport

Now that you can tell when you are in rapport with yourself and when you're not, you need to learn what to do about the times when you are incongruent. Many communications and self-help programs talk about "breaking through" and "overcoming" your own resistance. All of us sometimes ignore or suppress one or more of their parts temporarily so that we can get something done. However, when there is a part of you that is resisting, most people report that when you try to break through it, it just resists even more. If you're in conflict with a friend or business associate and they "break through" your objections, you probably don't feel good about it. Most people feel ignored, trampled, or worse, and your inner parts will, too. You need a better approach to deal with inner conflict.

Perhaps you've sat down to write a report, but you find yourself staring at the sunshine streaming in the window. Your mind keeps wandering to thoughts of hiking in the woods, or going to the lake. If you try to stop these thoughts, they're likely to sneak back in as soon as you are distracted from suppressing them. This type of internal conflict is unpleasant and detrimental to your success in any venture. It's like trying to drive your car in one direction with a tow truck pulling in the opposite direction. Some people get the idea that having conflicting parts means that they are disturbed. Not true. Our various, sometimes conflicting parts are only evidence of the potentially wide range of behaviors that make us complex, unique, and special individuals. It is also true that reducing internal conflict improves mental health and, over the long term, probably physical health as well.

While developing discipline for ourselves is a powerful skill for personal evolution, ignoring or overriding parts of ourselves is something different. When you've suppressed a part of yourself, that part frequently returns—often even stronger. There's a lot of energy behind some aspect of yourself that will return time after time, no matter how much you try to suppress it.

Paradoxically, you can gain more control over your wandering thoughts by temporarily acknowledging them and paying *more* attention to them. By giving in to thoughts of the woods or the lake, you can realize that this expresses an important need that you have ignored for too long; that a part of you realizes that you badly need the rest and enjoyment, the solitude and exercise that the woods or the lake could offer you.

Once you acknowledge that this distracting part of you wants something very worthwhile for you, you can make a firm promise that you will go to the woods or the lake the next weekend, or perhaps even that evening. When you make a firm promise like this, typically the distracting part will be content to wait until the weekend, secure in the knowledge that you will keep your promise, and not need to intrude into what you're doing now. In this way, all the energy that is involved in such a part of you becomes an ally rather than an adversary. In the same way that people are your greatest resource and you will do what it takes to have them as allies, all aspects of yourself can be your allies, working together in your best interests. The allies on the inside are as important as those on the outside.

Even when there is no inner conflict, you'll want to build the strongest relationship possible with the most important person in your life . . . you. To strengthen the relationship with yourself, you can use the same steps you learned to use with someone else in the previous chapter. Just as in building strong relationships, with others, the first step is to set a goal that is mutually respectful and satisfying. What goals do you have for the relationship with yourself?

The next step is to bring other parts of yourself more into the forefront of your goal planning, to make them more important so that you'll acknowledge and utilize them more. If you pay more attention to a playful part, for example, you can make all your activities more playful.

Then you can set relationship goals with this part of yourself just as you did with someone else, using the Goal Achievement Process. Include these planning steps for your inner relationship—think about what you want in positive terms, imagine what you can do to make this happen, know what evidence will show you you're succeeding, plan when and where you want this to occur, be aware of all the benefits and consequences of this, and make whatever adjustments are necessary.

When we gain greater harmony within ourselves, we may be thinking of particular parts that are most appropriately expressed in particular contexts, but often we are not talking about a particular situation, but about our entire lives. The way to begin a great relationship with yourself is to be clear about what you are doing with your life and your mission. Notice what words you say to yourself that make you feel wholly "on purpose." Ask yourself what it feels like you're here on earth to do. See yourself as a person who just naturally moves in the direction of fulfilling this mission.

Aligning with Your Inner Voice

In the previous chapter, you learned how to align with another person physically to gain rapport. You can use a similar inner alignment process to build a strong relationship with yourself. The complete process is called Aligning Perceptual Positions, developed by Connirae Andreas. You'll be learning one important step in this process here—aligning with your inner voice.

Many of us have critical inner voices. At certain times, we tell ourselves, "How stupid!" or, "I can't believe you just did that again!" or, "You should have done better!" Usually these voices are loud and fast, or have harsh and sneering tonality.

Some of us have inner voices that cause trouble for us in other ways. Perhaps a voice mostly judges, blames, and criticizes others. "If that guy weren't such a jerk!" Some voices create distance between ourselves and others by analyzing everything. "What's really going on here is *x, y,* and *z.*" Sometimes a voice repeatedly forecasts a negative future: "I'll never be able to learn to succeed."

If we really listen to these voices, we can discover something very interesting. These voices are almost never located where our own personal voice is created when we speak—in our chest, throat, and mouth. Instead, these voices almost always seem to be coming from another location, and the voice is usually directed *toward* us instead of out from us. Often these voices feel as if they are located outside our body, perhaps above us or to the right or left. Even when voices are located inside our body, they are typically at one ear, or at the back of the head or the forehead, or some other location. If these voices were fully aligned with us, they would sound just as our own voice sounds when we speak, with the breath moving up out of our chests, through our throats, and out through our mouths and lips. Internal voices are almost *never* aligned in this way, and if we take the time to realign with them, many positive changes occur spontaneously. The voices typically become softer and more pleasant to listen to, a friendly part of ourselves, instead of a critical antagonist. The next exercise can give you an experience of this kind of inner alignment.

EXERCISE 26: CREATING INNER ALIGNMENT

1. Troublesome Voice. Think of a time when an inner voice criticized you, or troubled you in some other way, and put yourself back into that situation. When you're there, listen to the voice and notice what it is saying, what it sounds like, where it is coming from, and where it is directed.

2. Move Voice into Throat. Now slowly allow that voice to move into the area of your body where your own voice comes from when you actually speak. Notice how the voice naturally changes as it moves closer and closer to coming out of your own chest and throat. Most likely, the words it says, the tonality, and the volume will change in some way.

3. Notice Differences. When it has fully moved into your throat area, into the source of your own voice, notice how it is now different. Usually the voice will have become softer, and the tonality will have become more like a friendly aspect of yourself. Sometimes the words will have changed from critical accusations to factual data or helpful suggestions. The words may have changed to a clear statement of how you feel, what you think, or what you want.

4. Check for I-You Structure. Troublesome voices usually begin with the word *you,* followed by a judgment, such as "You dumb _____." With this kind of voice I'm talking to myself *as if* I were speaking to another person—I say "you" instead of "I." When these voices move into your body, they often change spontaneously to a simple statement that begins with "I," followed by "feel," "see," "hear," "think" _____. "I don't like what happened." "I want to get a different response from you." If your voice has not already changed in this way, invite it to do so, and notice how that changes your experience. Invite your voice to make statements beginning with "I": "I think _____," "I feel _____," "I want _____."

5. Future Planning. Think now about the kind of future situations where you want to have this kind of inner alignment. Put yourself into one of these situations and quickly go through the above four steps again, noticing how this realignment makes you feel more whole and resourceful, and makes the situation easier to deal with.

Most people feel much more resourceful when they realign with an inner voice. People often say that they are clearer about what they think and feel, and that this clarity makes it easier to take appropriate action. Others feel a sense of relaxed openness and wholeness instead of confusion, frustration, and tension.

A few people, however, find that doing this process leaves them feeling uncomfortable. Should this happen to you, it indicates that you need to experience the complete process of Aligning Perceptual Positions to gain full and comfortable alignment.[1] For now, you can just put the voice back where you found it.

The Importance of Deep Personal Congruence

The more we study what it takes to be successful, effective, and feel fulfilled, the clearer it becomes that our personal congruence is of primary importance. Often what holds us back is not our lack of ability or skill, but ourselves. If we have dreams of what we want our lives to be, but feel unworthy, we will probably stop ourselves from doing the things that are necessary to reach those dreams. Most of us occasionally have emotional reactions or responses that get in our way. We might have fears that keep us from taking appropriate action. Feeling intimidated, jealous, self-righteous, or insecure are a few of the emotions that can interfere with the direction or path we have chosen for ourselves. Sometimes this is easier to see in others. You may have a guess about what stops some of your business associates from working well with you or others. We can all benefit greatly from noticing this in ourselves as well.

Most of us have tried at some time in the past to just override these parts of ourselves. We have experienced that trying to shove aside our fear, anger, or insecurity doesn't really work. We have the greatest opportunity for success and fulfillment when we seek to respect and welcome all parts of ourselves to come together into a unified whole.

The methods we introduced in this chapter can assist you in becoming more inwardly aligned—having a more harmonious relationship with yourself. If you would like to go farther in gaining inner harmony, the recent breakthrough work of NLP Comprehensive cofounder Connirae Andreas can be of great assistance.[2] Her Core Transformation Process has been called the flowering of NLP and can assist you in coming to personal congruence in a profoundly compassionate way. What you thought were your flaws become your valued friends. When we are whole, all of us is available to manifest our life's dreams.

Developing Your Physical Congruence

Aligning with your own internal voice is a powerful way to enhance your personal congruence. Similarly, aligning your behavior so that it is consistent with your values will lead to greater self-rapport, inner harmony, and self-fulfillment. People often say that they want the "good life" and will sacrifice to get it. If sacrificing means to you sometimes doing things that are difficult, or that you're unsure of doing, that's probably often necessary to be successful at anything. However, if you think you have to ignore and deny large parts of your values to have success, you'd better reconsider. Some people sacrifice their marriages or relationships with their children or their physical health in the name of success. If you really don't value those people and activities, then you might be able to ignore them and remain congruent. However, when you value something, you want to embrace it and spend time with it, fully including it in your life.

Demonstrate how you honor your own values by aligning with them. Spend time pursuing them. If you value your physical body, do something adequate to take care of it. If you value quality time with your children, find it. If you want intimacy with your spouse, create it. You have to know, acknowledge, and respect what is really important to you before you can do anything about it. There isn't some quick technique to achieve this process of alignment with yourself. It's more a matter of awareness—knowing what your most valued goals or purposes are, and acting in alignment with them. Once you have some awareness, then it's a matter of building trust in and with yourself. If you have broken rapport with yourself too frequently, it may be more like regaining the trust of a friend after it's been severely tested. It may take time and patience and humility, and the rewards will make it worthwhile.

Making Yourself Feel Good

The third aspect to building strong personal congruence is associating good feelings with yourself. Aligning your inner voice and aligning your behavior with your values will go a long way toward doing this. In addition, it's a good idea to treat yourself well. Treat yourself to things you can do for yourself—now, today. Good athletic shoes, cologne, or chocolate cost little compared to how they let you know, now, that you appreciate yourself. A massage, a weekend getaway, a movie series, or season tickets are other ways we can show that we appreciate ourselves. Understand that what is important for our personal treats is not the spending of money for the sake of it, or showing off, or buying something because we're supposed to, or because everyone else is doing it. If it's not something that *you* really want, it won't be of value. The goal is to find things to do for you that serve as reminders of how much you care for all of yourself.

By simply paying attention to the goals and values you have for yourself, aligning with your deepest needs and wants, talking kindly to yourself, as if you were your own best friend, and doing things big and small that make you feel good, you can develop incredible personal congruence through your entire life. With personal congruence, you know that everything you do will have the full support of all parts of yourself. This will be communicated to others before you even open your mouth, and it will contribute greatly to your personal success.

Reviewing What You've Learned

In this chapter, you've learned some of the secrets behind the power of persuasion. Learning to listen can provide you with the

specific information you need to offer compelling value to others—
the key to all successful communication.
Specifically, you've learned:

- Techniques of persuasion that motivate others to do what
  they want
- How persuasion and values relate to one another
- How to find the values of others by asking the right questions
- How to work with submodalities and use them with motiva-
  tion strategies or thinking strategies to persuade others
- The importance of personal congruence in powerful persua-
  sion and how to regain rapport with yourself

There are no single magic words or phrases that can help you to
become more persuasive in your life. The simple art of listening is
often the most important aspect of persuasion. Remember, by elic-
iting the information you need to successfully match others' values
with what you have to offer, you can generate the greatest amount
of influence with a potential customer. This allows you to discern
for yourself if what you have to offer will be of benefit to your
client. Above all, though, is your personal congruence, your alignment with yourself. This is not only the most dependable foundation
for influencing others, it is the very foundation of your whole life
and your mission in life.

CHAPTER EIGHT

Eliminating Your Fears and Phobias

Using Dissociation to Gain Confidence

Fear is normal. Sharks, undertow currents on beaches, spooky nighttime neighborhoods, vicious dogs, gang gatherings, and nuclear warheads can generate appropriately fearful feelings within all of us. Some part of us recognizes their dangers. The anxious feelings that we experience get us to avoid taking unreasonable risks and motivate us to change things.

Sometimes, however, people become afraid of situations and things that are not, in and of themselves, truly dangerous. These are often termed phobias. *Phobia,* the Greek word for fear, is a name for any strong avoidance of something unpleasant in the environment. Examples include public speaking, heights, storms, visiting the doctor, flying on airplanes, driving on freeways, meeting with superiors, sales cold calling, interviewing for jobs, and dealing with in-laws. Think of any situation and you can probably find someone who is afraid of it. These are not necessarily "rational" fears. If you mentally exaggerate the danger of a situation or become apprehensive of situations that others aren't frightened of, you may have a phobia or irrational fear. Psychologist Gerald Rosen states in his book *Don't Be Afraid: A Program for Overcoming Your Fears and Phobias*[1] that "researchers at the University of Vermont discovered that 1 in 10 Americans suffer from a serious fear. If milder anxiety problems were tabulated, the percentage figures would likely be higher.'' According to Rosen, the Vermont investigators studied a number of the identified phobias for five years to learn more about the natural course of phobias. The research findings identified that most childhood phobias were short-lived and disappeared without any particular treatment. This finding may be similar to your own experience, if you've raised children. One year a child is scared of the dark; the next year, strangers; and the next year, dogs.

Unlike the fears of childhood, adult phobias don't just go away on their own. Over half the adults in the Vermont study had failed to improve over the five years. Fully one third of these individuals began to experience worse fear. Although only one person in ten may suffer from a serious fear, all of us have fears that keep us from performing at our best, and hold us back in life. Whether it's a fear of public speaking, or of being rejected when asking for a date, fear of a meeting or of making cold calls, everyone has fears that are out of proportion to the actual danger in some situations.

Since everyone has suffered from fear at some time in his or her life, you probably are well acquainted with the feelings of anxiety, panic, or discomfort that can accompany this state of mind. What you might not know is that there are ways of replacing your fears or even lack of self-confidence with the ability to take action comfortably. This is an ability that you already have, but haven't yet used appropriately.

Remember, in NLP we say, **The map is not the territory.** The map of New York doesn't look much like what you see when you're in the middle of Manhattan staring up at the skyscrapers. Your feelings come from *how* you *think* about people, events, circumstances, or things, not the people, events, circumstances, and things themselves.

Connirae Andreas, NLP trainer and coauthor of the NLP book *Heart of the Mind,*[2] once worked with a woman who was petrified of public speaking. Connirae asked her to consciously notice the internal picture she was making when she felt fearful. The woman realized that she imagined being surrounded by people with giant critical eyes as she gave her presentation. When Connirae had the woman detach and *watch* herself, all her scared feelings disappeared. She then could see that her audience was just a normal group of people. She *literally* took a different point of view, and this changed her internal map.

The methods in this chapter will teach you how to choose to take new perspectives on memories and experiences that have caused you to feel fearful, phobic, or uptight. As a result, you'll become more self-confident, resourceful, and effective.

Creating New Perspectives

People have been talking about "points of view" for centuries; however, most people have always thought about this expression as metaphorical rather than literal. You can literally view something from any point in space. Each different point of view will give you somewhat different information and feelings. Remember the exercise in Chapter One where you experimented with seeing yourself on a roller-coaster ride, compared with the experience of actually being on the ride, hurtling down the track? When you looked out of your eyes from your own point of view we called that association. When you saw yourself on the ride, we called that dissociation.

Dissociation enables you to distance yourself from your feelings as you take on the perspective of an observer. By using Exercise 29, "The Fast Phobia Technique," you, too, can learn how to immediately decrease the fears that might be holding you back in your life, such as the fear of saying what you'd like to express at a meeting, making a cold call, making a public presentation, or any *personal* fear issue that may hold you back.

When people are afraid of some situation or thing, they usually imagine the frightening situation and then step into it and experience it as though it's actually happening at that moment, associated. However, when they imagine the same situation but watch themselves, they will have only the feelings of the observer. Dissociation enables you to watch yourself have any unpleasant experience and handle it without fear as long as you remain a detached observer.

The Physiology of Mental States

When you use a dissociated image, your observer perspective is not the only part of you that can help you control your mental states. Your posture also contributes to these different mental states of dissociation and association. Try the following quick experiment. Remember, NLP is about *experience,* not just head knowledge. *Doing* the exercises is the best way to use this information. Sit in a straight-backed chair about four or five inches from the back of the chair. Lean back comfortably against the back of the chair and feel your shoulders move back even a bit further. As you do, let your eyes relax and defocus. Let your chin rise slightly, and let your head move back. Feel your body become still. Notice how this posture, this physiology, begins to change the perspective that you take on the world. Notice the feeling of detachment that goes with this posture. This is the physiology of dissociation.

Now scoot back in the chair, so that your lower back is touching the chair and lean forward slightly. Looking around in both directions, imagine what you would need to do with your body in order to catch a ball if it were tossed to you. This physiology is more in the situation. This is an associated physiology.

Notice that when other people are adopting this kind of physiology, they are more fully engaged in whatever is going on. Your physiology can have a lot to do with your ability to either associate or dissociate. When doing any process or technique that uses association or dissociation, you'll want to adopt the appropriate physiology for each step of the technique.

It's very useful to recognize dissociation in contrast to association when you're communicating with others. When people are dissociated, they're apt to be analyzing the experience and thinking about what is going on rather than being involved in it. When they are associated, they will be "in" the experience and feeling it fully.

How to Access Your Mental States

Let's do another short experiment. Think of two memories from your past, one pleasant and another unpleasant. Take a minute to reexperience each of these two memories in whatever way that you naturally do. Notice how you recall those experiences, whether you relive them, associated, or whether you simply observe your experience, dissociated, and see yourself in a movie or slide at some distance.

Whichever way you recalled those pleasant and unpleasant memories naturally, go back and reverse them. If you were dissociated in the unpleasant one, step into the image and notice how that changes your feelings. If you were associated in that memory, step back out of your body, and see yourself dissociated, and notice how that changes your feelings.

Now, think of how you recalled the pleasant memory. If you were dissociated in the pleasant memory, step into it and experience it like it's happening now. If you were associated in the pleasant memory, step out for a moment, and see what it's like to watch it.

When you're associated into a memory, you will tend to have all the feelings that you had in the original event, whether pleasant or unpleasant. When you are dissociated, you will usually have only the feelings of a detached observer. Having gone through this experience, it's clear which ways you'll want to use to remember events. You'll want to remember positive experiences in an associated way and negative ones in a dissociated way.

One example of how not to use these skills is the story of a woman who had a wonderful time at a party on New Year's Eve. For hours she had fun, she danced . . . she even sang for the group, and was the funniest person there. At about two o'clock in the morning, just before everybody left, someone walked by and bumped her arm while she was drinking a cup of coffee. It spilled all down the front of her white dress. She jumped up, horrified, and said, "The whole evening is ruined!" A few months later, at the grocery store, she met someone who was at the party that night. When he began to talk to her about it, she interrupted him, saying

in an exasperated voice, "Please don't talk to me about that party—
that was a terrible night!"

This woman had the experience of being the life of the party for
hours and then had the whole thing ruined by one negative moment.
Instead of enjoying all the pleasant memories of the evening, she
associated into the experience of the spilled coffee at the end of the
party and dissociated from all the hours of fun she'd had. That's not
a very wise way to remember a party, and it's not a useful way to
go through life.

Consider people who get depressed. They're often people who
dissociate from their *positive* experiences and *associate* into the
negative ones. Now consider people whom you may know who are
typically on an emotional roller coaster. They're up one minute and
down the next. These are the people who associate into almost all of
their experiences, pleasant or unpleasant, and who seldom dissociate. There are also people who tend to experience much of life from
an observer position. Usually they are attracted to professions that
require analysis, including sciences such as engineering or computer
programming. They are often more oriented to concepts, information, and things than they are to other people.

If you really want to enjoy your life, you will want to associate
into your memories, so that you can enjoy all those pleasant feelings
and use them as positive resources that support positive attitudes for
future results.

The physiology of pleasant feelings is also much healthier for
your body than the stressful physiology of unpleasantness. Typically your body reacts to unpleasantness with a "fight or flight"
physiology. This is useful in escaping a truly dangerous situation,
but in ordinary, unpleasant situations it only results in tension,
higher blood pressure, and all the other physiological stress responses. It's bad enough that you had to experience all those bad
feelings for the first time; why experience them over and over again?
When you dissociate from an unpleasant memory, you can still see
yourself unhappy over there, so you can still be aware of what you
don't want to experience in the future. You don't lose any valuable
information, and you can still remember important lessons from
those experiences. All you lose are the bad feelings that tend to limit

your thinking and creativity when you need it most. By dissociating from unpleasant memories, you can remain resourceful and creative, better able to deal with the difficulties that life presents. Learning to choose when you associate or dissociate gives you a profound way to change your life. The next step is to begin to teach your unconscious mind, so that you can exercise this choice automatically. If you already experience this kind of automatic choice, the next exercise may be unnecessary for you. However, it's enjoyable and could still make an important difference in your life.

EXERCISE 27: ASSOCIATION AND DISSOCIATION

I. Association

1. Physiology. Utilize the physiology of association. Lean forward, look from side to side, feel whatever feelings you are experiencing now, and feel a readiness to move, to act in response to whatever happens next.

2. Associate into a Pleasant Memory. Now think of a pleasant memory and take the time to associate into it fully, so that you are there inside it again, looking out of your own eyes, seeing what you saw, hearing what you heard, and enjoy feeling all the good feelings you originally had in that situation.

3. Repeat Step 2. Use several other pleasant memories, one at a time, while maintaining the physiology of association. Pick pleasant memories from widely different contexts—work, play, home, some athletic, some sensual, self-satisfaction and recognition from others, etc. Associate into each one completely, so that you can enjoy feeling those positive and resourceful feelings fully.

4. Ask Your Mind to Associate Only Positively. Now close your eyes, and ask your unconscious mind if it would be willing to be a positive resource for you by automatically allowing you to associate into all positive memories, whenever you recall them. Recognize that in nearly all cases, this will be a wise choice that will enable you to enjoy life more and to be more resourceful in the face of life's inevitable difficulties. Take the time to be sure

Continued

that this inner message has been heard and responded to positively. Pause for a moment and relax.

II. Dissociation

1. Physiology of Dissociation. Utilize the physiology of dissociation. Lean back in your chair, and feel your shoulders move back even a bit more. Let your chin move up a bit as your head also moves back, and let your whole body become still.

2. Dissociate from an Unpleasant Memory. Now think of a moderately unpleasant memory and take the time to fully dissociate from it. See yourself in that memory, as if watching a movie on a TV set. It can help to make the movie black and white, or to move that TV set farther away, and let the movie become dimmer and less clear. If you have any trouble dissociating, imagine viewing it through a plate of thick Plexiglas. Enjoy that feeling of being a detached observer, yet interested and curious.

3. Repeat Step 2. Use several other moderately unpleasant memories from a wide variety of contexts—unpleasant experiences at work, play, home, with others and alone, disappointments and mistakes, etc. Dissociate completely from each one, in turn, so that you can enjoy that feeling of being a detached observer, yet interested and curious.

4. Ask Your Mind to Associate Only Positively. Now close your eyes and ask your unconscious mind if it would be willing to be a positive resource for you by allowing you to automatically dissociate from all unpleasant memories whenever you recall them, recognizing that in nearly all cases that will be a wise choice and enable you to enjoy life more and to be more resourceful in the face of life's inevitable difficulties. Take the time to be sure that this inner message has been heard and responded to positively.

There is another useful way to process unpleasant memories so that they become positive resources, and that is to run them backward. Use the next exercise to find out how useful this can be.

EXERCISE 28: RUNNING A BACKWARD MOVIE

1. Unpleasant Memory. Think of a moderately unpleasant memory, and run a movie of it, however you recall it now. As you watch and listen to this movie, notice whatever unpleasant feelings you have. Run it clear through from beginning to end.

2. Run a Movie Backward. Now step into that movie at the end, and run the entire movie backward, in color, and very fast, taking only about one and a half seconds to do this. It will be just as if you were *in* the experience and time is running backward very fast. Do this two or three more times if you want to.

3. Test It. Now run that same movie that you ran in Step 1, and again notice your feelings in response to it.

For most people, the original unpleasant feelings they had have been neutralized. Reliving the experience backward quickly changes the order of the experience in your brain in such a way that the fear is eliminated. You just can't have the fear anymore. It's as if doing this process in your mind pulls the fear out of the situation. Being in a situation backward means that you actually jump into the ending and imagine that you are doing everything backward, walking backward, talking backward, moving backward, doing the entire process backward—as if you were starring in a video playing on your VCR that was programmed in a fast "reverse" mode, and you end up at the beginning of the experience before it occurred.

When this process doesn't work, it's because the person only made a movie of themselves going backward, watching themselves do it, instead of actually being inside it, getting the sensations of moving backward. You need to actually relive it backward. It might help to imagine you are being flipped back through the experience by a giant rubber band, feeling the sensation of moving very fast toward its beginning.

Combining dissociation with running the movie backward provides a method that is even more powerful than either method alone—one that is powerful enough to neutralize even the most intense phobia or traumatic memory. This method was developed by Richard Bandler[3] as an improvement on an earlier method he developed with John Grinder.[4]

An insurance salesman had a fear of elevators. If his client's office was above the third or fourth floor, he had to take the stairs or avoid the visit altogether. This fear really limited his income—though it did give him plenty of exercise climbing stairs. When he was asked where he got that fear, he didn't have a clue. He couldn't recall the first time, but said as far as he knew he had been afraid of elevators his entire life. He recalled as a child being afraid to go up in the elevator to the dentist's office on the seventh floor of a building and having to take the stairs instead. He still shuddered when he thought about it. To help him overcome his fear, he was asked to imagine that he could see himself on the elevator going up. He watched a black-and-white movie of that seven-year-old boy going up in the elevator, filled with terror and panic, as though he were watching the scene from a distance. In addition to seeing himself in the elevator, it was very important that he hear that upset little boy crying and struggling as well. His internal dialogue was appropriate for dissociation, for detachment from his fear. He used sentences such as "He's frightened over there; that little boy is frightened."

After he watched his little boy self go up in the elevator and then get off at the top floor knowing he was safe again, he then associated into the situation in a special way; he jumped into the end of the scene and rolled through the whole movie backward, very fast, from the end to the beginning. He did this in full color, and he did it very quickly, taking only about one and one half seconds from the end back to the beginning.

At the end of running this movie backward, he popped out at the beginning before the event ever occurred. He is still doing fine after six years. Right after doing the technique, he tested his fear by riding a glass elevator to a thirteenth-floor restaurant, where he enjoyed a glass of wine in celebration.

Relieving Trauma Through Visualization

The same technique can work on any traumatic memory, even if it didn't result in a phobia. One man had had a particularly difficult life experience. He'd gone home early from work one day to share with his wife the exciting news that he had just gotten a promotion that he didn't expect. When he got home, he walked into his backyard, where he knew his wife would be gardening. Tragically, he found her dead from a heart attack at the age of thirty-five. This scene had remained with him and powerfully affected him. Whenever he thought of her, or their ten years of marriage, he would vividly picture his wife lying in the backyard, and he would relive the shock of the experience all over again. To help him change the nature of this traumatic experience, he watched the same experience as though he were watching it from a hundred feet up in the air, *seeing himself* walk into his backyard and finding his wife dead. He saw himself sit down, put his face in his hands, and sit for a few minutes, and then saw himself crying at the arrival of the ambulance. At the end of this movie, he jumped into it and imagined he was sucked back through the entire experience in one and one half seconds, just as if he were being pulled back by a giant vacuum cleaner. This disconnected the shock and fear from this memory, and he began to be able to remember his life with her more easily. Only then was he able to associate into the many pleasant memories he could recall with his wife.

The same technique also works exquisitely on post-traumatic stress disorders (PTSD), which many Vietnam veterans and police officers face. Any time a person has an intense and instantaneous fear or other unpleasant response, whether you'd think of it as a phobia or not, this process can be very useful.

What Phobias Really Are

These are two things to keep in mind when you have any kind of fear. First of all, some people with phobias think there's something wrong with them, that they are crazy, or that it's stupid to have the fear. Actually, if you have a phobic response to something, it means your brain can learn very quickly. Phobias are typically the result of a one-time learning experience. For example, one woman had a snake phobia because a snake had been thrown at her by some other kids when she was a little girl. Somehow, outside of her consciousness, whenever she saw a snake or thought about one, she would imagine that dangerous and frightening snake flying at her through the air. That single experience had created a fear that had lasted for over twenty years. After all, she *never* forgot to get scared when she saw a snake. This was powerful proof of her ability to learn very quickly.

The second important thing to remember is that fear is a *communication* from your unconscious mind. Your unconscious mind is attempting to communicate to you that danger is present and that you need to be careful.

In the next exercise, "The Fast Phobia Technique," it is important to explicitly go through each of the steps carefully. You'll notice the similarities between it and the two previous exercises. After you have experienced the impact of those two exercises, you are now ready to assimilate them into one process. Using this technique, you'll be able to change a fearful experience into a detached memory. This method is appropriate for any situation, memory, or event where you want to eliminate strong negative feelings. It can also be used on less intense unpleasant memories. You may want to have someone assist you in going through this process with a very strong unpleasant memory.

EXERCISE 29: THE FAST PHOBIA TECHNIQUE

Although this method will work well with very intense fears or phobias, we highly recommend that you *learn* the process thoroughly, using a *moderately* fearful situation.

1. Fearful Situation. Take a minute and think of a situation that makes you moderately fearful. This could be making a cold call, making a presentation, or any other situation that makes you afraid. Think about it just enough to get a little bit of the feeling of fear. You want to be sure that you can get access to the part of you that creates the fear.

2. Movie Theater. Now, in your mind's eye, imagine you are sitting in a large movie theater. See yourself up on the screen in a still picture just *before* you had the fearful response for the first time. (If you can't think of the first time you experienced this fear, think of the most intense time that you have had this kind of fear response.)

3. Leave Body. Now imagine floating out of your body and go up into the projection booth, so that now you can look out and see yourself watching yourself on the screen. (For a height phobia, instead of going up into the projection booth, just imagine you moved back ten rows in a theater.) Stay in this projection booth until you are instructed to leave it.

4. Watch a Movie. As you watch yourself watching yourself, begin to run a black-and-white movie of what actually occurred in that fearful situation, and see yourself going through that experience. Continue to watch that movie from the projection booth, until you reach the end of the situation when the trauma was over, and you can tell from your movie that you're safe again. At this point, stop the movie and make it into a still picture of yourself after the trauma was over with.

5. Run the Movie Backward. Now leave the projection booth, step into the still picture on the screen, and go through the experience backward, in color, just as if time were reversed and you were being sucked back through it by a giant vacuum cleaner. Do this very quickly, in about one and one half seconds. Do this step several more times if you believe it would be helpful. When you're finished, actually physically get up and move your body around. Shake your arms and take a deep breath.

6. Checking. Now, think of the experience again, and notice your response. In your mind, rate the fear on a scale of 1 to 10, with 10 being the worst. If it's more than 2, repeat the entire process, being careful to do each step thoroughly.

Continued

It is important to be cautious as you test the change you've just created in the real world. For example, if your fear was of heights, you might go to a fairly high place, look out a window, and notice how your fear has changed. Test yourself gently and carefully, with respect for your own personal safety. Use appropriate caution in dangerous situations. The fear has probably kept you out of these situations, so you don't have much experience in how to cope with them. Some situations do have inherent danger, so it's important to respect this and learn how to deal with them cautiously and resourcefully.

The Need for Rapid Change

Most people have a hard time believing that an intense fearful or unpleasant response can be changed so quickly and easily. Many people mistakenly believe that change has to be long and tedious. The only reason that change usually takes a long time is that the methods used have been primitive and inappropriate. With appropriate understanding and methods, change can occur more quickly.

In fact, you can't change slowly! Your brain learns very fast. If you watched one frame of a movie every day for five years, it would be hard to tell someone the plot. It would be impossible—you can only get the meaning of the movie when you watch the frames go by very fast. As Richard Bandler says, "Trying to change something slowly is like having a conversation at the rate of one word a day."

People often ask, "How often do I need to practice this process to make it work?" Once you've done this process thoroughly, you should never need to do it again. The change is permanent. You learned to have this unpleasant memory or phobia very quickly, and you can learn to change it just as quickly.

We have described and demonstrated what the Fast Phobia Technique does, how it works, and what it is useful for. In NLP, all the techniques are carefully described in terms of what they are useful for and what they do. It is equally important to point out what they don't do, and what they should not be used for.

If you were to use the phobia process on pleasant experiences, those, too, would become neutralized, and this would not be helpful. If you were to use this process on all the good experiences in a relationship, the good feelings would vanish, and the relationship would probably end.

You can usefully use the phobia technique on a sudden shock or other traumatic responses to the way that a person died, as in the example provided earlier. This traumatic response to the event of death is quite different from the loss of the valued relationship and all the wonderful experiences you had in relationship with that person.

If you were to use the phobia process on the loss experienced by a grieving person, it would either have no effect, or it would make it worse, because the mental structure of grief is exactly the opposite of a phobia. In a phobia, a person *associates* into a very *unpleasant* memory; in grief a person *dissociates* from a very *pleasant* memory. Since the structure of the two problems is opposite, the process to remedy the two problems is also opposite. This provides an inkling of some of the other uses for association and dissociation in other NLP techniques.

The Three Perceptual Positions

So far you've explored two thinking perspectives: association and dissociation. You found that by utilizing these two perspectives appropriately you can create impressive change in your life. There is also a third perspective that you can use to greatly increase both your personal effectiveness and the wisdom with which you live.

First, we want to relabel being associated or dissociated. Being associated can also be thought of as being in *self* position. You are experiencing things through your own eyes, feeling your own physiology, thinking about things with your own values and through your own mental filters. This *self* position is one perspective on the world. Dissociation provides you with another perspective in which you are an *observer,* watching yourself. It's a neutral, detached point of view. This allows you to consider a situation in an objective way.

The third and new perspective we want to offer you is being in *other* position, in which you take on someone else's experiences. The ability to take *other* position is particularly important and useful when you have a disagreement or dispute with someone else, so that you can literally "see it his way." Seeing a situation the way someone else does doesn't mean you have to agree with it, and it doesn't mean that you have to abandon how you see it. It can give you the additional vital information you need to find a common ground to begin to resolve the issues that have divided you.

Being in *other* position is like being inside the experience of someone else, sometimes called empathy. It's the point of view you adopt when you step into the shoes of another person and experience something through their eyes, their mental filters, their personal history, and their physiology. Taking *other* position is something most people do naturally and automatically with someone they love deeply. That wonderful feeling of connection and being together comes partly out of this alignment with the loved person's views, desires, and perspectives.

When we ask someone to look at something through our eyes, we're requesting them to take *other* position, our position, on a particular issue and try on our experience of it. We're asking them to empathize deeply with us. Very few people learn to do this in a thorough and congruent way, yet the ability to take *other* position gives you a powerful and useful new perspective on your behavior or on any situation.

To get a clearer idea of *other* position, think of being in a movie theater, watching a favorite film on the screen—you naturally adopt a character's feelings, and become him or her in your imagination. For example, if someone were being chased, you have all the sensation of being pursued, your hands sweaty, your heart racing, in spite of the fact that you are sitting safely in the theater. That's truly taking *other* position.

Effective actresses and actors are known for their rich ability to step into the shoes of their character and become that person. One famous actor said that he actually *became* the character in his own mind's eye. He would see the world differently, he would understand it differently, and he would even do things spontaneously that weren't necessarily something he himself would do, but would certainly be something that character would do.

Gandhi wrote that in preparation for a negotiation he would consider situations through the eyes of the Hindu, the Moslem, and the British. He would think of actual people that he believed represented these particular points of view and adopt their body postures to truly understand their thinking on the issues.

One of the people who worked with Gandhi said that before a particular negotiation, Gandhi walked about his house holding his hands like the Briton he was going to meet with, while thinking through each of his interests. This is a clear reference to *other* position. Gandhi also said that he considered his negotiation outcomes through the eyes of the world—an *observer* perspective—before proposing them. Much of his wisdom resulted from his skill at taking different perspectives. When you take *other* position, you get new and useful information about how someone else experiences a situation.

Perhaps the best way to realize the importance of *other* position is to think of situations in which it is absent. Think about how common it is—yet how limiting and damaging it can be—to make decisions from only one perspective. For example, companies that pollute rivers or air, or that cut down rain forests for short-gain profits, are making decisions strictly from their own perspective. Think of an abusive or autocratic boss that you might have had. Wasn't that person stuck in making decisions from only their own *self* position, without a thought to your experience?

You can probably think of many other unpleasant examples in your life when someone didn't attempt to take *other* position, and understand what it was like to be on the other side of the situation. How much simpler and more pleasant it would have been if both parties had really entered the experience of the other. Use the following exercise to deepen your ability to take *other* position and enter into the experience of someone else.

EXERCISE 30: TAKING *OTHER* POSITION

1. Conflict Situation. Think of a moderately difficult specific situation in which you had a disagreement or conflict with someone else.

2. **Self** *Position.* Run your movie of this situation from your own point of view. Imagine that you are going through this situation again, looking out of your own eyes, reexperiencing what actually happened. Notice what you hear and feel—all the information that is available to you. When you come to the end of this episode, rewind the movie and stop it just at the very beginning of this conflict situation.

3. Study the Other Person. With the movie stopped on "pause" at the beginning, look over at this other person. Notice his breathing, his posture, his facial expression, the way he moves and speaks, the tone and tempo of his voice, all the nonverbal information that tells you what this person's experience is like. You can also review all your experiences with this person, and all that you know of his likes and dislikes, his attitudes, his personal history, everything that contributes to who he is.

4. Take **Other** *Position.* Now let your awareness float up out of your body and around to align with that other person, perhaps looking over his shoulder, so that you can begin to see what he sees, and hear what he hears.

Begin to take on his likes and dislikes and personal history by saying to yourself, "I am a person who . . ." and follow it with all of the traits and characteristics you know about.

Allow your awareness to enter his body, and take on his posture and movement, and all the other nonverbal behavior you noted earlier. As you continue to become this person even more fully, feel what it is like to really be this person.

5. Run a Movie from **Other** *Position.* Now run that same movie of the conflict situation again, seeing it from his perspective. As this other person, how do you experience this same conflict situation? What feelings do you have? What are your wants, hopes, and fears? What are your positive intentions, and how are you attempting to cope with this difficult situation? What do you notice about how your own behavior looks and feels to this person as you run this movie to the end? What else can you learn about this person's experience?

6. Return to Self Position. Allow your awareness to float up again and return to your own body. Take all the time you need to fully return to being yourself before opening your eyes, leaving all the elements of this other person's identity there with him.

Most people who take the time to thoroughly do this exercise learn a great deal about the other person, and about how they themselves appear to this other person. Usually this information has important messages about what to do to begin to find a basis for agreement and resolve the conflict.

In the previous exercise, you learned how to leave your *self* position and enter *other* position to experience this position fully. Earlier you learned how to take an *observer* position with respect to your own experience in order to dissociate from unpleasant feelings and become more resourceful. However, there is yet another way to use *observer* position: to observe the interaction between yourself and another person. Use the following exercise for an experience of how this can be useful.

EXERCISE 31: THE NEUTRAL OBSERVER

1. Conflict Situation. Return to the same conflict situation you used in the previous exercise.

2. Self Position. Again, take *self* position in this situation. You don't have to run the whole movie this time, as long as you put yourself back into the situation fully.

3. Other Position. Now take *other* position in the same way. Again, you don't have to run the whole movie, as long as you fully become this other person in this situation.

Continued

> *4. Take* **Observer** *Position.* Now move out to a position from
> which you can see and hear both you and this other person clearly.
> Make sure this observer is the same distance from where you see
> yourself as it is from where you see the other person. Also make
> sure you are observing from a place that is eye-level with yourself
> and the other person—not higher or lower.
>
> *5. Run a Movie as Observer.* Now run the entire movie, watching
> and listening to the situation unfold as an observer, as if you were
> observing these two people for the first time. From this neutral
> perspective, pay close attention to the interaction between the two
> of you. Notice particularly how what one does stimulates or trig-
> gers the other, how one person's behavior stimulates feelings in
> the other, and vice versa. Learn all you can about this interaction
> from this *observer* position. How do you feel in this position as
> you observe this interaction?

In this exercise, many people gain important and useful understanding about how their own behavior triggers responses in others,
and vice versa. Beyond this, they often experience a deep compassion for both of these people who are so caught up in the dispute.

A Basis for Wisdom and Genius

All three positions—*self, other,* and *observer*—provide unique
information and understandings. When you are able to shift between
the three at will, the combination of all this information provides a
basis for true wisdom.

Robert Dilts, one of the developers of NLP, said, "*Excellence
is a passionate commitment to something from self position. Wisdom is the ability to consciously move back and forth between self,
other, and observer positions.*" The more fully and completely you
can do that, the more you will enhance your own personal effectiveness. You'll also enhance your own ability to maintain a resourceful thinking process, whether you are negotiating or giving a
presentation, approaching a new customer, or responding to your
child. Finally, as you use these processes, you'll increase your

mental flexibility and your ability to deal powerfully and positively with a variety of people and situations.

The ability to take a total *self, other,* or *observer* perspective is rare in our world. Einstein, Gandhi, Mozart, Disney, and many other geniuses wrote about these points of view and indicated that they actively used these different perspectives as a part of their thinking processes. For example, Einstein used the perspectives of *self* and *observer* to create his theory of relativity. He imagined what it would be like to be riding on the end of a light beam at 186,000 miles per second while "another" Einstein watched him from *observer* perspective. These thoughts were the basis for the theory that transformed our thinking about the structure of the universe.

Walt Disney also used these different perspectives in his imaginative process for creating stories. He switched positions with his audience while he was planning and designing because he wanted to be able to look at the story from their point of view. Because the ability to consciously dance between these perspectives is so valuable, take the time to go through Exercises 30 and 31. If you do it fully, you'll discover the usefulness of adopting each of these perceptual positions.

Practice Your Techniques

Perhaps the best way to understand how valuable these three perspectives can be is when you're dealing with conflict resolution, negotiation skills, and customer-service skills, or when your organization seeks to build effective teams. In these situations, it is ideal for you to consciously move between *self, other,* and *observer* perspectives. It will empower you to plan and act with wisdom and self-confidence in relationship to others.

Take time right now to think of a situation involving others where you feel fearful or you would like to have more choice. For example, you may be afraid of dealing with someone in a confrontation. Or maybe you're afraid of asking for that promotion that you feel that you deserve. Perhaps you're afraid of approaching that intimidating client. Whatever your fear is, take a few minutes to transform it to personal effectiveness using the perceptual position skills that you've learned here. You can have much more control over your feelings of fear and anxiety than you may have ever dreamed possible.

Reviewing What You've Learned

Learning to eliminate your fears and phobias is as simple as learning a few easy NLP techniques. To review what we've discussed in this chapter, you have learned:

- How to use dissociation, or the process of watching yourself, to distance yourself from your feelings about unpleasant events
- How to access your associated and your dissociated mental states, to enjoy pleasant experiences and neutralize unpleasant ones
- How to run a movie of an unpleasant event backward to neutralize it
- How to apply the Fast Phobia Technique to help you remove your fears quickly
- How to consciously use the three perceptual positions—*self, other,* and *observer*—to improve your relationships and provide a basis for wise and creative decisions

Eliminating fears and unpleasantness is a valuable goal, one that can release your abilities and allow you to move forward confidently. However, these goals are trivial in comparison to the wisdom you can gain from utilizing the three perceptual positions in every arena of your life. Remember that the exercises are just that: devices for you to flex and strengthen your "mental muscles" for all the tasks you undertake. The more often you use these exercises, the more supple and flexible your mind will be.

CHAPTER NINE

Building Self-Confidence

*Great art of every form rests firmly on a foundation of technical
skill. For example, ballet requires mastery of the plié and pirouette.
For me, NLP comes as close as anything I have discovered to
providing the technical foundation of the art of the whole human
being.*

— LARA EWING, *international management consultant*

Understanding Your Self-Evaluations

Just as fears and anxieties can get in the way of your achieving
success, the bad feelings that some people experience from self-
judgment and criticism can also hold you back. Nothing can weaken
or derail you as effectively as the sting of negative self-evaluation.
People typically use two main mental processes to put themselves
down: making internal pictures of failing or messing up, and hearing
an internal voice that reminds them of what they're doing wrong.

Have you ever thought about an upcoming presentation you had
to give and found yourself making pictures of getting up in front of
the group and looking nervous and making a fool out of yourself?
Have you ever said something to someone and had a voice fire off
inside your head that said, "You dummy—whatever possessed you
to say that?" Most of us have had experiences similar to these where
we became our own worst enemy. These mental processes set us up
to fail ahead of time.

Consider Bill, a man who had a big problem with negative
self-evaluation. He said that he'd been feeling blue and depressed
for over a year. In exploring his thought processes, he discovered
that he was making pictures of all the things he didn't do well,
and then commenting internally about how awful he was—using
both of the troublesome processes mentioned above. When he was
asked, "What about all the things that you do well?" he responded

that he knew that his successes were in his brain, but he just couldn't focus on them. Using the techniques in this chapter, he discovered new choices in both his internal pictures and internal dialogue so that his depressed feelings were replaced with feelings of self-confidence, helping him to become a more dynamic and successful member of his work team and in his life.

Locating Your Critical Voices

Let's work with internal voices first. Think back to a specific situation when you noticed that an internal voice was being critical or was making disparaging comments about you. First, put yourself back into that situation and briefly relive it. As you recall that experience, pay special attention to that critical voice.

In Chapter Six you learned how to change the location of a troublesome voice so that it became aligned with you and became integrated into you. This time we want to teach you a different approach. The voice might be loud or soft, or fast or slow. The tonality of the voice might be sarcastic or strident. It might sound like your own voice, or it might sound like someone close to you who's been critical of you in the past—for example, a parent, or older sibling, or other relative. Notice your emotional response as you listen to the voice.

Now, experiment with different tonalities. Notice what happens if you speed the voice way up or slow it way down—like you are changing the speed on a phonograph. Make the voice sound like the cartoon characters Elmer Fudd or Mickey Mouse or a computerized recording. Try making it playful, teasing, or seductive. Notice how your emotional response changes as you change the speed, tonality, or tempo of the voice, even though the words remain the same.

Discovering Positive Intentions

Now let's discover the *intention* of this voice that is critical, by asking what it's trying to do for you that's *positive*. One of the NLP

Presuppositions is that **underlying every behavior is a positive intention** for us, or we wouldn't continue doing it. You can assume that this critical voice has some positive purpose that it's attempting to accomplish for you, and it's important to find out what that positive intention is.

So again, hear that voice in your mind being critical of you, and ask the voice—just as if it were another person:

> "What's your intention for me?"
> "What are you trying to accomplish for me?"
> "What purpose do you have in mind when you are being critical of me?"

After you have asked one of these questions, remain silent and listen to what the voice says in response.

Common answers to this question are:

> "I'm trying to keep you from making a fool of yourself."
> "I want to protect you."
> "I'm making sure you do what's right."
> "I want you to be all that you can be."

After you hear an answer from this voice, notice your response to this intention.

You probably don't appreciate what this voice says to you or the tonality it uses, but do you appreciate the voice's intention? If you have difficulty accepting that what you're hearing is positive, keep asking the voice until you do find an intention that you can agree with. For instance, if the voice says, "I'm trying to get you motivated," you can then ask, "And when you're trying to get me motivated, what does that do for me?" The voice might say, "Well, when you're motivated, you get things done and make more money." To this you might respond, "And when I'm getting things done and making more money, what does that do for me?" Then the voice might answer, "You'll be a success and feel good about yourself." That's an intention that most of us can certainly appreciate and be glad to have a part of us striving for.

If the voice initially says, "I want to punish you," you probably won't agree with that intention. When you ask again, "What will it accomplish for you to punish me?" the voice might reply, "Then you'll pay attention to me and remember what I say." After again asking for the positive intention, the voice might reply, "I want to keep you out of situations where you'll fail and feel bad." Here at last is an intention most of us would agree with, except that it's stated in the negative. What this voice really wants is the positive— for you to succeed and feel good.

Once you have determined the positive intention of a critical voice, the first step is to agree with it and thank the voice for having it. Affirm that you value its intention for you. "I'm glad you have that positive intention for me. Thank you for wanting this for me." When you do this, you have achieved a crucially important step. Because both you and the voice agree on the positive intention, you are no longer adversaries. Now you have become allies who can work together to resolve the problem that remains: that the way that the voice is trying to get its outcome—nagging and criticizing—is causing you misery. In fact, this nagging and criticizing may even be causing you to fail—the reverse of its positive intention, which is to help you succeed.

Negotiating with Your Critical Voice

Since you and the voice both agree on the positive intention, you can now explore other, more comfortable, and perhaps more effective ways of getting the results you both want. The next step in this process is to ask the voice the following: "If there were additional ways to get this positive intention met that were at least as good as—and perhaps better than—what you are now doing, would you be interested in trying them out?"

That's an offer that your voice can't refuse. If the voice doesn't agree to have more and better choices, then it obviously does not fully understand the offer. Sometimes a voice thinks it would have to give up what it's doing now, or would have to use a choice that it doesn't agree to. If the voice refuses, simply restate the offer and clarify it. You want to search for additional choices, and you will only be satisfied with them if the voice fully agrees they will work better than what it is now doing. Proceed to the next step only when the voice agrees to a joint search for new choices.

Now we need help from your creative part—the part of you that plans and comes up with new ideas. Ask your creative part to generate lots and lots of ideas about how the voice can meet its positive intention for you, and have the voice choose three different additional ways to meet its intention that the voice likes—at least ways that will work as well as, or even better than, what it's currently doing. What you want are new ways of behaving that will build up your self-confidence, rather than drag you down. As the creative part generates hundreds of possibilities, you and the voice select only those you both agree will be a significant improvement.

Here's an example of how this process works. John complained one night that he had been feeling a bit blue and depressed lately. As he explored this issue, he discovered an internal voice that was saying, "You're a bad person." When he asked the voice "What's your intention in saying that?" the response was, "I want to get you to pay attention to how you come across to others. You've been really negative toward others lately, and you should stop doing that."

John was surprised at that answer, yet when he thought about it, he could verify that the voice was right. He had been negative toward others recently. He responded with, "And when I stop being negative toward others, what will that do for me?" The answer to that was, "You'll have more self-respect and feel better about yourself." Following that he asked, "What does having more self-respect do for me?" The response to that was, "When you feel good about yourself, you will be positive with others and the result of that is more friends and better relationships."

John considered this all to be valuable information. He realized that he had gravitated toward habitually noticing what was wrong in his life, as well as in others' lives. He realized how much value there was in having a voice that wanted him to feel self-respect so that he could improve his relationships with others.

He moved on to asking the voice if it would be interested in additional behavioral choices in getting that intention met—other choices besides telling him, "You're a bad person"—which actually made the problem worse. After getting agreement to that, he had his creative part generate ideas of new behaviors he could do. The three choices that the voice liked and agreed to do were to breathe deeply and smile before responding to others; notice and comment on what the other person is doing that is positive; and offer encouragement to John about what he's doing well, noticing the positive aspects of his behavior. At the conscious level, John realized that these choices would certainly work much better for him than an internal voice that was critical.

You can also negotiate with the voice about *when* it offers you corrective feedback. Feedback during a performance usually disrupts and interferes with it, while the same feedback later is much more useful. Ask the voice to give you feedback and suggestions *after* you've completed your performance. Many top performing athletes will hum a tune or repeat a positive phrase over and over in their minds to keep their internal voices from interrupting them, so that they can keep their confidence levels high. These athletes have found themselves much less likely to listen to a voice that might offer criticism if they have a pleasant internal sound during a performance.

What follows is an adaptation of a process called "Six-Step Reframing" developed by Richard Bandler and John Grinder.[1] The following summary is provided as an exercise. As with all the exercises in this book, the more often you do it, the more it will become an automatic part of your thinking and responding.

EXERCISE 32: REFRAMING AN INNER VOICE

1. Critical Voice. Think of a situation in which an inner voice criticized you. Put yourself back into that situation and listen carefully to the sounds that the voice says, and the voice tone, tempo, and rhythm in which it says those words.

2. Positive Intention. Ask this voice, "What is your positive intention?" or, "What is it that you want to achieve for me by criticizing me in this way?'' and then listen to what the voice says. Keep asking this question until you can completely agree with the positive intention you hear.

3. Acknowledge and Thank. Acknowledge the positive intention, agree with it, and thank the voice for having this positive intention for you.

4. Ask the Voice to Join in a Search for Alternatives. Ask, "If there were additional ways to get this positive intention that were at least as good as—and perhaps better than—what you are now doing, would you be interested in trying them out?'' Wait for a full "yes" response.

5. Creative Part. Ask a creative part of you or a part that plans to assist you to generate lots and lots of possible behaviors. The voice will choose three of the best ones, ones that it likes and believes will work as well as, or better than, what it has been doing.

6. Future Planning. Actively imagine carrying out each of these in turn, in the appropriate situation, to find out how well each works. If some don't work as well as anticipated, back up to Step 5 to generate more choices. When you have three new choices that you both like, ask the voice if it will be willing to actually use one or more of these choices in the appropriate situations.

After you have become fluent with this process, you can skip past steps as long as you are careful to preserve the function of each step.

For instance, if a voice has good advice, but you don't like to listen to it because the tone is scornful and abusive, you can say, "I appreciate what it is that you have to tell me, but I assure you that I'll be much more willing to listen to you if you use a soft friendly tone of voice like my friend uses. Are you willing to do that?''

If a voice notices all your mistakes after they happen, you can say, "You know a lot about the kinds of mistakes I'm likely to make in this situation, and when I'm likely to make them. Would you be willing to act as a friendly prompter and tell me what to do ahead of time, so that I can succeed more and more often?''

Reframing is a very streamlined and effective process that can be used for a wide variety of internal negotiations. The same principles are also very effective in negotiating or mediating between people or organizations. First, establish agreement on positive intent, or goals. Then, and only then, explore possible alternatives or solutions as a team.

Now that you've tuned into your internal voices and the kinds of things you say to yourself, you'll find it easy to listen to the speech patterns that get in the way of your personal effectiveness.

The Problem with Negations

In Chapter One, we pointed out the impact of negative statements: that they make you think of exactly what you don't want to think about. And when you say negative statements to others, it makes them think about what you don't want to think about. The same process has a big impact on self-confidence.

Repeat the following statements internally and become aware of the pictures and feelings they generate:

"Don't think about how badly you could screw up in the meeting."

"Don't be concerned about what your boss thinks of your report."

"You won't need to worry about what could go wrong on your vacation."

As we pointed out in Chapter One, by transforming these statements into statements of what we do want, our self-confidence can be much improved. It can also help to change these positive statements from "you" statements into "I" statements. "You" statements seem to come from someone else, and because of our past history, we will often hear them in an unpleasant tonality. "I" statements come out of ourselves, so we feel more the source of power and ability, and we are more likely to hear them in a positive tonality.

"I wonder how well I'll do in the meeting tomorrow?"

"What will my boss like best in my report to him?"

"I wish I knew what will be particularly right during my vacation."

Changing Universals

Another common internal language pattern that can seriously interfere with feeling self-confident is overgeneralization. Statements such as, "I never do anything right"; "I'm a crummy, rotten parent"; "Everybody always rejects me"; "I might as well give up—I'm just a failure" are common confidence deflators because they also contain hidden negations. "Never" means "*not* ever," "crummy," and "rotten" mean "*not* good," "rejection" means "*not* acceptable," and "failure" means "*not* successful."

As you say one of these statements to yourself, what happens to your emotional state? You feel hopeless. Besides negations, all these statements contain something else that is very harmful. Each one has an *all* or a *never* in it, what linguists call universal generalizations. If *everybody* rejects me, I really am in a difficult situation, and it makes perfect sense to feel helpless. If I *never* do anything right, I must really be a failure. The next time you make a universal generalization, you can use the following method for questioning your self-talk. As you go through the example, notice how your internal images change.

If you say to yourself: "I never do anything right," answer with: "Really—*never*? You mean there's *never* been a time when I did something right? What specifically did I do that didn't turn out well?"

Then you might realize, "I've done some things right. Actually, I've done many things right. Only sometimes do I goof up."

Notice how challenging your self-talk begins to change both the content and the submodalities of your internal pictures. By asking yourself these kinds of questions, you can go from universal generalities about yourself to a specific situation that is unsatisfying, so you can focus on it and change it.

Here's another example: "Everybody always rejects me." Notice the picture you produce when you take on that statement. Ask yourself: "How many people are in your picture when you say that?"

Probably there are hundreds—or none. Then ask yourself: "Who specifically is rejecting me?"

Then you might realize: "Actually, it's just Mary Lou (or whomever) who is rejecting me."

It's much easier to respond to one person rejecting you than to hundreds. The thought of having only one person rejecting you leaves you with a much greater amount of your self-confidence intact. By now you might be realizing that one important function of your internal voice is to create internal pictures and movies that can positively impact your emotions, helping you stay resourceful, capable, and confident.

Building Affirmative Self-Talk

Affirmations are statements about you that are framed in the positive—in other words, what you want to have happen rather than don't want. They are stated in the present or future tense as if they are already occurring or will be soon.

Equally as powerful as putting your statement in present tense is to use the "ing," or gerund, form of the verb. Note the difference in your mind between "I feel" and "I am feeling" or "my voice sounds" versus "my voice is sounding." The gerund form of the verb puts more action into your experience so that it becomes more real to you, and helps you associate into it, as if it were happening now. This action form also makes internal still pictures into moving pictures with much more information in them.

One other criterion is worth mentioning. If you make a statement in an affirmation that is contradictory to how you perceive yourself, you will think of it as unreal. If you think of it as unreal, either it won't work or it will boomerang.

For instance, if you realize that you have often been inconsiderate to others, the affirmation "I am considerate to others" will be a waste of time. However, if you change it to "I can learn to be considerate of others," that won't conflict with your conclusion that you have often been inconsiderate.

Here are some examples of useful affirmations:

I am learning things easily.
Each day I can become more kind and loving toward others.
I am a worthwhile person who is caring toward myself.
I can learn to behave responsibly.
I can be loving toward myself.
I can enjoy acting honestly in my dealings with others.

You first need to take the time to construct an affirmation that is important to who you want to be and become. Then you need to say it to yourself and check in your internal experience whether the result is what you want. If not, rewrite your affirmation until you can respond to it fully and congruently, or do some negotiation with the part that "boomerangs" it.

Affirmations can assist you in building a different internal dialogue, the kind of dialogue that will help your confidence in certain situations. Often, when you get into situations where you're not sure of yourself, your internal dialogue is not very supportive of you.

Benjamin Franklin used affirmations on a regular basis to improve his feelings about himself. He had thirteen virtues that he constantly worked toward. These virtues were temperance, silence, order, resolution, frugality, industry, sincerity, justice, moderation, cleanliness, tranquility, chastity, and humility. He even had affirmations about these virtues written on a piece of paper that he kept inside his pocket watch, so that every time he looked at his watch he had a positive reminder about improving his life. This was one way he consistently improved his confidence levels.

Although Franklin's affirmations worked for him, affirmations can boomerang on some people, and actually make the situation worse. Many of us have more than one internal voice, and some of them are very sarcastic and skeptical. If you say a nice affirmation to yourself, and another voice responds sarcastically with, "Oh, right,'' you'll probably end up with some images that are not at all supportive of what you want to have happen.

If you pay careful attention to your internal experience, you can easily tell whether an affirmation is doing what you want it to accomplish.

For instance, if you say to yourself, ''I can learn to be more considerate of others,'' what internal response follows in your mind? You could have a series of images of being more attentive to others, or asking others who are considerate how they do this, for example, and feel good about this direction in your life.

On the other hand, you might hear an internal voice snickering, and then see an enormous collage of all the times you were inconsiderate to others, and feel bad. If you had a response of this kind, you can always use the reframing technique you learned in the last chapter to change it. The positive intention of the snickering part is probably to keep you from false optimism and the disappointment that typically follows. However, until you make such changes, don't use affirmations, because you have just found out how they will boomerang on you.

We have already mentioned two criteria for affirmations: State them in the positive, and place them in the present or immediate future.

Turning Frustration into Flexibility

The next exercise can give you more options for your behavior by systematically visualizing alternative behaviors. This method can be especially useful when you find yourself frustrated and stuck in situations where it would be more useful to be relaxed and have other alternatives to try.

During a negotiation training, a manager complained that she wasn't as flexible as she would like to be when dealing with her boss. She mentioned that she was typically very talkative and expressed her opinions openly with people, but she was disappointed that she didn't do that with him.

She recounted an experience in the recent past where she had been called to his office and was told about some drastic changes in her job duties as manager of a typing pool. She sat silently and didn't have the courage to give her boss important information that he was lacking—information that would have changed the decision he made. She felt passive and uncomfortable in that situation and behaved very nonassertively. She wished she had felt more self-controlled, centered, and intelligent.

To help her feel more like this, she tried the technique of making mental movies of three different behaviors she could do in that situation. In the first picture, she saw herself breathing deeply and repeating to herself, "Mind—alert, body—calm." In her second picture, she imagined switching to *other* position to gain empathy with her boss. In her third picture, she was asking first what his intentions were in changing her job duties, and then offering the information that he needed to revise his decision.

When she actually stepped into these movies and rehearsed doing these three choices in her boss's office, she discovered that her first choice, controlling her breathing to relax, worked best to get her to a comfort level, so that she could follow up with the third choice. The second choice, though often a useful one, did not help her as much in this particular situation.

As her cue to engage in this new behavior, she pictured her boss talking to her from across his desk. Then she fully imagined doing this process and having a voice say, "I'll do that one. I can handle the added responsibility." Her feelings about herself and dealing with her boss changed dramatically after doing this technique.

EXERCISE 33: FRUSTRATION INTO FLEXIBILITY

1. Unresourceful Situation. Find a situation in the past where you weren't performing as resourcefully as you wanted to. First, step back into the situation just long enough to become aware of the feelings you're having. Then label your feelings. Give them a name, like "confused," "frightened," "anxious," "spacy," "fearful," etc.

Continued

2. Observer *Position*. Now, detach from that event and comfortably watch yourself behaving in the way you behaved at the time. As you watch this movie, you'll be gathering information, both consciously and unconsciously.

3. *Choose Feeling*. As you watch this scene, ask yourself what emotion or feeling you'd like to be experiencing in that context and label this feeling perhaps "centered," "grounded," "assertive," "calm," "excited," "persistent," etc.

4. *Review New Behaviors*. Keeping that positive emotion in mind, look up and see yourself doing different behaviors in that scene that could give you the feeling you want. Take the time to see yourself doing at least three behaviors in that situation that are different from what you did in the past, making at least one of your choices outrageous and humorous—something that you wouldn't have considered in the past. You don't ever have to do it, but thinking about it will add to your flexibility. Rehearse variations of each of these, and revise them accordingly. Take all the time you need to do this thoroughly.

5. *Rehearse New Behaviors*. Now associate into the behavior you thought of first and imagine you're in that situation behaving that way so that you become aware of your feelings. How intensely does this behavior create the emotion you want?

Now just set that choice aside, and step into the second behavior you imagined, experiencing what this choice is like, and checking the intensity of the emotion you want in that choice.

6. *Compare Choices*. Which one of these two choices gives you the stronger emotion, or seems like the best choice? Code this one as the current front-runner and then set it aside.

Now step into the final choice again, checking the intensity of the emotion created. Compare this choice with the front-runner and choose your favorite.

If none of the three is very satisfactory, go back to create even more choices until you have one you really like. After choosing your favorite new choice, hear an enthusiastic internal voice saying, "This is the one I'm going to do."

7. Future Planning. Now, make this new choice automatic by thinking of an external cue that will be present as the situation begins. For example, if the situation is public speaking, the cue could be seeing a group of people seated and waiting for you to speak, or seeing a podium in front of you. If you choose talking with your boss, the cue could be seeing or hearing that person. If you choose dealing with an angry client on the phone, the cue is hearing angry tones on the other end of the line. First imagine the cue, and then put yourself right there in the situation behaving in the new way you have chosen, to program that new behavior into the future situation by doing this.

Creative Visualization

In this exercise and in many previous exercises, we have used a two-step process that we haven't explicitly commented upon. When visualizing a goal or a future behavior, it is useful to do it from *observer* position. From this position it is easy to be a "film editor," rapidly running lots of different scenarios, cutting out sections that don't work well, adding in new segments, until you have a movie that looks good from *observer* position. From this position you also have some pretty good information about how it would feel if you stepped into it, because you can see the expression on your face and the faces of the other people involved as the finished movie runs.

For this *observer* movie to translate into actual behavior in the real world, it's essential to associate into it and take *self* position, living through it to find out what it is like to be inside as it unfolds. As you do this, you are doing three things: First, you are testing, to be sure that this scenario really is as good as it looked from the outside. Second, you may find that you still want to make a few minor revisions as you go through it, or you may find that you didn't plan for an important contingency and have to back up to the movie-editing booth and start over. And last, you are rehearsing the actual doing of this new behavior, programming yourself to respond automatically to appropriate cues in the ways you have outlined in your *observer* movie, adding in the feelings, tastes, and smells that make experiences fully real and compelling.

In all the foregoing, we have assumed that the person is competent, and only needs the confidence to feel comfortable and motivated to exercise this competence. This is clearly true, for example, in stage fright. You know that the person has the ability to speak fluently in other situations, but in front of a group he somehow isn't able to speak coherently.

Although self-confidence is a foundation for exercising our abilities, sometimes we lack confidence for a very good reason: We don't yet have the competence to do something well. For example, someone may lack confidence because he has never done it. Have you ever heard a speaker who was confident, but who bored you because he wasn't competent to present the subject matter?

What does it take to become competent, or really good at something? Think of any task you can already do really easily and skillfully—such as driving an automobile. Remember the first time you drove a car? You probably felt a little overwhelmed at all the things you had to do consciously in order to make the car go down the street, especially if that car had a stick shift. You were sitting there trying to steer, looking out the windshield, looking in the rearview mirror, coordinating the clutch and the gas, and trying to remember the rules of the road at the same time. Perhaps you killed the engine two or three times before you ever got it going. After a while, you became competent at driving, but the task still required most of your conscious attention. Now, some time and experience later, you can probably get in your car and drive fifty miles or so on the interstate without even thinking about what you're doing, or where you're going. You've developed a part of you that can drive the car automatically, and presumably safely, without having to consciously think about it. Every time you learn something well, you go through the same stages of learning:

Unconscious Incompetence. Before you think of trying to learn something, you're not conscious of how incompetent you are at this skill; you didn't even think about it.

Conscious Incompetence. When you begin to learn a new skill, you become quite aware of your incompetence.

Conscious Competence. After some practice, you can become competent at a skill, but much of it is still very conscious—you have to think about what you're doing.

Unconscious Competence. Ultimately you can reach a point where you have learned the skill so well that it becomes unconscious. You just do it without having to consciously attend to it.

Knowing that we will inevitably go through this sequence any time we learn something, we can be accepting and tolerant of the inevitable mistakes we will make along the road.

Many of us set such incredibly high standards for ourselves that we stop ourselves from attempting something new, because we know we won't do it perfectly at first. Think of what your life would be like now if you had stopped yourself from trying new things when you were young. Imagine that as you were learning to walk, you pulled yourself up to a chair, took a wobbly step forward, and fell, and you thought, "Well, I'm not going to try that again; I must have looked like a real jerk." Life wouldn't be very interesting for you if you had done that; you'd still be crawling around on all fours. At those youthful stages, you kept on trying until you got things to work. NLP visualization processes won't immediately make you perfect, but they will prepare you thoroughly and get you going effectively into the situation in which you can continue to learn. Keep in mind that whenever you're learning something new, using the ongoing feedback you get is one of the most important elements to learning.

Another NLP Presupposition is that **there's no such thing as failure, only feedback.** Robert Dilts has a friend who is an inventor. He tries out lots and lots of things that don't work. Once Robert asked him, "How do you keep from feeling discouraged when you try so many things that don't work?" The inventor replied, "Oh, when something doesn't work, I just realize that it's a solution to a different problem."

Yet another NLP Presupposition is that **every behavior is useful in some context.** When you program in a new behavior and it doesn't work well, that's just an indication that you need to try something different in that context. Every time you try something that doesn't work, that gives you good information about what else might work. As someone once said, "Good judgment comes from experience. Experience comes from poor judgment."

Building Your Self-Confidence Daily

One way to make sure that you are consistently creating new behavioral choices and building your confidence is to build the Frustration into Flexibility Process into your life as a daily exercise. Here's how.

Before drifting off to sleep at night, run a movie of your day and the activities you did during the day. Stop when you come to a scene in the movie where you're not fully pleased with your behavior. Review that scene to gather information about what happened and what your goals and intentions were. Then replay that movie with you behaving in a way you're pleased with, a way that gets you better results. Adjust that scene until you find a behavior that is just right. Then picture or hear a cue that will be there in your external environment and imagine you are right there in the situation doing this new behavior. By doing this process, you will be building a new, and more resourceful behavior for the future.

This is a way to constantly review your actions and change those behaviors that don't work for you. This takes what you might have considered failure and turns it into feedback—feedback about changes and improvements that you can make. Utilizing this daily review in the way just described can give you an incredible sense of self-satisfaction in the way you act in the world—a great confidence booster!

Hopes and Expectations

In studying the various kinds of visualizations that are taught for changing behaviors, it is surprising to discover that sometimes people get amazing, exciting changes from visualization, while others visualize changes with little or no results. There is a major difference in those who are successful in making changes.

Let's explore your own thought processes to find another dimension of how this works. Think of something that could happen tomorrow. For example, imagine you have planned an outdoor excursion for tomorrow and the weather report says that it will be a nice day. Say to yourself, "I hope it will be sunny tomorrow," and notice how you represent hope inside your head through pictures, sounds, and perhaps words. Now say, "I expect it to be sunny tomorrow," and notice how you represent an expectation inside your head.

As you contrast these two experiences, pay attention to the following details. Do you have one or two pictures? Is the picture still, or is it a movie? Notice the location, brightness, clarity, amount of color, dimension, framing, etc. Are you looking through your own eyes, or are you somehow an observer to what is going on? Also note any auditory sounds or words in your thoughts. Do you have one or two voices, or many? Note any other distinctions like location, direction, speed, tonality, or intensity of any voices or sounds. Especially notice how these submodalities are different depending on whether you hoped something would happen or expect it to happen. How strong is your belief that it will be sunny tomorrow when you compare hope and expectation? Make either a mental or written note of the qualities that are associated with expectation for you, because they can be quite important in programming in new behaviors.

Many people represent an expectation as one picture. It may begin dissociated, but usually ends with being associated—looking through your own eyes. Often the picture is true color, bright, clear, and with movement in it. Any auditory is usually distinct and clear, perhaps with a matter-of-fact voice saying, "Of course, that's going to happen." Expectations feel real.

In contrast, most people represent hope as two pictures—of what might happen and what might not happen, with a voice saying "maybe, maybe not." Sometimes hope is one picture, but one that's distant, fuzzy, without motion and not very colorful. Thinking about something using those qualities leaves you doubtful about whether it will happen or not, whereas expectation is usually much more solid and real in your mind.

With that background, follow along with this process. Begin by forming an outcome that is related to having more confidence in a specific situation. How do you want to behave in the context you have selected? Perhaps you want more confidence in a job interview. After thinking of how you would like to behave in that situation, perhaps you decide that you want to look calm and somewhat relaxed, with dry armpits, flexible posture, a pleasant smile on your face, an ability to be articulate, a smooth confident-sounding voice, feeling poised and in control. If you really want to be thorough, write down your outcome in depth. Carefully examine it to make sure it's something that you really *do* want and that it's worth having. Ask yourself, "Is there any reason why I shouldn't have this outcome?" or, "Do I have any reservations about having it?" At this point, you may want to negotiate with any reluctant parts.

Once you have the outcome firmly defined, relax yourself into a receptive state of mind. Now begin visualizing your outcome using the submodalities for expectation that you discovered earlier. This is the most important part of the process. By using the submodalities of expectation, you are giving your mind a very powerful message that this will happen. Using the example about being confident in a job interview, you could run an entire interview through from the beginning to the end, creating it the way you expect it to happen with the confidence built in by using your submodalities for expectation.

Visualize your outcome as an expectation until you feel complete with it, and then let it go and expect it to happen. By using this process regularly to create outcomes for yourself, you will be maintaining an active involvement in your own personal evolution.

Reviewing What You've Learned

In this chapter, you have discovered many techniques you can use to build your self-confidence. Specifically, you have learned how to:

- Make a critical voice into a helpful ally by discovering its positive intention
- Brainstorm ways for your voice to fulfill its positive intention in more useful ways
- Restate your negative self-talk in the affirmative, as a specific, positive "I" statement of affirmation
- Turn frustrating situations into opportunities for choice through creative visualization
- Create solid and convincing positive expectations

You've learned that your brain is always doing the best it can, and that you can count on it to do what it has learned how to do. You can use your brain's own language to change its programming so that you can create more of what you want for yourself. Schedule a time each day with yourself on your calendar to do these powerful techniques to build your self-confidence. No one else can do it for you. *You,* and all parts of you, deserve it.

CHAPTER TEN

Creating Self-Appreciation and Self-Esteem

We become what we think about.

—EARL NIGHTINGALE

The Virtues of Self-Appreciation

What is self-esteem? Perhaps it can best be defined as an objective and favorable impression of one's self that influences all of one's experiences. That's quite a statement, and yet just about every psychologist, counselor, and motivator, successful businessman or -woman, psychiatrist and mental-health professional will agree that self-esteem is the bottom line for peace of mind and personal satisfaction.

Of course, the more positive self-esteem you have, the better your life will be. Positive self-esteem is a pervasive attitude that can make you feel good about yourself, truly appreciate yourself. It makes you feel like you really belong, just as you are, right now. It can make you feel safe and personally empowered to begin changing. It can give you the energy to tackle new challenges, to courageously look into unexplored areas of your life, and to add richly to the texture and flavor of all your experiences.

Take a moment and think of a time in your life when you felt particularly good about yourself. No matter how long ago it was, go back to that time in your life and see what you were seeing, hear what you were hearing, and feel what you were feeling. Notice how good you felt then, and how good you feel now, just thinking of it. Think of what your life would be like if you could choose to feel good about yourself and even more loving of yourself, whenever you wanted to, simply by choosing to do so. The question is: What stops you from choosing it? What stops you from choosing high self-esteem? Most people don't choose it because they simply don't know the specific steps to create it.

Although virtually all human-performance professionals agree on the value and importance of personal self-esteem, in reality only a rare few can teach us *how* to achieve it. Everyone talks about self-esteem, but no one seems to know how to teach us effective ways of achieving it.

Fortunately, this is where the achievement-oriented technology of Neuro-Linguistic Programming really shines. With NLP you can easily learn the specific steps for using your brain to powerfully affect your self-esteem, which in turn will impact your level of personal achievement.

Will Power and Self-Esteem

Will power has very little to do with improving your self-esteem. You don't have to strain your mental muscles in order to change the way you think of yourself. Frankly, will power is not enough to create self-esteem. You've probably discovered this for yourself the hard way, many times, and yet you may need to see it spelled out: All the will power in the world will not create an objective and favorable impression of yourself that influences all of your experiences. Using your will power to create self-esteem is an exhausting effort that simply does not work. What you need is know-how.

With NLP we know that high self-esteem is due to your inner map or representations of yourself. In other words, self-esteem is not due to the reality of how you actually are but to your internal representations of yourself, to the way you *think* about yourself. Change your internal representations of yourself, and you change your self-esteem. You do not have to strain yourself; you simply *think* it. It's as simple as that.

Form and Content

NLP knows that the way we visually think of ourselves determines a great deal of what we feel about ourselves. Specifically, the form and content of our inner pictures of ourselves are the visual building blocks of high and low self-esteem.

Like any other experience, the intensity of a person's self-image is determined by visual submodalities, the visual elements that provide the structure or form of any image. Typically, a self-image that looks small, dark, and far away will seem less intense and less real than a self-image that is large, bright, and close up. Since the form is different, the intensity is different.

On the other hand, the content of a person's self-image determines whether the intensity is positive or negative. For example, if the "you" in your self-image is distorted or ill-formed in some way, you will probably feel much differently about yourself than if your self-image is positive, whole, and complete.

The Content of Low Self-Esteem

Low self-esteem is typically associated with a self-image that is visually very intense in form and very negative in content. For example, Jean, a professional woman in her early thirties, found herself unable to attain the financial security of which she knew she was fully capable. She worked very hard, but something always held her back. When she took a few moments to examine her internal self-representations, Jean discovered that she maintained a self-image that was negative and upsetting. Jean literally saw herself as unnaturally twisted and hollow. But that was not all. She literally saw this vividly colored snapshot, large, bright, and extremely close to her face.

Since the content of her self-image (a twisted and hollow-body image of herself) was upsetting to look at, and the form was intense (large, bright, and close up), Jean felt emotionally upset whenever she thought of her personal worth, and, consequently, she maintained very low self-esteem.

Naturally, no matter what her colleagues would say about her work, no matter what accolades and rewards she would receive, Jean did not believe she was a valuable human being. She simply did not see herself that way. Whenever she compared the pictures she saw in her mind's eye with what others said about her, Jean believed what she saw, and she felt very badly about herself. The combination of the intense form and the negative content left Jean feeling pretty low. The resulting lack of self-esteem interfered with her ability to create the kind of financial security she truly wanted.

The Form and Content of Very High Self-Esteem

Very high self-esteem, on the other hand, is typically characterized by a positive self-image that also has submodalities that are visually very intense in form. For instance, when Jean completed "The Autobiography," an NLP exercise that you will learn in this chapter, she finally saw herself differently than she had ever seen herself before. Jean saw herself as whole and complete, life-size, and smiling with radiant self-confidence. This self-image took on the intensity of a large, bright, colorful motion picture. This combination created feelings of high self-esteem. Today she not only feels good about herself, Jean thinks of herself as solidly on the road to the financial freedom she desires.

The Structure of Self-Esteem: Variations of Content and Form

Since content can be positive or negative, and form can be intense or not, there are four variations of content and form. As you saw in the example of Jean, the subjective structure of very high and very low self-esteem is as follows:

1. Very high self-esteem is made of intense form and positive content.
2. Very low self-esteem is made of intense form and negative content.

3. Mildly high self-esteem is made of a positive self-image that is represented in a very mild form. In such a case, your mild sense of self-esteem could be improved by simply changing the form, by intensifying the submodalities. The form of the positive self-image could get more colorful, larger, brighter, become a motion picture, or take on whatever submodality changes make it more intense for you. The positive content would remain the same, while the form is intensified to make it more powerful.

4. Mildly negative self-esteem is made of a negative self-image that is represented in a very mild form. In this case, both the form and the content need to be changed. First, the negative self-image can become positive by changing the content of what is seen, and next the mild impact could become more powerful by changing the form of what is seen.

The pictures we maintain of ourselves in our mind's eye can be intensely negative or intensely positive or anything in between. With your NLP knowledge of the impact of submodalities and content, the choice is yours.

This exercise provides yet another example of how your inner thoughts, which are made of images, sounds, and feelings, can support courageous behavior and lead to independence, achievement, and choice, or can make you fearful and ineffective. What makes the difference is your personal ability to choose to change your inner thoughts, your self-image. When you know how to deliberately change your inner representations of yourself, when you know how to change by choice, you can effectively improve your level of self-esteem, right now.

EXERCISE 34: DEVELOPING YOUR SELF-ESTEEM

1. Self-Image. Take a moment to get an image of yourself in your mind's eye. Just think of what you look like. Is the form mildly or powerfully intense?

2. Adjust Content. Is the content positive or negative? First, make sure that the content is positive. Look for any physical distortions and instead see yourself as you really are. Notice anything in that image that seems negative, and change it into a positive representation by thinking of a more positive aspect of what you see represented. For instance, if you see yourself as slow-moving, and the meaning of this could be that you're slow-witted, or tend not to get things done, realize that taking time also means that you are not impetuous, and think things through thoroughly before taking action.

Use any of the other methods you have learned in this book to make the content of your self-image into a positive and accurate representation of your strong points, your best skills, attitude, and abilities. See yourself looking whole and complete, as you look when you have just accomplished a strongly desired goal.

3. Adjust Form. Now allow this self-image to become a large, bright, close, 3-D colorful movie of yourself. By now you will have already discovered other submodalities that you can use to make this image even more powerful and compelling for you.

4. Compare Feelings. What difference do you feel when you compare the self-image you just created with the one you originally thought of? Most people who take the time to actually do this simple exercise discover that their sense of self-esteem is powerfully affected by the different form and content of images they have of themselves. When their self-images are both positive and intense, they feel greater self-esteem.

How Self-Esteem Can Change Your Life

People who maintain high self-appreciation are fundamentally no different from you. It's not that they never feel down or upset or depressed. They do experience these unpleasant emotional states from time to time. Of course, self-esteeming people are human. The difference is that they are simply aware that their emotions provide deeply important information about how they're living their lives. They take such emotion-based information seriously and then consciously make appropriate changes in the way they think and, therefore, the way they behave in the world. With NLP know-how, you can think of your emotions as feedback that gives you the opportunity to change your life, change your representations, or both.

For example, a young businessman named Fred found that he was unable to feel comfortable with himself, and he did not know why. He had recently begun to feel sad and depressed. Some of his friends told him that he should speak to a psychiatrist about the problem. Other people told him he should take a long vacation. Still others said he should try to totally immerse himself in his work. This state of affairs went on for a week. When Fred realized that his feelings would probably not change on their own, he made the decision to take charge of his emotional life. That is when he began to use his feelings as feedback.

Specifically, Fred compared his sad and depressed feelings with his feelings about his work, his home, and his intimate relationships. By doing this he realized that he enjoyed the life he had created. His home life was rich and satisfying. His uncomfortable feelings did not stem from his life-style or relationships.

Since Fred had some knowledge of the NLP approach to emotional reactions, he looked at his inner representation of the depression, and he noticed that his feelings resulted from a very specific image he found in his mind's eye. Fred had unwittingly created an image of a large black wall, standing directly in front of him. This image was the source of his feelings. It was making him feel sad and mildly depressed.

Once he was aware of the black wall, he used his NLP know-how to simply change the color of the wall from black to white, which, in his case, allowed the wall to crumble into dust before him, leaving him feeling a sense of openness, inner strength, and security. This simple procedure was all he needed to do to get the results he wanted.

To reiterate, with NLP technology and procedures, when self-esteeming people feel upset, they know they are empowered to skillfully change their inner representations, their emotional lives, and consequently their behavior, by choice. The secret of self-esteeming people is that they have the know-how to change themselves if and when they want to.

Being Versus Doing

John Bradshaw, the author of *Healing the Shame That Binds You,* said, "You are a human being, not a human doing; you are a human being, not a human performance."[1] When you learn to separate who you are from what you do, you can more easily notice that your being is fundamentally good. Your behavior—how you act—is simply effective or ineffective at achieving the results you truly want. Knowing that you are not your behavior avoids many troubling emotions like regret, self-blame, and shame, leaving all your energy free to examine how you are living and to change behaviors and responses that you are not satisfied with.

Many people's self-images only utilize *observer* position. They see themselves as an outside observer would. It can be really useful to enrich your self-image by adding *other* perspectives. A particularly useful *other* perspective is seeing yourself out of the eyes of someone who loves you. Other people often see us differently than we see ourselves, and loved ones often see things that we might never notice on our own.

Recently a self-employed businesswoman attended an NLP-based self-esteem seminar. When Eileen came to the seminar, she wondered how people could possibly love her for herself. When she saw herself from the perspective of someone else, someone whom she knows really loves her, she saw through her behavior to her essence, to who she really is. She had never done that before. Perhaps the greatest impact of doing this is that she now likes herself a lot more, and she accepts who she is and what she is. She said, "I am a lot less critical of myself. I'm more comfortable and relaxed with myself and with others. This definitely affects my business relationships, too."

Another example of using this process comes from a multitalented entrepreneur and business consultant. Trent is now in the process of expanding his business to the international level.

Again, after one experience of this technique, of seeing himself through the eyes of someone who loves him, he said that it helped him to develop self-love in areas he did not think were possible, and even in areas he did not know were needed. He said, ''It created a fullness of being in my personality and in my body; an integration. Self-love really does it. This process has had an incredible impact on my business and will affect every other area of my life.''

The next exercise, entitled ''The Autobiography,'' is adapted from the NLP book *Solutions* by Leslie Cameron-Bandler,[2] and can give you a rich experience of seeing yourself as a loved one does. You can use this exercise several ways, but some work better than others. For example, you could simply read it to yourself one time, thinking that should be enough. This would probably be the least effective method. A better way would be to memorize the general procedure, find a place and time when you're sure you won't be disturbed, and mentally recall the entire exercise. An even more effective way would be to record the exercise on tape in your own voice and go through the procedure whenever you have time to listen to it. Still another method, and probably the best way, would be to have a trusted friend read it aloud to you, pausing to let you complete each step and resuming when you have indicated that you're done. That way, you can enjoy the experience while knowing you will have someone you trust to share it with when you have finished.

EXERCISE 35: THE AUTOBIOGRAPHY

1. Become Completely Relaxed. Find a comfortable and quiet place in which to proceed with this exercise. Your favorite chair will do. It's a good idea to do this exercise sitting up rather than lying down. You want to feel very relaxed, and yet remain alert and attentive.

It's time to relax, now . . . breathe . . . let your body relax. Breathe slowly . . . and deeply . . . and fully . . . it's all right to make noise when you breathe. Imagine that you have nostrils on the bottoms of your feet . . . and you can breathe air up your legs and into your lungs. Fill your body with good, fresh air. And while you're breathing comfortably and slowly and fully, think about what it's like to really appreciate yourself, as you are. As you feel your body relax, just let go of any bodily and emotional tensions you may have. Take a moment and check your body for any "holding feelings" you may be experiencing and let them go. Let them go, completely.

2. Think of Someone Who Loves You. Before beginning this process, think of someone who you know loves you. Think of someone who, you are certain, without a doubt, loves you: a friend, lover, husband, wife, parents, child, whoever; simply notice who it is for the process you are about to learn. If you can't think of anyone who you know loves you, then think of a person who you assisted in some way, and you know that person deeply appreciates you. Whether you think of someone who you know loves you or of someone who you know deeply appreciates you, in either case, simply notice who he or she is for now. You'll make good use of this personal resource later on.

3. Write Your Autobiography. Now, imagine that you are sitting at a desk writing your autobiography. You may be using a pen or a pencil, or perhaps a typewriter or a computer keyboard. In some way, you find yourself writing your autobiography, telling the story of your life. You're quite comfortable as you write your autobiography. You can feel and see the desk and the chair you're using. You may notice, right away . . . in a few seconds . . . or perhaps later on, how the words that describe your life begin to gently occur to you. And as you write, you become aware of the thought of someone who you know loves you . . . or appreciates you. You begin to think even more clearly about that person who you know loves you.

4. See the Person Who You Know Loves You. Now, take your time to notice that, across the room from where you're writing your autobiography, you can see someone standing on the other side of a glass door, the person who you know loves you. And as you see this person who you know loves you or appreciates

Continued

you, you become aware that he or she is looking at you, observing you. And you decide to describe this person in your autobiography, and the part he or she has played in your life. Take your time and describe this person, what you see and what you feel about this person. Even include what you hear yourself saying to yourself about the person who you know loves you. Write all of this down into your autobiography. Take all the time you need.

5. See Yourself from Another Perspective. Now that you have a full sense of what it's like to describe the person who you know loves you, gently allow yourself to leave your body at the desk and float your awareness across the room through the glass door, and notice what it's like to stand next to the person who loves you. Take your time to look through the glass door and observe yourself writing your autobiography. Just stand there and notice what you look like from this perspective of being behind the glass door. And notice just how much you currently appreciate yourself. Notice your actual feelings about yourself as you look at yourself through the glass door. You may notice a great deal of self-appreciation, or you may only notice a little. Whatever you notice, simply accept this experience.

6. See Yourself Through the Eyes of Someone Who Loves You. Now, gently and tenderly, allow yourself to enter into the body of the person who you know loves you. Take all the time you need to do this in a comfortable and easy way. And when you are completely in the body of the person who you know loves or deeply appreciates you, look through that person's eyes at yourself as you write your autobiography. See yourself through the eyes of someone who loves you. Notice what you look like over there writing your autobiography. And notice how you move and breathe. Take enough time to fully appreciate the qualities and special aspects of yourself that you are aware of, perhaps for the first time, as you see yourself through the eyes of love. And since you're in the body of someone who loves you, notice the thoughts you hear being spoken about you and the feelings being felt about you. Notice the tone of voice of the positive, appreciative thoughts you hear as you see yourself over there, writing at your desk, from the perspective of someone who you know loves you.

7. Return to Your Own Perspective. When you are fully aware of the qualities and special aspects of yourself that make you who and what you are, gently, tenderly, allow your awareness to leave the body of the person who you know loves you, and float back, through the glass door, across the room, and back into your body at the desk writing your autobiography.

8. Write About Your Experience. You can take your time, now, to write into your autobiography what you just experienced by seeing yourself through the eyes of love or appreciation. As you write about what you experienced, be sure to describe several of the qualities and special aspects you noticed in yourself when you saw yourself through the eyes of love.

9. Think of the Future. As you write this experience into your autobiography, begin to think of your future—both of future experiences you expect are coming, and also of those unexpected experiences that may surprise you. Think of all the places and times in your future . . . tomorrow, the next day, weeks and months and even years from now, when you'll want to be easily able to review, recall, and remember this precious experience of seeing yourself through the eyes of love, noticing your specialness and deeply appreciating who and what you are in the world.

10. Return to the Present Moment. Now, begin to return to your full awareness, your full consciousness. At your own pace, gently become increasingly wide awake and alert. Come all the way back to this present time and place, feeling much better than before. Notice the sounds of the room. And you can notice the feelings in your body. And in a moment, you can open your eyes as you gently return to your full conscious awareness and stretch your arms and legs. Welcome back.

11. Notice the Changes. Now that you have had the chance to actually experience the self-appreciation that eludes so many people, please take your time and comfortably notice how this exercise has changed your inner representations of yourself in subtle and not-so-subtle ways. Notice the ways in which you can now actually see yourself from a new, more appreciative, and loving perspective. The experience you just went through has provided you with the kind of deep personal self-appreciation that is often a first step toward totally supporting and encouraging yourself.

Self-Appreciation: A Step-by-Step Approach

One useful definition of the self-esteeming person is that he or she is someone who is empowered to see the big picture, including the picture maker. And that's exactly what you did in the NLP Autobiography exercise above, seeing yourself from a uniquely loving perspective. You saw yourself through the eyes of love.

Viewing yourself within the big picture, from this self-appreciative perspective, assists you in more fully accepting yourself as you are. It is now more possible to let go of a variety of unnecessary inner struggles and more fully accept and love the fact that a tree is a tree, a flower is a flower, and you are who and what you are.

Not long ago, a professional consultant in his late thirties took an extended course in understanding the fundamentals of NLP. He wanted to discover for himself whether or not the technology of NLP could live up to the claims he had read so much about. During the course, he fully participated in the exercise called The Autobiography. Later he said, ''I had no idea of the power of seeing myself through the eyes of love. I now see things about myself that I never knew existed. I really feel more in touch with my personal value and the positive impact I have on others. This experience will be valuable in every aspect of my life. I will never forget it.''

Even after using this NLP technique only once, you can notice just how much more self-appreciative you've already become. And since the true depth of your self-appreciation is improving and expanding, please take the time now to be sure to preserve, for your future, all of your ways of thinking about yourself that allow you to develop new and better learnings and understandings as you continue to open yourself to greater and greater self-esteem. Now make a promise to yourself to do the exercise again soon with another loving, appreciative person in your life so that you can further benefit from it.

Distinguishing Self from Others

Another aspect of self-esteem is recognizing your individuality. The self-esteeming person commonly uses "I" statements rather than "you" or "we" statements. With high self-esteem, a man or woman might say, "I feel wonderful today," rather than, "Some days, you know, you just feel wonderful," or, "This is a wonderful day." This is because the self-esteeming person easily distinguishes himself or herself from other people, things, and concepts.

Using "I" statements ensures your ownership of your own experiences, wants, and needs, and this will empower you to stand up for your identity, to know what you feel and what you want. You will be able to say, "I am myself. I am this person and no one else. I love myself, imperfections and all."

The self-esteeming person also believes in other people's rights, and allows and encourages others to have their own identity, to express what they feel and what they want. Self-esteem lets you have differences, express your differences, and be different. When you have self-esteem, you actually feel safe to be yourself, just as you are. You honestly feel safe enough to be yourself, a separate individual with your own personal ideas, feelings, goals, and values. Being a separate individual means being able to express yourself, which can boil down to the ability to say yes and no.

Without the ability to say no, all your yeses are basically meaningless. If you are compelled to say yes, then you are without choice and will lack the self-esteem that comes from choosing your life.

The same is true if you must say no to everything that comes along. In either case, if you are compelled to say yes all the time, or if you are compelled to say no to everything, these compulsions both lead to lack of choice and result in low self-esteem.

Today, a lot is being said about a kind of lack of choice called co-dependent behavior. The First National Conference on Co-Dependence (held in Scottsdale, Arizona, in 1989) defined co-dependence as "a pattern of dependence on compulsive behaviors and on approval from others in an attempt to find safety, self-worth and identity." Self-worth and identity are simply other descriptions of self-esteem. Clearly low self-esteem, placing little or no value on your own being, leads to fewer and fewer choices. This lack of choice often characterizes co-dependence and other addictive or compulsive behaviors.

Interestingly, when someone feels that she is without much value, she tends to miss or ignore many of the choices available to her: Feeling worthless leads to fewer choices. Fewer choices lead, in turn, to repeating behaviors, even when they are not effective. Ineffective behavior patterns lead to fewer successes in life. And a lack of success leads to feeling worthless, completing the vicious circle of low self-esteem.

For example, a middle-aged businesswoman named Claire said she had recently made several important decisions to create more independence in her life, and yet she felt like a complete failure. She said she was sure she was co-dependent because, whenever she was by herself, she could not feel comfortable or be productive. She tried everything she could think of to increase her self-esteem, but she invariably felt like a failure in literally every area of her life. Feeling like a failure made Claire play it safe. She therefore produced less and received little recognition from herself and others. All this increased her feelings of worthlessness.

On an intellectual level, Claire knew perfectly well that she was not a failure. Many people would have happily traded places with her life situation. But deep down inside, on an emotional level, she was still convinced of her worthlessness.

When Claire took the time to trace her feelings of low self-esteem to her internal representations, she discovered a very large, imposing image of her mother shaking her head in obvious disappointment and disapproval. Claire realized that her feelings of being a complete failure, and the lack of choice those feelings engendered, were directly related to this image. Many therapeutic approaches would explore the historical roots of this image, and sometimes this can be useful in changing the image to something more positive. However, with NLP we have many ways to change a troublesome image directly. Using submodalities, Claire learned she could change the size of her mother's image. When she made it large, she felt worse, but when she made it small, she felt much better. After experimenting in this way, she found that when she made this image of her mother small, far away, dim, flat, and black and white, it no longer affected her at all. When she did this, it took away the image that made her feel bad, but it didn't automatically put something more positive in its place. Feeling "not bad" wasn't enough; she wanted to feel good. In order to accomplish this, she learned the NLP Swish Pattern, originally developed by Richard Bandler.[3]

The Swish Pattern

Here is one example of how the Swish Pattern works, and its immediate impact. During a short presentation on NLP to an audience of particularly interested individuals, the subject of personal achievement and public speaking came up. Surveys show that the fear of public speaking is the number one fear in America. More people report being afraid to stand up and speak in front of an audience than report being afraid of anything else, including heights, dogs, the dark, or death.

In the course of the discussion, Tom, a middle-aged business-man, raised his hand. He said he had a demoralizing fear of public speaking. He had been afraid of talking in public for as long as he could remember, and this fear had prevented him from participating in certain business functions. Whenever he thought about the possibility of expressing himself in public, he would feel upset and anxious, and this had always slowed down his ability to achieve his goals. Even from the safety of his seat, he found it very difficult to express himself and his particular needs. When he was asked if he would like to be a demonstration subject, he said he couldn't, because he couldn't bring himself to stand in front of the group. Tom was a perfect demonstration subject for the Swish Pattern, because at the end of the process, it would be easy to test whether it had worked by asking him to come up to the front of the room.

The NLP trainer spoke to Tom, who remained seated in the audience. He asked Tom what he saw in his mind's eye whenever he thought of speaking in public. Tom said he saw a large, bright image of a lot of people looking at him. Interestingly, the people he saw in the audience all seemed to have eyes the size of light bulbs. Whenever he saw that image, his stomach muscles would tighten up and his mouth would go dry.

Next, the trainer assisted Tom in creating a positive image of himself, a "wonderful Tom" who was the kind of person who no longer responded to audiences the way he currently did. Then, as the audience watched, listened, and learned, Tom put this image of the "wonderful Tom" into a sparkling dot, placed the dot in the center of his image of the audience with light-bulb eyes, and rapidly replaced the audience image with the "wonderful Tom" image by having it become big and bright. Then Tom was asked to see a blank screen and repeat this simple process ten times, seeing a blank screen at the end of each process, and doing it faster each time.

When the trainer was convinced that Tom had thoroughly and effectively run the Swish Pattern several times, he invited Tom to come to the front of the room and talk about the results. As Tom walked to the front of the room, and comfortably and confidently faced the audience, he said, with some surprise and disbelief, that he now felt fine speaking in public. The audience broke into applause.

The Swish Pattern not only handles self-defeating behavior and other blocks to self-esteem, it also orients your brain for greater and greater self-esteem as it enables you to look into a brighter future. This pattern deals with present, past, and future issues and concerns related to self-esteem all at once, because that "wonderful you" image literally builds a piece of positive self-image.

Mary, a forty-two-year-old woman who was training to be a therapist, used the Swish Pattern to resolve a lifelong issue. Mary's unresolved anger and fear, which were related to her father's early abandonment, had prevented her from standing on her own feet and achieving more of her potential. When she thought of what was stopping her from being her personal best, she suddenly became aware of an image of her father's fist coming at her. Accompanying that image, she also heard his voice saying, "I don't want you." The combination of this image she saw in her mind's eye and the voice was more than enough to create deep feelings of worthlessness, accompanied by anger and fear.

As with Tom, Mary was asked to take all the time she needed to visually create an image of herself being the kind of person who had already solved the issue she had had with her father's attitudes, beliefs, and actions. Then Mary allowed herself to see the "wonderful Mary" become a sparkling dot floating in space. She placed the sparkling dot in the center of the image of her father's fist. Then she rapidly replaced the fist image with the "wonderful Mary" image by allowing it to become big and bright, until it filled her mind's eye. Every time she replaced her father's fist image with the "wonderful Mary" image, she heard the "wonderful Mary" saying, "I feel good about myself." The sound of "wonderful Mary's" voice echoed around Mary's head. Within a few minutes, Mary had completed the Swish Pattern several times and experienced a profound inner transformation.

Months after doing this, Mary wrote, "I now have an inner freedom and joy and see myself alive and radiating in the future. And as I see me, I experience a greater strength to be in the moment. I have an even deeper love for myself." Her relationship with herself and her memory of her father had completely changed. Shortly after this transforming experience, she became self-employed and severed a long-term, unproductive relationship with a married man.

Now you are invited to go on a similar journey of profound learning and personal change for yourself in the next exercise.

EXERCISE 36: THE SWISH PATTERN

Take whatever time it takes you to complete each step of this exercise thoroughly, comfortably, easily, and at your own pace.

1. Identify the Cue Image. Think of a time in your life when you were being particularly hard on yourself, when you lacked self-esteem. A time in your life, maybe recently or maybe very long ago, when you lacked the self-esteem to take the steps toward the personal achievement you truly desired. A time when you felt unable to be the best you could be. Or you may think of something you anticipate happening, something in your

Continued

future that, when you think of it, makes you feel unpleasant, or helpless.

Actually allow yourself to be *in* that experience seeing what you're seeing, feeling what you're feeling, and hearing what you're hearing. Let the unpleasant feelings that you associate with that time in your life become even more intense. As those feelings become stronger within you, notice the part of your body in which you feel those feelings most strongly.

Now, as you are aware of these feelings, you can also begin to notice what you are seeing in your mind's eye. Become aware of what you see that is associated with this feeling. The image may make complete sense to you, or it may not. In either case, simply notice what you see internally. And also notice what you may be hearing—something being said to you, or by you, that may also contribute to these unpleasant feelings.

Now set that unpleasant image and those sounds aside temporarily.

2. Distraction. To help you set the experience aside, say your telephone number out loud. Now, just for fun, and to distract you for a moment, try saying your phone number out loud again but backward this time.

3. Create a Resourceful Self-Image. Now take a minute or two to create in front of you an image of yourself, the way you would look if you had already solved the issue that affects your self-esteem. This is a future "you," a "you" who is just a few steps ahead of you, a "you" who has already learned how to solve the issue that has troubled you. This future "you" has solved the issue with methods that are yet to occur to you. And this "you" knows you will succeed because he or she already has. This is a "you" who has been through everything you've been through and a bit more. He or she thinks of you with love and kindness and knows you will succeed.

See this "wonderful you," right in front of you, a large, bright, and colorful image of yourself having many resources to handle the issue that has blocked you. A "you" who has many additional choices, many different ways to handle whatever you were seeing in the unpleasant image. Be sure the "wonderful you" is not perfect, and has a sense of humor.

And most important, notice that you feel powerfully drawn to him or her. Just by looking at him or her, you have a strong feeling of wanting to become that person. If you don't feel powerfully drawn to become more like the ''wonderful you'' image, take whatever time you need to make that image more real, more believable, more of whom you want to be. You can do this by enriching the submodalities of the image. For example, you can make the image larger, brighter, more colorful and moving. Another way to create a compelling ''wonderful you'' is by asking yourself the following question: If the ''wonderful you'' image were powerfully compelling, what would it look like? This ''what if'' question will immediately allow your brain to create a more powerfully attractive ''wonderful you'' image.

And now that you feel strongly drawn to become that future you, notice that the ''wonderful you'' is speaking in a sincere and frankly honest tone of voice, saying, ''I feel good about myself.'' The words ''I feel good about myself'' come toward you and begin to encircle your head, going all the way around your head. Listen to the words going around your head . . . making a slight echo, as though your head were within a large, golden bell. And as you hear the words, ''I feel good about myself,'' allow the good feelings to begin to wash over and through you.

4. Practice Expanding the Resourceful Self-Image. Now, take the image of the ''wonderful you'' and put it into a tiny sparkling dot floating in space in front of you. Allow that sparkling dot to rapidly blossom and get larger and larger—until it becomes life-size again and you can see the ''wonderful you'' . . . right in front of you . . . large and bright and colorful. And you hear the ''wonderful you'' saying, honestly and frankly, ''I feel good about myself'' . . . and those words encircle your head, as though your head were within a large, golden bell, and you feel the good feelings wash over you. Now see a blank screen in your mind, like in a movie theater. Repeat this process several times, until it is automatic.

5. Place the Resourceful Self-Image Dot into the Cue Image. And now place that tiny sparkling dot in the center of the cue image that you discovered in Step 1.

Continued

6. *Exchange Images (Swish Them)*. Now, as the unpleasant image fades and gets smaller and disintegrates, the sparkling dot containing the "wonderful you" swiftly gets bigger and brighter and bigger and brighter until . . . swish . . . the "wonderful you" image overwhelms the unpleasant image, filling your mind's eye, so that all you can see is the "wonderful you." As you see that image of yourself, large, bright, and colorful, right in front of you, saying, "I feel good about myself" . . . you hear the words encircle your head and slightly echo . . . as though your head were within a large, golden bell . . . and you let the good feelings wash over you.

7. *See a Blank Screen*. Now see a blank screen in your mind, as though you were looking at a blank screen in a movie theater before the movie begins.

8. *Repeat Ten Times*. Now do Steps 4–6 a little bit more quickly. Place that tiny sparkling dot in the center of the unpleasant image, again. Now, as the unpleasant image quickly fades and gets smaller and disintegrates, watch as your self-image rapidly gets bigger and brighter and bigger and brighter until . . . swish . . . the "wonderful you" image overwhelms the unpleasant image. And the "wonderful you" is large and bright and colorful and is saying, "I feel good about myself" . . . and the words encircle your head and echo as though your head were within a large, golden bell . . . and you let the good feelings wash over you. Then you see a blank screen, just like one you might see in a movie theater.

Repeat this whole process four more times, doing it faster each time. Then repeat the process three more times, being sure to see the blank screen between each one. And finally, run the process two more times, as fast as you possibly can. When you do it really fast, you may not consciously be aware of the images as they exchange places. Doing the process ten times will be more than enough for most people. However, for some people once or twice is enough; others might need to do it twenty times. How many times do you need to do it until you can no longer feel those unpleasant feelings?

9. *Multiplying the Resourceful Self-Image*. Since self-esteem is an objective and favorable impression of yourself that influences all your experiences, it will be most powerful if you are seeing an inner positive image of yourself everywhere you look—in the past, present, and future. Imagine that you can physically hold the "wonderful you" image in your hands. Simply reach out and get hold of it with your hands. When you touch it, it will begin to glow. Now, multiply that image, by making thousands of images of the "wonderful you," one behind the other, like a very large deck of cards, glowing and in color.

Now leave one of the images right in front of you as you take all the rest of them and toss them up high into the air. Watch all those images of the "wonderful you" begin to come down and settle all around you in concentric circles, all around you for as far as you can see in every direction . . . in your past, your present, and your future. Imagine that there are rows after rows of circles of "wonderful you" images and you can hear all of them like a chorus of loving, honest voices saying, "I feel good about myself." And you can allow the good feelings to wash over you and through you.

10. Testing Your Work. Now that you've run this pattern several times, it's important to test your work. So take a moment now and notice what you feel when you try to get that original, unpleasant cue image back in mind. If you are unable to get the unpleasant feelings at all, or you have a tough time even seeing the unpleasant image, you've succeeded.

If you have any unpleasant feelings when you think of that cue image, simply repeat the pattern, paying careful attention to each step, until the unpleasant feelings vanish.

The Swish Pattern is a very simple and effective way to create an objective and favorable image of yourself that produces immediate results in specific troublesome situations. One of the interesting features of this technique is that you won't know ahead of time exactly what you will do the next time you encounter a situation that is similar to one that used to be troublesome. Whereas many NLP processes create a specific set of behaviors to deal with a situation, the Swish Pattern relies on the person's unconscious mind to creatively deal with it, a stunning confirmation of the NLP Presupposition that **people already have all the resources they need.**

One way to think of the Swish Pattern is that it creates a very powerful motivating self-image of who you want to become. This powerful motivation organizes and focuses all your conscious resources on the problem situation and figures out how to deal with it. The self-image you build with the Swish Pattern also influences all of your experiences: past, present, and future.

The Swish Pattern presented here uses size and brightness to exchange the two images. You can also use color/black and white; close/far; 3-D/flat; snapshot/movie or any other pair of submodalities to exchange the images. Since different people respond more strongly to different submodalities, using one of these alternate ways of doing the Swish Pattern will be more effective for certain people than the one presented here. It is also possible to adapt the Swish Pattern to the auditory system, exchanging a cue sound and a self-image voice.

If the pattern that is presented here was not effective for you, even though you did it carefully and repeatedly, it is likely that one of these alternative ways would work much better for you.[4]

Fear of Criticism

For most people, one of the biggest obstacles to simply being themselves is fear of criticism. Since our relationships with other people are the source of our most special joys—as well as the source of other important things like food and work—we all feel a need to fit in and get along with others. Being criticized by others can often be perceived as very threatening and dangerous. To protect us from others' criticism, we often warn or criticize ourselves. Have you ever heard a voice in your mind telling you that you cannot complete a particular task, or that you will fail to perform at a desired level, or that you are simply stupid or incompetent? All of us do at times. In the last chapter, we presented several specific strategies for handling these self-critical voices.

Transforming Self-Consciousness

A closely related unresourceful state of mind is painful self-consciousness, usually due to feeling criticized or "discounted" by actual others, rather than an inner critical voice. Many people feel self-conscious if they discover that they are the object of another person's criticism. But many people are able to feel self-conscious even when they are alone. Since someone who is completely alone can feel criticized and consequently self-conscious, this clearly illustrates that it is our thinking that creates our self-esteem, not external factors.

Take a moment, right now, and try this thought experiment. Think of a time when you felt particularly self-conscious. It might be a recent experience of self-consciousness, or it might have happened a long time ago. In any case, think of such a time and see what you were seeing at the time, hear what you were hearing at the time, and feel what you were feeling at the time.

If you have fully re-created the experience of being self-conscious, you are probably feeling somewhat self-conscious right now. Let's use that feeling to make some changes. Where in your body does the feeling of self-consciousness reside? Just take a moment and notice.

Now, relax and allow the feeling of self-consciousness to get a bit stronger. Let the feeling get so strong that it becomes an image you can see in your mind's eye. Now, take whatever image you are looking at in your mind's eye and make it smaller, dimmer, black and white, and move it farther away. Do you still feel the same? Do you feel different? For now, it is not important to judge the value of how you feel—just notice how you feel.

Now, do this: Take the same image and make it larger, in color and very close up. How do you feel now? Typically, people who try this thought experiment report a powerful increase in their bodily feelings of self-consciousness. Now make that image smaller, dimmer, black and white, and far away again, so you can feel more comfortable. By changing the intensity of the image, through intelligent use of submodalities, you can make yourself feel more or less self-conscious. Which way of thinking about that experience would you like to keep in mind?

Habits of Self-Esteeming People

Typically, a person with low self-esteem who doesn't know how to feel good about himself would react defensively if someone else were to find fault with his performance, values, or goals. He would feel hurt and helpless if he were criticized by almost anyone. Therefore, he might verbally "slap back"—try to find fault in some way—in an effort to maintain his own self-esteem. Or he might feel devastated by such a critical comment and be unable to listen to the rest of the other person's views. He wouldn't be able to notice that everyone has his or her own unique perspective and model of the world. He wouldn't be able to objectively compare another person's opinion with his own. And unfortunately, some low self-esteeming people might actually ignore their own feelings and values, and try to please the criticizing person by being "agreeable," no matter how unfairly they were treated.

In contrast, a person with high self-esteem feels good about himself, and in the same challenging situation would be empowered to listen to and evaluate the accuracy of the other person's point of view. He would not feel compelled to accept or reject the other's perspective. By accepting himself as he is, he would feel free to accept the fact that each of us has a different, and personally valid, model of the world. If, however, he felt he were being abused in some way, the high self-esteeming person would feel comfortable saying so and take appropriate action to create a win-win solution whenever possible.

It's been said that one of the key differences between successful and unsuccessful salespeople is their ability to dispassionately react to repeated rejection of themselves and their product. On a daily basis, salespeople must be able to effectively face and overcome rejection or they won't remain in sales for long. And since income from sales is often directly related to the number of people contacted each workday, the more rejection you can comfortably handle, the more success you are likely to achieve.

Utilizing Criticism Comfortably

You've already seen how your own internal criticism can rob you of confidence, and you have learned two different ways to make these voices into positive allies: (1) by aligning the location of a voice in Chapter Six and (2) by reframing it in Chapter Eight. Next, it's important to learn how to deal with other people's criticism, because that can be equally devastating, and it is often a big issue in the workplace as well as at home.

Tom, the head of training and organizational development for a large bank, was feeling quite down on himself because of something that kept happening at work. His boss, the CEO of the bank, was critical of him, and he didn't know how to react to his criticism without becoming defensive. Tom would get a gut-wrenching pain in his stomach whenever his boss was being critical. Then he'd become defensive, feel depressed, and end up being unproductive for the rest of the day.

To solve his problem, he tried using a technique based on the *observer* perspective from Chapter Seven. In his mind's eye, he stepped back and saw himself and his boss and ran a movie of his boss criticizing him. This allowed him to listen to what his boss was saying without getting that gut-wrenching feeling and becoming defensive. He then compared what his boss was saying he had done with what he remembered he had done. His boss kept saying he wasn't a team player because he missed parts of certain meetings. Tom thought about this and said to himself, ''But I only miss the part of the meetings that don't directly relate to my department.'' As he thought about this more from this *observer* position, he realized, ''But it must seem to the others that I'm not supporting them; they don't have a way of knowing what I'm doing when I'm not there.'' He realized that part of his boss's criticism was valid feedback—he just hadn't been able to hear it before, because he became defensive so quickly.

Tom then thought about how he wanted to respond to his boss. He thought of an appropriate response and then ran a rehearsal movie of himself interacting with his boss, paying close attention to his boss's reaction. He also imagined himself either attending the meetings or explaining to the management team why he would be missing from them. This helped to program his mind to follow through and make use of the feedback that his boss had given him. When he was through, he realized that he was feeling much more positive about his boss as well as himself.

Reprogramming Your Brain

What Tom hadn't yet realized was that by rethinking how he responded to criticism in this particular way, he had reprogrammed his brain so that in the future, whenever he would be faced with criticism from anyone, he'd step back, evaluate the criticism, think of an appropriate response, deliver it, and consider how to incorporate any useful feedback. You can reprogram your brain as Tom did by practicing the following technique.

EXERCISE 37: RESPONDING COMFORTABLY TO CRITICISM

1. Criticism. Begin by recalling a recent criticism that you reacted badly to; you weren't satisfied with the way you responded. Pick a moderate criticism for ease in learning this technique. Back up the experience to just before it happened.

2. **Observer** *Position. See yourself* about to be criticized by that someone and, as soon as that other you recognizes that it's criticism, watch as *that* "other you" dissociates. As that "other you" begins to receive the criticism, you can imagine him stepping out of his body or feeling himself protected by a Plexiglas shield around him. It can be helpful to see the critical words being printed out in a cartoon balloon.

---

3. Movie of Criticism. Watch as that "other you" makes a detailed movie of the meaning of the criticism, so that he can understand what the criticism is about. If that "other you" doesn't have enough information to make a clear movie, see him asking the critic for more information, until he has a clear understanding of what the critic is saying.

4. Movie of Your Experience. Now that that "other you" has the critic's view of the situation, what he perceived, watch as that "other you" makes a movie of what *you* remember happening in the same situation, and compares your movie with what the critic saw.

5. Compare Movies. Do the movies of the incident match or mismatch? They might match, match only partially, or completely mismatch. After all, they are different perceptual positions. If they mismatch, watch yourself ask the critic for more information. That "other you" is attempting to understand the criticism.

6. Choose Response. Based on that "other you's" comparison of the movies, decide on an appropriate response. There are many different possible responses, depending on the circumstances, and the amount of match/mismatch between the two movies. He might say, "I'm sorry," or, "My intention was to let you know I was concerned," or "From my viewpoint, it looks very different." Or he might respond, "That's an interesting view of what happened," or, "Perhaps I could have done that differently," or even, "Thank you for expressing your opinion." Watch as he chooses a response that is appropriate in this situation and lets the other person know that he is thoughtfully receiving their communication. As you see yourself responding to the critic, notice what reaction you get. You can modify what that "other you" says, and how that "other you" says it, until you're pleased with the results.

7. Future Planning. Next, decide if you want to change your behavior based on the information you've just received. If so, see yourself in a similar situation using different behaviors in the future. This process is a way of programming yourself so that you'll have these new behaviors automatically available when you next experience that type of situation.

Continued

8. Repeat Practice. To make your responses even more automatic, individually review two or three different future situations in which you're likely to be criticized, and where you will want to be able to use this new way of responding. Repeat Steps 1–6 of this exercise with each of these so that the sequence becomes even more automatic.

9. Integration. When you're finished, actually reach out and bring that part of you that learned this new strategy into your body, so that whole process of evaluating and responding to criticism becomes fully a part of you now.

This process for comfortably responding to criticism is effective for detaching from criticism and discovering what useful feedback is available, whatever the source. It can also be used when you think that someone might criticize you or when you criticize yourself. Knowing that you can use this process to remain open to communication and respond appropriately can do wonders to increase your self-esteem.

The Value of Criticism

Without the NLP Responding Comfortably to Criticism strategy, you may react without a choice to criticism. If you have to react in a defensive manner whenever you are criticized, you will be blind to whatever useful information that criticism may contain. **Every behavior is useful in some context.** This very important NLP Presupposition means that even criticism has value. In fact, all criticism has useful information. If you use the Responding Comfortably to Criticism strategy and do not react defensively when someone criticizes your beliefs, values, or behavior, you will be able to listen carefully and evaluate objectively whatever was said and use whatever you learn for your own purposes.

If the criticism is accurate, and you are objective about it, you can respond by comfortably agreeing with the speaker, "I see what you mean." Your agreement, however, does not necessarily mean that you intend to change anything about yourself. You might change, you might not. The choice is up to you. What you have learned is that you and the other person can see eye to eye about some things, and whenever you communicate with that person, you can emphasize the nature of your agreements.

If you find that you are simply unable to understand what the other person is talking about, you can comfortably say, "I can't yet see what you're saying; please be more specific." By objectively asking for more detail, you increase the likelihood of learning a great deal more about the speaker and yourself. You can simply compare whatever the other person tells you with your personal experience and discover exactly where you agree and disagree.

Finally, on the other hand, if you disagree with the speaker, you can comfortably do so by objectively saying, "I don't see it that way." And you will have learned that you and the speaker see the world significantly differently concerning some things. With this information, you will be better prepared in the future to communicate with that person in a form that makes more sense to him or her. These are the communications of a self-esteeming person.

Reviewing What You've Learned

In this chapter, we have presented several useful processes for building self-appreciation and self-esteem. Specifically, you have learned how:

- Self-esteem is simply the result of the images you make in your mind that you can change: the content in the image for the positive or negative feelings and the submodalities of the image for the intensity.
- A powerful resource for high self-esteem is to take *other* position and experience what it is like to be someone who loves and appreciates you and add these experiences to your self-esteem.
- The Swish Pattern is a way of building positive self-esteem and a way to create new, resourceful behaviors for particularly troublesome situations.

- You can protect your sense of self-esteem by learning how to utilize criticism comfortably, which allows you to listen to criticism, evaluate it objectively, and decide what you want to do in response.

Self-esteem is not something that you're born with, or something that just happens to you. You play an active role in creating and maintaining your self-esteem, so create the best for yourself.

CHAPTER ELEVEN

Securing a Positive Mental Attitude

The Impact of a Positive Attitude

Most us think we know the importance of a positive mental attitude—an attitude of mental toughness to get us through the hard times. Most of us will never have it put to the test the way NLP Comprehensive trainer Gary Faris did a dozen years ago.

Gary went out running after an NLP seminar in Santa Cruz, California. At thirty-eight years old, he was training to compete in the masters running category for the quarter mile. That day, he decided to run down a paved farm road with lush green artichoke fields on either side. Out of nowhere, a pickup truck came barreling down that road at over sixty miles an hour behind him. The driver hadn't seen him because of a small rise in the road. He tried to brake, but his truck was still moving very fast when it smacked into Gary, throwing him 120 feet into a field.

At first, the emergency-room doctors weren't sure he would even live. They performed the first two of six operations Gary would eventually need to have. When he was out of danger, a few of the emergency-room doctors visited him. On the positive side, they told Gary the only reason he was still alive was because he was in such excellent physical condition. Then they told him he'd never walk normally, and certainly would never jog, much less run.

For the next two years, Gary was in sports rehabilitation. He rebuilt his damaged body, overcoming incredible physical pain as well as the doubts of his doctors. Today, Gary runs and trains regularly at a competitive level.

What happened? Had Dr. Bernie Siegel, the author of *Love, Medicine, and Miracles,* been there, he might have pointed out that the doctors were just using the best statistical evidence available to them. When Gary was wheeled into their emergency room, they didn't know that he would turn out to be an exceptional patient.

Gary is someone who has used NLP to overcome a life-threatening injury. You've already read how we use NLP to study the superachievers in the world, how we find the qualities that make these people's accomplishments possible and then teach these same qualities to others. Gary used the same principles in rebuilding his body, mind, and spirit.

Gary has always been an athlete with an interest in sports fitness. After the accident, though, he had new, very personal, and very compelling motivation for studying sports-injury rehabilitation. Rather than complaining about the unfairness of life, or making a list of whom he could sue, or considering how big a disability check he might be entitled to, Gary decided to search out the core characteristics of those athletes who'd gone through successful rehabilitation. After all, he reasoned, things like this have happened to other athletes. What had they done? Particularly, what had the ones who had completely recovered done? Gary was living the NLP Presupposition: **If one person can do something, anyone can learn to do it.** And he was determined to learn.

Even as he participated in his painful physical-therapy sessions, he talked to people in the same predicament. He read about famous athletes and what they had done. He looked beyond their stories and reasons to examine their underlying mental attitudes. His tenacious efforts paid impressive dividends. Gary eventually found six distinct mental patterns or characteristics that were possessed by every successfully rehabilitated athlete he had met or read about, and he set about applying them to himself.

When Gary shared his findings with sports-rehabilitation specialists, he was gratified at the positive reception he received. Eventually, his research was published in professional journals.[1] When he shared his discoveries with his NLP colleagues, he was surprised and delighted at the calls, letters, and conversations it stimulated. As others used Gary's insights with business clients, health professionals, and even elementary-school students, they found that these six mental patterns applied to a wide range of situations, all as different from one another as parenting, pole vaulting, and politics. These six mental patterns turned out to be core characteristics of any positive mental attitude. Whether we looked at athletes, entrepreneurs, or executives, the more solid their mental attitude, the more they utilized these six elements. Jack Schwager, author of the acclaimed best-seller, *The New Market Wizards,*[2] thought these characteristics were so important that he included them as one of the significant keys in becoming a successful commodity-futures trader.

The Six Characteristics of a Solid Positive Mental Attitude

Let's examine these six characteristics of a positive mental attitude. As we do, keep in mind that no single characteristic is more important than any other. These six characteristics are presented in a sequence, but it's the simultaneous interaction of all of them working together that creates the synergy for a solid positive mental attitude.

1. Inner Motivation

The first element Gary discovered was the inner-motivation direction these rehabilitating athletes used. These athletes were moving *toward* a very specific goal and *away from* certain unpleasant consequences. These were not "Hollywood" movie or "new age" images of a general desire to win, or be the best, or avoid making a fool of oneself. These athletes had personal, specific, and compelling visions of desirable goals or unpleasant consequences. For example, a promising young high school swimmer was coming back from an injury. She not only wanted to regain her health, she also wanted to compete to win a college scholarship. She was motivated and directed *toward* her goal. In another case, a forty-two-year-old man was in rehabilitation to keep an arthritic condition from getting worse. His motivation was to get *away from* a possible consequence of an often debilitating disease. However, the best athletes use both *away from* and *toward* motivation. They vividly imagine specific undesirable consequences worth avoiding, and then very desirable and worthwhile goals that draw them forward. By doing this, they get the maximum motivation.

II. The Value of High Standards

The second element Gary noticed about these athletes in rehabilitation was that they were dedicated to regaining full strength and health. This became their guiding goal, their first and final standard. Their attitude was that anything less was unacceptable. In fact, many of them not only wanted to regain their full strength and health but wanted even more. They wanted to be in even better shape than they were before their injuries. They knew what they were capable of and wouldn't accept anything less. These athletes were measuring their ultimate results against these inner standards. They could have settled for a more reasonable standard, but none of them did. They had to be their best.

We often read or hear about this athletic obsession to be the best. Consider this for a moment. If you demanded the best from yourself, and right now you didn't have it, that could be a setup for a letdown. These athletes also needed a way to expect the best, even though they didn't have it now, in a way that motivated them to work for it to happen in their futures. The third and fourth elements provide the keys for doing just that. Here is where it begins to become clear how critically important it is for these six elements to work *together* to create a solid positive mental attitude.

III. Chunking Down Goals

The third key element these athletes all had was their ability to focus on the process of rebuilding their health and athletic fitness one small step at a time. In NLP terms, they were able to decide what "chunk size" they paid attention to. Have you ever thought about the total effort required to overcome a serious injury—the pain, the frustration, the time, the incredible efforts required just to get back to where you started? Or how about guiding a major project in business—coordinating departments, keeping people motivated, tracking important details, and tying up loose ends? If you were to think of all the work involved in either project all at once, it could easily be overwhelming. On the other hand, if you take either project in "bite-size chunks," that is, one step at a time, then you can stay on track and complete it. For Gary Faris, he had to survive before he could stand, stand before he could walk, and walk again before he could run.

However, these athletes chunked much smaller than that. The ability to do five movements rather than four before they became exhausted, or an additional quarter-inch range of motion in flexing a foot became the achievable goals for the day.

"Chunking down" a difficult or demanding enterprise in this way has two added advantages. First, it enables them to focus on small tasks that they can actually do now. Second, Gary and the other athletes he studied got great satisfaction from completing each of these small steps. With specific measurable chunks to complete, these athletes experienced succeeding at every small milestone on the way to their complete goal of full strength and health. Each step along the way became a new goal with its own satisfactions of achievement. Being able to focus on specific achievable goals, and the satisfaction of succeeding at each one, maintains the motivation to continue.

IV. Combining Present and Future Time Frames

The fourth key element successfully rehabilitated athletes had in common was how they thought about time, which combines two skills. The first skill is that when concentrating on the small chunks and daily tasks, successful athletes are in the present moment. They think about the single task they are doing right now. Arnold

Schwarzenegger has said of his training that doing an exercise movement once with awareness was worth ten times an exercise done while distracted.

Athletes could easily get distracted and discouraged when they think about the uncertainty of the future. For example, if they project ahead doubtfully, asking questions like, "Will I be able to reach my previous capabilities?" or, "Will I be a success?" they may begin to imagine problems and barriers that weren't even there—until they thought of them. These questions can create a negative orientation and deflate motivation. It's much more empowering to ask, "What can I do now to reach my next milestone?" When they experience their present situation fully and get involved in making it better, they take actions that bring out their best. The same is true for all of us.

The second of the time skills is just the opposite of being fully in the present moment. It's the ability to think vividly and fully in the positive future. Sometimes a future orientation is much more beneficial and motivating than being in the present moment. An athlete in rehabilitation after an injury will go through some very painful times. At those times, it's much more helpful to think ahead to experience fully the rewards all your hard work and pain will bring you. While you're visualizing a healthier body, increased range of motion, and being back doing what you love, the pain and effort in the moment seems an insignificant price to pay. While your body is rebuilding and relearning in the present moment, you're already enjoying the future. That attractive, long-range goal keeps pulling you forward, solidly maintaining your motivation in the present.

Successful motivation actually combines these two skills. At the same moment that you are concentrating on achieving the small task at hand, you can see that big, bright picture of your future accomplishment drawing you forward.

V. Personal Involvement

The fifth element of successful rehabilitation and a positive mental attitude is the athlete's personal involvement. Gary found that the more athletes actively participated in their own rehabilitation plan, the more they helped themselves, and this, in turn, greatly improved the possibilities of their full recovery. Even if it was something as simple as placing ice on an inflamed area, the act of doing for themselves reinforced their sense of participation.

Sports medicine, just like everything else in this technological age, has grown very complex and detailed, with legions of experts and authorities. These doctors, physical therapists, athletic trainers, nurses, and sports psychologists have often spent most of their professional lives learning their skills. Their authority is earned, but sometimes this onslaught of expertise encourages athletes to passively place themselves in expert hands. Gary's research indicates that this is a mistake. Neither passive acquiescence nor rebellious resistance is a reliable path back to personal excellence. Athletes, and the rest of us, need to work actively with our highly trained experts to produce the kinds of results we want.

If you think about this for a minute, it makes sense. Have you ever been on a team and then had to sit on the sidelines of an important game or meeting? It may have even been appropriate at that time. Yet even if you were excited by the final outcome, you still probably felt separated from it, as if there were a glass wall between you and the action. You were there, but you weren't playing. You weren't really part of it. When we participate, we influence what's going on. We can feel the difference. It increases our personal commitment and focuses our intensity. It makes us more determined and active, which leads us to more personal involvement, and a bigger stake in our own future. Taking actions for ourselves, no matter how small, is important.

VI. Self-to-Self Comparisons

The sixth and final key element for successful athletic rehabilitation, and for building a solid positive mental attitude, is how these athletes judged their performance—the kind of mental comparisons they made. Sports commentators, newspaper statistics, and their fans regularly encourage athletes to compare themselves and their actions to others, living and dead. If they come out on top, they get to feel good; if they don't compare favorably, they're supposed to feel bad or somehow inadequate. This same tendency is very strongly ingrained in many of us. Early in life we noticed, or had blatantly pointed out to us in school, that some kids were smarter, some were more athletic, some were better-looking, and others were more popular than us. We might have been high on one scale, but if we checked another, we often found ourselves low. As we entered the world of work, this tendency to compare ourselves with others continued and, in some cases, even increased. We met people who were more aggressive, or clever, or better at office politics or computers or something than we were. As adults, we often make these comparisons unconsciously and automatically. We compare ourselves to movie stars, to the latest business mavericks, to our neighbors and their life-styles, or to anyone else in sight. We're encouraged to do this at work and at home by the media, and we continue to do so because we don't know the cost.

Recovering athletes know the cost. They know it is critically important *not* to fall into this mental habit. They know that because of their current injuries, they won't "measure up." They may even compare poorly with amateur athletes. This could be seriously discouraging, and they know it. Instead of comparing themselves to other athletes at any level, Gary Faris found, the really successful ones looked solely at their *own* progress. They made what NLP calls a "self-to-self" comparison. They asked themselves questions like, "How far have I progressed since yesterday, or since last week? Since last month? Since last year?" All of us can learn to do this, too. We can learn to measure our progress with our own development, whether in athletics or at work and at home.

This is one of those insights that not only applies to a positive mental attitude but to all aspects of life. Some of the best motivational speakers have asked, "What would you do if you knew you couldn't fail?"—a provocative and stimulating question to be sure. Yet anyone who has tried, learned, and then mastered a sport, a profession, or a musical instrument knows that countless failures are at the base of any success. Do you remember when you took up golf, tennis, the guitar, or something like it? Your mind was probably full of images of succeeding. You probably saw the ball gliding through the air almost effortlessly, or heard beautiful musical notes floating up from beneath your fingers. You may have even been lucky enough to experience that beauty and excitement the first few times. Then reality came home to roost. Beautiful things were possible with your instrument of choice: a club, a racket, a stringed instrument, or a keyboard. However, the cost was a long apprenticeship and dedication to your chosen craft. Many of us decided the musical instrument was too difficult, yet we stayed with the equally difficult golf or tennis or another sport. It has now filled years of our lives, offering us both deep frustrations and transcendent rewards. What was the difference between what we gave up on and what we stayed with? With Gary's NLP research as our guide, at least part of the answer is in how soon we experienced progress. How soon did that ball glide through the air? How soon did we experience our first inklings of competence, a genuine sense of progress? This sense of progress comes from comparing our beginnings with our current achievements. In other words, a self-to-self comparison.

But every day the media, well-meaning teachers and coaches, and even other students remind us and our children that there are people who are better at some things than we are and others who are worse. If a child shows promise at gymnastics, some parents immediately start making Olympic plans. If a child's drawings show a natural talent, some people start making comparisons to Picasso at the height of his ability.

Since our society makes so many self-to-other comparisons, there must be something positive about it, and there is. The accomplishments of others show us what it has been possible for a person to do. They are also valuable models for how to do it. By studying their mental patterns and physical behavior, we can learn not only what is possible but how it is possible.

However valuable, there is also a great danger in self-to-other comparisons. When a person sees the vast difference in ability, he may conclude, "I could never do that," or, "She must just have a natural talent." If your child shows little promise the first time he or she studies math or science, a second chance may not come along because comparisons come crashing in. The premature conclusion is reached that "I'm just not good at that." All of this can be very discouraging. It certainly could extinguish the creative joy of accomplishment that encouraged a very young Picasso, Mary Lou Retton, that slow math student Albert Einstein, and even basketball superstar Michael Jordan to exceed themselves again and again.

Remember: The royal road to results is measured by our *own* progress. When our children have this self-to-self comparison in mind, they can look to others' accomplishments for inspiration, for models of excellence, and for sources of high-quality information on their own improvement, not as targets of envy or jealousy. They will learn to delight in the success of others, for they are guides and models to their own possibilities. Later, they are very likely to be the models of success for a future generation. They will truly value their own success, for they have taken the full measure of it. Teaching your children to make self-to-self comparisons is probably one of the greatest gifts you can give them.

The six elements of successful athletic rehabilitation and a solid positive mental attitude are: inner motivation, the value of high standards, chunking down goals, flexible time frame, personal involvement, and self-to-self comparisons. Together these six elements create an unconscious and compelling mental image for success. With them, a positive mental attitude is assured. Without them, other achievements in life can become difficult.

Positive Attitude in Action

Let's look at a few different examples to show how these elements work together and what happens when they don't. The first is a thirty-one-year-old man who seriously hurt himself while playing on an intercompany softball league. As soon as he started rehabilitation, his first question was, "When will you be finished so I can get back to my job?" This single question spoke volumes about his mental patterns and emotional makeup. His only thought was that of returning to work. That's an admirable goal in itself, and indicates a *toward* motivation. However, it's also so general that it doesn't specify whether he'll be walking or in a wheelchair, limping or healthy. It's also a very big goal; it's a big chunk to chew on. He doesn't have any plan that chunks down his goal, and he wants a promise from someone else about how long it will take him. Also, notice that in his language he shows a lack of personal involvement; he's passive. "When will *you* be finished," he asks. He wants his physical therapist to do it for him. He doesn't realize he needs to take an active role. If he doesn't change this attitude, it's likely that his rehabilitation will end up being long and possibly unproductive.

Another case is a star high school football player who was injured midseason of his senior year. On arrival at the hospital, he vows to be back on the playing field the next game. When his doctor and coach impress upon him the seriousness of his injuries, the young athlete becomes despondent. His teammates' encouragements are met with, "What's the use?" He complains that the "rehab" exercises are too painful, and he refuses to do them, or does them halfheartedly. It isn't until he receives a call from a college recruiter asking how soon he'll be back playing football that this young man becomes interested and involved in his own recovery and rehabilitation. Effective motivation requires a personal and compelling vision either *away from* an unpleasant consequence or *toward* a specific desirable goal. When the young man found that he couldn't continue to play football that season, he lost his compelling motivation. When he did the rehab exercises, he had no compelling future to distract him from his pain or provide a motivation to move beyond it—until the recruiter called. Then the five remaining elements that were already there, combined with his new compelling motivation, were enough to motivate him to work diligently toward recovery.

These six elements are clearly present in the most celebrated comeback stories in sports. Most Americans paid no attention to European bicycle racing until a young American with a French sounding name won the toughest, most grueling bicycle race in the world—Le Tour de France. Winning in 1989, Greg LeMond set international bicycling records on a new course. He returned to the United States a hero, opening up a whole new arena of athletic excellence to young Americans. Taking a well-deserved rest and recreation break with his family, he went hunting. In the now-famous freak accident, he was shot in the chest and leg, and quite seriously injured. Even after extensive surgery, several shotgun pellets were still left in him around his heart because it was too dangerous to remove them. An athletic success story, an American hero, and a victim of circumstances, Greg LeMond could have rested on his laurels as well as his recovery. Nearly everyone would have been proud for the young athlete to simply recover and give inspirational speeches. Not Greg LeMond. Over the next two years he took charge of his own rehabilitation program that set him on a course to exceed his own previous best. As Greg moved from his hospital bed to home, and from walking to cycling again, any other comparisons besides his own progress would have been ludicrous. For a long time, any child could have beaten him. Yet he continued, increasing his workout time and his stamina. Sports commentators and media skeptics talked of his "pipe dreams," his futile efforts, and his coming public humiliation. He continued to hold in his mind his own personal and compelling vision of what he wanted. Even when he won a new place in the Tour de France, many commentators, while delighted with his obvious spirit, offered to look away rather than record his embarrassment. In the final leg of that race, Greg LeMond and his cycle barreled down the famous Champs-Élysées, shotgun pellets still around his heart, making the fastest time in the history of the race and securing for him his second victory.

This same solid positive mental attitude serves as a foundation for success in business. Morrie Mages was a Chicago businessman who has become a folk hero. Years ago, on Maxwell Street, at an open-air weekend flea market, Morrie sold shirts out of the trunk of his car. Then he started to sell athletic equipment. In a few short years, he had developed his salesmanship and deal-making skills into one of the largest retail sports stores in Chicago. At "the top of the heap," as he would say, this big man, big spender, and big lover of life enjoyed his success as Chicago enjoyed his flamboyant life-style. And then, quicker than it had come, he lost it all. Many men would have "disappeared" or claimed they retired. Instead, Morrie went back out on Maxwell Street, once again selling out of the trunk of his car. Like those great athletes who came back from injuries, Morrie Mages also came back. Today, his superstore is one of the biggest and most famous retail sports stores in Chicago.

Even with this short description, Morrie offers us clues to his use of the six elements of a solid positive mental attitude. We don't know if he had a motivating vision of his future superstore when he started, but once he got it, he obviously kept it in mind. While some people would have been too embarrassed to go back to selling on the street, Morrie was like the exceptional athlete, imagining the future enjoyments of his efforts, rather than dwelling on his current painful circumstances. A retailer his whole adult life, he knew you sold one customer at a time, specifically, the one right in front of you. This is an excellent example of paying attention to the small chunk-size task in the present. Finally, while the accomplishments of others were all around him, and may even have distracted him at times, he ultimately had to return to his most personal source of progress, himself. A warm, open man with a big voice and an even bigger heart, looking at him you wouldn't guess the past hardships. But that's the way it is with people whose positive attitude is there not just for the hard times, but for all times. That kind of attitude will help you throughout your life.

Attitudes are a choice. They may not come in bottles or little colored pills from your local pharmacy, but attitudes are real. We've all experienced times when a negative attitude has stuck a project in the mud before it even had a chance to get going. We've also experienced how a positive attitude has brought people together and made miracles happen. The following NLP technique is especially designed to assist you in integrating into your own life the six elements of a solid positive mental attitude you've learned about in this chapter. This is your chance to choose to have an attitude that can make a difference in the quality of the rest of your life. This process is similar to the technique you used to change your motivation strategy in Chapter Two. Now, we'll use it to make the successful athlete's positive mental attitude a natural part of your thinking and behavior. Let this NLP technique make a difference for you.

EXERCISE 38: EMBRACING A POSITIVE MENTAL ATTITUDE

Find a quiet place and a time when you will be undisturbed for twenty or thirty minutes.

1. Choose a Situation. First, think of a specific situation in your life where you'd like to have a more solid positive mental attitude. If your answer is everywhere, then think of a specific situation where you would like to have it first. It could be a familiar situation from your past that you anticipate happening again, and that you want to be different next time. Or it could be a future situation you anticipate coming up soon. Whichever you choose, in your mind's eye go to a moment just before that situation began to happen so that your new positive mental attitude will already be there just *before* you need it.

2. See Yourself. Begin by literally imagining seeing yourself, another "you," just before the beginning of that situation. You will watch that "other you" who is going to learn this process. You will have to be completely satisfied by what you see and hear before the learnings of this "other you" become yours.

3. Motivation. Watch as that "other you" notices what is worth avoiding in that experience. Then see that "other you" truly attracted *toward* the specific results you want in this situation. See both what you want to avoid and the desirable things in vivid, colorful, exciting, and compelling movies. You're literally creating your own future; you're setting a motivation direction and establishing inner goals.

4. High Standards. Now, holding that "other you" image in your mind, go on to watch him refine his goal by establishing a high standard for success.

Think: "Anything less is unacceptable." See that "other you" over there filled with the desire for complete success, almost like a magnet, drawing him farther on course. You'll know that this value is there when you begin to see a relaxed determination in his body and the joyful sparkle in his eyes.

5. Chunking Down Goals. Notice as that "other you" practices first seeing "the big picture" and then focuses on one specific aspect that he could achieve now. See that "other you" experience satisfaction at completing each step on the way toward the overall goal. Just watch and listen to this as if it's a movie in front of you.

6. Combining Present and Future Time Frames. Notice how that "other you" can easily stay in the present when concentrating on small chunks and tasks. And while that "other you" is working on something difficult or painful, that "other you" can also foresee the future to richly experience some of the ultimate rewards for the current discomfort and efforts. Watch as these time-management skills are spontaneously practiced over and over again by that "other you" over there. Enjoy the results you see.

7. Personal Involvement. Watch as that "other you" takes charge of his own life and gets personally involved in solving problems and moving toward success. See how that "other you" shows increasing feelings of determination and intensity with more participation.

8. Self-to-Self Comparison. Watch and listen as that "other you" asks, "How far have I progressed since yesterday? Since last week? Since the first phase? Since I began this?" See that "other you" pleased and encouraged by this measurable improvement.

9. Adjustment. Now, let a mist float by so you can't see that "other you" for a few moments. While he is in that mist, the wisdom of your unconscious mind can integrate these skills with all other aspects of your thoughts, feelings, and life in a way that will most effectively produce a solid positive mental attitude for *you.* Each person is unique in the way that they can best make use of the six elements of a positive mental attitude. Every person needs to make adjustments in exactly how they carry out these elements in the real world. Most of these adjustments will occur unconsciously, so there is no need for you to consciously figure out anything. Just watch the mist as all parts of you consider how best to make use of the information this "other you" has learned.

As this process of integration is completed, the mist will slowly

Continued

clear so that you will see that "other you" in full possession of this new attitude in a way that pleases you. If this takes only a few moments, let it. For some people, most of the elements were already in place, waiting to come together now. For others, these are tremendous new learnings, and giving them adequate time to thoroughly integrate is the most effective means to making them permanent.

10. Check. As you look at that "other you" with the positive mental attitude, would you like to become that person, having those skills and attitudes? If not, have the mist come back and again envelop that "other you" so any other qualities that are important can be added now.

11. Integration. When you are satisfied that you want to become that "other you," have that "other you" come toward you and into you, so these skills are inside you and become fully part of you. Some people find if they actually put out their hands and draw that "other you" into their chest it enhances the results. Some people feel a tingle or some other pleasant feeling as this happens. Whatever way you brought that "other you" completely inside, you've completed this process and you've now got these skills in you.

12. Future Planning. The only thing left is to decide when and where you want to be especially sure that this set of positive mental attitudes will be active. When will you want to have this attitude most strongly? Notice your response as you think of that future situation, and enjoy the feeling of having more choices as a result of this positive attitude.

After completing this exercise, many people want to know how they can spread this change through the rest of their lives. They want to know if they have to do the process on all their past memories and future expectations. In the early days of NLP, we sometimes had to do an NLP technique dozens of times to go through a sufficient number of old memories to get the feelings or attitudes to generalize well. Using more recent developments in the field, it has become possible to change years of unpleasant feelings, useless attitudes, and limiting beliefs in a matter of a few minutes. All that is needed is a state of powerful personal resourcefulness ready to go and a knowledge of how a person organizes time. In the next exercise, you can discover how you organize your experiences in a time sequence, or what we call your personal timeline.

Your personal timeline is a fundamental way that you organize the events and experiences that you have had in the past and hope to have in the future. As just one example, if your future is close in front of you, then when you set goals they will be right where you can see them all the time. You'll be more motivated to reach them than if your future were way off to the side in your peripheral vision where you can barely notice it. Many other applications of timelines and how to change them for specific outcomes are described elsewhere.[3] For now, we want to utilize another aspect of a personal timeline: its continuity.

The timeline delineates exactly how your life is a continuous succession of events experienced by the same person—you. An attitude or other personality characteristic of any sort, whether it's positive or negative, is something that persists through time. Most of us go through all kinds of different situations, experiences, and thought processes and still maintain the same sense of ourselves and attitude of mind. Most people relate to this idea most easily when thinking about a bad mood or negative attitude, but the process is exactly the same for a positive one. According to our NLP understanding, our brains have coded our current attitudes or moods on our timeline, whether they're positive or negative. If we want a positive mental attitude, then that's the code we'll need to add.

EXERCISE 39: FINDING YOUR PERSONAL TIMELINE

Allow at least ten minutes to do this exercise. First find a comfortable position, and take a minute to relax.

1. Daily Task. Take a second or two to clear your mind. Begin by thinking of something ordinary that you do fairly regularly, like brushing your teeth or reading the newspaper. This should be something relatively neutral, something that you don't have strong feelings about.

Continued

2. *The Past.* When you have something in mind, think of a specific time you did it a week ago; then think of a time two months ago, then a specific time six months ago, then a year ago, then three years ago, and finally ten years ago. When you have each of these, think of them all at once. Notice how they arrange themselves in your mind's eye as you think of all six at once.

For many people, their mental images form a line with the most recent memories closest and the more distant memories farther away. For many people, this line extends off to their left. For others, it goes behind them, and they have to look around to see their past. Some have their past on their right. Whatever way you do it is fine; it's the way your brain has found it useful to sort out the time of your life.

3. *The Future.* Where is your future? This time you'll do much the same thing as before, except now you'll find ordinary events you expect to happen in your future. Again, take something you do regularly and expect to do in the future. First, a week in the future, then two months, then six months, then a year, then three years, then ten years.

Now think of them all at once and find out how they are arranged in space to form the future portion of your timeline. Notice the direction these images take toward your future. For some people, their future extends out to their right. For others, it is right in front of them. A few have the future on the left. However you do it, take note of how your timeline extends into the future.

4. *Your Personal Timeline.* Taken together, your past and future form your timeline with you at the present. Your timeline might be shaped something like the capital letter *V,* with you at the base of the *V* and the left side of the *V* formed of your past memories and the right side your future expectations. Or your timeline might be like a straight or slightly curved line passing through you, with your future in front of you, and your past extending behind you. A few people even have curled or looping timelines. Whatever way yours is organized, you're now in possession of one of the most effective means of personal change ever discovered.

Reevaluating Your Past, Present, and Future

Now that you are able to envision your timeline, you can use this information to change the way you think and feel about yourself throughout time. That's the idea behind the next NLP technique, Richard Bandler's "Decision Destroyer," so named because he developed it to help people destroy poor decisions made earlier in their lives. This is done by teaching you how to put a better decision in your memories before the bad one, thus neutralizing it. We're going to use this same principle to put that solid positive mental attitude you just created into your past, present, and future. The result will be that you'll feel like you've had this great attitude for a long time already and will continue to enjoy it for a long time to come.

The following exercise will use your new solid positive mental attitude from Exercise 38 and your knowledge of your own timeline from Exercise 39. If you haven't already done the previous two exercises, do them now before doing the next exercise. Take your time. Follow the process and enjoy the results.

This exercise starts with a positive attitude or memory and takes it through all your life experiences, spreading it through your life so that it becomes even more fully a part of who you are throughout time. This is how solid positive mental attitudes are naturally created. With NLP, you can re-create your past to have what you've always wished was there, a storehouse of powerful and positive memories to draw on for your present success—where we all live, work, play, and create.

EXERCISE 40: THE DECISION DESTROYER[4]

1. Empowering Memory. To begin this NLP process, you'll first need to think back to an empowering, positive memory. It should be so empowering it affects your behavior even today. It's the kind of experience that convinced you of a quality about you, such as that you're athletic, or likable, or talented at something.

Continued

You just know it's true; you don't question it. These experiences often occur when we're young and in our teens, though they can happen at any time in life. This memory formed a positive imprint in your brain. When you have found a positive imprint memory, bring it fully to mind, reliving it as if it is happening to you now.

2. Ordinary Memory. Now think of an ordinary memory that doesn't affect your life much one way or the other, such as yesterday's errand to the grocery store, or opening your mail.

3. Submodalities of Empowering Memory. Compare these two memories to find out what submodalities create the power in your empowering memory. You might find that the empowering memory is bigger, more dramatic, more colorful, than the ordinary memory. Pretend that you were going to make a real movie of it, and notice its cinematic qualities: its visual and auditory submodalities. Notice the size, brightness, and location of inner images and sound qualities. Notice the visual and auditory qualities that make it the important memory it is. List them if this helps keep them in mind.

4. Creating the Positive Mental Imprint as an Empowering Memory. Now, think of the positive mental attitude you created in Exercise 38. Remember the moment after you brought it into you. Put your images of the solid positive mental attitude in the same mind's-eye location as your empowering memory. Give that positive attitude all the same qualities, all the same visual and auditory submodalities as the positive imprint experience you just thought of. Make your positive mental attitude into an empowering imprint memory for yourself.

5. Traveling Through Time. Now you're ready to take a transformational mental journey. Keeping your positive mental attitude imprint with you, imagine floating up out of your body and above your timeline, which you discovered in the previous exercise. You may go back just a few years, or you may want to go back to when you were quite young, looking for an early time in your past when you really could have used a solid positive mental attitude, a time when making changes would positively affect the rest of your life.

When you've found a specific past memory, slide down into

your past timeline at any time *before* that past memory, keepingyour positive mental attitude imprint with you. Now begin to move rapidly forward through your timeline. See, hear, and feel as that past event is transformed by your positive mental attitude imprint.

Now, continue to move rapidly through all your past memories toward your present. Experience how these past events are also instantly changed and enriched by your positive mental attitude imprint. Keep moving rapidly through your timeline all the way up to your present and stop there.

Now, see yourself with your positive attitude imprint, moving through your future experiences, transforming them as well. It's a great future, filled with enriching experiences, even better now because your new attitude is imprinted on it.

Some people like to cycle through this complete exercise several times in order to strengthen its benefits even further.

Reviewing What You've Learned

If you completed the exercises in this chapter, you have just created an empowering positive mental attitude for yourself and imprinted it on your past memories and future expectations. Essentially, you've just re-created your life with much greater possibilities of action. You can use this same technique to bring other resources of success and achievement to everything you've done and everything you will do, building an even more solid foundation for your future.

We're the totality of our experiences. When we learn to change our memory experiences, we change our lives. By putting a new attitude in our past, we give ourselves a new sense of our history, and new possibilities open up in our present. Old mistaken beliefs often fall away of their own accord, and a new sense of self emerges from deep within us—a self that is naturally optimistic, positive, and happy.

In this chapter, you've learned:

- The importance of a positive mental attitude
- The six elements that together create this attitude
- How to put a positive mental attitude into your life now
- How to change past decisions into positive resources and put those positive resources into your entire lifetime

Some people might say, "But it's all in your mind. You haven't done anything." And at this moment, that's a true statement. Yet how do you decide what you want to do? You get an idea, a desire, or a dream, or you come across something in the real world right in front of you and begin to see the possibilities. And that is the moment that your attitude makes all the difference. Your attitude is something you can choose. The chance to live the life you've dreamed of has arrived. Every dream that becomes an action does so because of an attitude.

CHAPTER TWELVE

Achieving Peak Performance

Mountain Peaks and Peak Performance

Mountains have always been special to people—almost always majestic and somehow mysterious. Mountains, especially those with the tallest and most jagged peaks, are symbols deeply important to the human psyche. On seeing a mountain, almost all of us think of climbing it. We imagine what it must be like to view the world from the top—from the peak.

The peak has been an American symbol of success for some time now; whether in business, sports, academics, or entertainment. This makes sense. Seeing things from a peak is inspiring. The view is unobstructed. The vistas of nature open up, and the horizon feels like it's an infinity away. The sights below appear smaller and more manageable. We feel ourselves on top of things. For most of us, our inner world of possibilities expands. It's as if we can see farther, not just into the distance, but into life. The unobstructed view encourages more sweeping thoughts and grander plans. It's not surprising that entrepreneurs, certain CEOs, and children seek high open places. They still want to see the world as full of possibilities.

We at NLP Comprehensive know the magic of mountains well because our main offices are in the beautiful city of Boulder, Colorado. Set in a wooded office park near a creek, we look out from the base of the Rocky Mountains. From our windows, we see the seasons change and gain the perspective that being near mountains brings. If you were to visit our offices or come to Colorado for NLP training, you would take Highway 36 out of Denver and head toward the mountains. At first they don't look much like mountains, but more like low gray clouds on the horizon. With each mile you drove, that gray uneven horizon would begin to loom larger, transforming itself into those grand mountains, their jagged peaks against the sky, the highest ones always tipped with ice and snow. As you drive past the farms and fields of grazing cattle and horses that border both sides of the highway, you'd leave behind your airplane ride, the airport, and the Mile High City. Finally, you would see the famous Flatirons, three dramatic rock outcroppings that mark the beginning of the Rockies, and at their foot, set in a lush green valley, the city of Boulder. Here, climbers from across the globe gather each summer to test their skills and determination—to climb the peaks and to find their peak performance within.

If you've ever climbed a mountain, whether it was a day hike or a competitive technical climb, you know it can take hours of effort. Day-to-day concerns are dropped by the trail as the task of climbing absorbs more and more of your concentration. On the way up, you go through every possible emotion: frustration, fear, elation, self-doubt, trust, and triumph. The climb condenses into a few hours' experiences that might ordinarily take place over weeks, months, or even years of "regular" life.

While climbing, there comes a point, perhaps about halfway up, when you evaluate your progress and your state of mind. You now know clearly what you've gotten yourself into. How much more is there to go? How much more are you willing to commit physically and emotionally? It's the same kind of feeling you get when you've been intensely involved in a project for months and months and find yourself once again working late. You reflect on how your efforts have brought you so far, and on how much more effort is still required to finish it. You can look back into the past, back toward your beginnings. You can see your accomplishments and the skills you've gained. And you can also look forward into your future, seeing the upcoming difficulties and required efforts as well as the anticipated goal and its rewards—all as real as a mountain peak.

Each of us is a unique combination of natural talents and resources. At some point in life, we pick out a path, or find ourselves already on one, and begin to climb. We may go it alone or travel with others. We may even elect to carry the load for several. Whatever path we picked, we know it is the one that we travel and unless and until we pick another, we will need to meet its demands and relish its rewards. Having journeyed this far with us, we know you are committed to following your path the best way you know how. We know you are someone who looks toward the peaks. By reading this book and pursuing this new technology of achievement, you've proved this to yourself. You could be watching TV reruns, but instead you're pursuing your own excellence.

In the last chapter, you learned how to gain access to a solid positive mental attitude. This attitude can be your bedrock, a foundation for your future accomplishments. Now, you may want to know, what is the difference that makes "the difference" between those who achieve and those who achieve their peak performance? Let's find out.

Modeling Peak Performance

Many others have studied peak performance, and their research provides a promising orientation to gaining greater levels of human excellence. Some of the best known work has been done by Charles Garfield. As a novice computer programmer for the Grumman Aerospace Corporation during America's drive to put a man on the moon, Charles watched in amazement as inspired men and women sought the best in themselves and others. Managers with ratings in the lower 50 percent were transformed into the top 15 percent in less than eighteen months. Though a recent college graduate, his life experience was wide enough to alert him that this was not the norm. He was in the presence of something extraordinary. Informal investigations gave way to a lifelong interest in achievement and a degree in psychology. Today, Dr. Garfield is one of the country's leading authorities on peak performance. In his book *Peak Performers: The New Heroes of American Business*,[1] he sets forth his original research into the qualities that produce peak performers. Using an approach very different from NLP, he has also discovered patterns of excellence. Like NLP, his work points to common thoughts, attitudes, and behaviors among high achievers.

Dr. Garfield found that the peak performers shared a set of key characteristics. They showed commitment to a mission larger than themselves, purposeful activity with real, measurable results, team building with team playing, course correction—having a path that is flexible and stays on course and changes management—maintaining momentum and changing with the times.

Studying Dr. Garfield's key characteristics of peak performers, you can see how the exercises in this book have helped you integrate many of them into yourself. In Chapters Three and Four, we showed you the importance of a mission and offered you exercises to discover and develop your own heartfelt life mission. In those same chapters, we introduced you to goal achievement conditions and the evidence for success, the basis for setting purposeful goals and measuring real results. In Chapters Five and Six, we introduced you to rapport and the power of persuasion and showed you how to build your team, both inside and out. In Chapters Two and Three, we showed you the importance of having a course of action and how to use NLP to keep yourself on track. As for change management, NLP is the most advanced communication technology available for creating and managing change. Each exercise you have done in this book has added to your flexibility and resourcefulness.

In addition to these, Dr. Garfield found a less tangible yet crucial characteristic. Whether he was talking to rocket scientists or people recovering from cancer, he found each and every one of them had a total belief in the *likelihood* of their own success. They believed in themselves. They believed they would make a difference. Dr. Garfield found this quality was sometimes brought out by new opportunities, as when President Kennedy announced an American would walk on the moon before the end of the decade. At other times, personal challenges, like an accident or cancer, has brought out the peak performer. Dr. Garfield wondered if peak performance was only the offspring of circumstances. When he found outstanding achievers in sports, the arts and entertainment, and business were internally motivated, he rejected that possibility. Ask yourself if only circumstances motivated basketball legend Michael Jordan, or celebrated American painter Jasper Johns, or world-renowned choreographer Twyla Tharp, or singer-songwriter Bruce Springsteen? Whatever their circumstances may have contributed, these people were internally motivated by their desire to make a difference. Garfield found this desire and ability to be at the top of the mountain, at our peak, was within each of us, without exception.

The Roots of Powerlessness

So how is it that so many of us know people who feel powerless? From television shows, newspaper stories, and individuals around us, we know that many people don't feel they have the power to change their circumstances, much less achieve their peak performance. Why is there such a wide gap between those with a sense of empowerment and those without it? Dr. Michael Lerner, of the National Institute of Mental Health, decided to find out. In the mid-1980s, he directed a research project to discover the roots of people's sense of power over their own lives. He and his staff interviewed thousands of people from every aspect of American life: high tech, blue collar, service, professional, government and self-employed. He asked them how much power they experienced in and over their lives. He published his research findings in an academic book entitled *Surplus Powerlessness.*[2] The results of his research study are startling and deserve a much wider audience.

First, and not surprising, he observed that we live in times of unequal economic and political power. Second, his findings showed that in most people's minds the perception of this inequality of power was far greater than it actually was. Dr. Lerner found that many people felt they had very little power to change things and thus created a "surplus of powerlessness" in themselves He called this "emotional powerlessness" because it was their feeling about their situation, not the reality. Third, he provided compelling evidence that most people had a deep identification with their powerlessness. Even as their feelings of powerlessness corrupted their lives, isolating them, and making them distrustful of others and limiting their fulfillment, they would not challenge it. Instead, they acted as if it was inevitable or told him it was what they deserved.

As it turns out, Dr. Lerner's startling discoveries are supported by Dr. Garfield's own work, in which he searched for the changes in people with average levels of performance who became peak performers. He found they often described themselves or their capacities as having greatly enlarged. Dr. Garfield concluded that too many people restrict their potential, thinking much less of themselves than their possibilities. When their circumstances quickly and dramatically changed, this often acted as a trigger that released people from their old limitations, and they found themselves larger than they thought they were. To put it in NLP terms, their limitations were not in their capabilities or in the world, but in their beliefs, thoughts, and feelings about themselves.

Providing specific NLP techniques in this book that can help you integrate the key characteristics of peak performers has been deliberate on our part. We wanted to highlight the differences between theory and application, between ideas and action. So much valuable information on many areas of human excellence is available: how to eat to become more healthy, how to exercise for optimal results, the key characteristics of winners, study skills for school success, and the methods of top negotiators, to name but a few. We do not lack for peak-performance possibilities or living models of excellence. What has been lacking is a reliable method for getting these great ideas into human action. You know what you should eat to be healthier. Do you do it? You know that exercise is good for you. Do you willingly, even excitedly, get to it? For most people there is a wide gap between what they know is good for them and what they do. Often there is just as wide a gap between what people dream and desire for themselves and those they love, and what they actually do to achieve it. Closing this gap and making dreams and desires into realities truly represents the promise of NLP. One of NLP's goals is to offer everyone the opportunity to achieve their best. Throughout this book, we've offered an abundance of NLP techniques to enrich and enhance your life. Human excellence is born within each and every one of us. With it we can achieve whatever we want. With NLP, we anticipate you'll feel empowered to take the actions to make your lives more what you want them to be. All of us, regardless of our level of success, can make our lives and the lives of others much better.

Every time we teach an NLP training, we witness more people putting aside their powerlessness and engaging the greater capabilities and qualities that have always been within them. People from all walks of life enroll in our trainings: managers, students, salespeople, doctors, nurses, mental-health professionals, therapists, lawyers, entrepreneurs, educators, and the just plain curious. They attend for a variety of reasons: to improve communications, accelerate learning, enrich relationships, increase results, and learn new skills. As they apply NLP techniques to successfully reach their individual goals, time and time again, we have seen a much bigger change take place. While the business people came to NLP for an edge, and the teachers came to NLP for educational strategies, and the therapists came to NLP for more effective change techniques, about halfway through the training all of them had expanded their possibilities to include their own self-development. The formerly shy teacher had decided to open her own business. The self-contained computer programmer decided to do volunteer work at a crisis center. The entrepreneur decided to teach NLP techniques to everyone she works with instead of just using them herself. The business manager had found that NLP management skills apply equally well to parenting. Again and again, our participants' horizons have been expanded. They have found more of themselves by getting in touch with their potential. It was always there. It was always believed in. More important, it needed to be prompted in a way that they would believe.

The Total Belief of Peak Performance

So let's return our attention to that less tangible, yet crucial characteristic of the peak performer that Dr. Garfield identified: a total belief in the *likelihood* of his or her own success. While a single technique in a book is no substitute for an NLP training, your concentrated attention to the following NLP process can pay you substantial rewards. We will use the Swish Pattern again. This is the same technique you used in Chapter Nine to enhance your self-esteem. It is a useful technique any time you want to change a habit of mind. The Swish Pattern is one of the easiest NLP techniques to learn, and also one of the most profoundly powerful. That's because it uses the problem itself to trigger you automatically to become more of the kind of person who no longer has the problem. The more you practice this technique, the more uses you'll find for it. Right now, let's use this process to give you more resources and feelings of empowerment.

EXERCISE 41: THE SWISH PATTERN FOR SELF-EMPOWERMENT

1. Identify the Cue Image. Begin by thinking of a specific time when you felt powerless. While some people immediately think of a dramatic example from their lives, picking a more ordinary moment with a familiar feeling of powerlessness can be even more effective. That's because when you change that everyday feeling of powerlessness, all your similar life experiences will also change. Make sure it's a real and specific memory, a time when you felt you didn't have the ability to make things better.

For a moment, step back into that memory and see what you saw out of your own eyes, just *before* you felt that sense of powerlessness. This is the cue image we'll use later. Now set this cue image aside temporarily.

2. Create a Resourceful Self-Image. Now, in your mind's eye, see an inner image of yourself the way you would look if you'd already overcome this problem. See that "you" in your mind's eye, empowered and resourceful. It's like a studio photograph of "you" without a background. You don't need to know how you got that way. You can just see that "you" exuding the qualities of empowerment, perhaps by the sparkle in the eyes and a confident smile, for example. Take all the time you need to let this self-image develop fully. Make sure that it's real to you, and that you feel powerfully drawn to become this resourceful self-image. Enjoy that image of "you."

3. Practice Expanding the Resourceful Self-Image. Now, put this resourceful self-image in your mind's eye into a tiny, sparkling dot in front of you. Allow that sparkling dot to rapidly expand and blossom, and get larger and brighter until you can see this resourceful "you" life-size in front of you. Then see a blank screen. Repeat this process several times, until it's automatic.

4. Place the Resourceful Self-Image Dot into the Cue Image. Now put that sparkling dot with the resourceful self-image in the center of the cue image that you got in Step 1.

5. Exchange Images (Swish Them). As the cue image quickly fades and darkens, allow the sparkling dot to rapidly expand and brighten as it reveals that resourceful image and it quickly becomes full and life-size.

6. See a Blank Screen.

7. Repeat Ten Times. Now repeat Steps 4–6 a bit more quickly. Place that tiny sparkling dot in the center of the cue image again. Now, as that cue image quickly fades and darkens, watch as your self-image rapidly gets bigger and brighter and bigger and brighter until . . . swish . . . the resourceful self-image overwhelms the cue image. Then see a blank screen again.

8. Multiplying the Resourceful Self-Image. Since this "resourceful you" image can probably serve you well in many other situations, it will be most powerful if you are seeing this positive image of yourself everywhere you look—in the past, present, and future.

So when you're unable to get the unpleasant feelings you used to have, simply imagine that you can physically hold the "resourceful you" image in your hands. Reach out and get hold of it with your hands. When you touch it, it will begin to glow. Now, multiply that image—make color Xerox copies—make thousands of images of the "resourceful you," one behind the other, like a very large deck of cards, glowing and in color.

Now leave one of the images right in front of you as you toss the rest of them up high into the air. Watch all those images of the "resourceful you" begin to come down and settle all around you in concentric circles, all around you for as far as you can see in

Continued

every direction . . . in your past, your present, and your future. Imagine that there are rows after rows of circles of "resourceful you" images all around you. And you can allow the good feelings to wash over you and through you.

9. Checking Your Work. Now that you've run the pattern several times, it's important to test your work. So take a moment now and notice what you feel when you try to get that original, unpleasant cue image back in mind. If you are unable to get the unpleasant feelings at all, or you have a tough time even seeing the unpleasant image, you have completed the technique.

If you still have any unpleasant feelings when you think of that cue image, simply repeat the pattern, paying careful attention to each step, until the unpleasant feelings vanish.

What you have just done is set your brain in a new direction. It's kind of like a railroad track switching system. Every time your brain is headed in the direction of feeling powerless and unresourceful, your "swish" will automatically switch your thoughts to take the track directly to self-empowerment. The more often you are encouraged by the world around you to feel powerless, the more practice your brain will get in switching you over to self-empowerment. The Swish Pattern helps you organize and access your unconscious resources so you can get in touch with your greater capabilities. The way you will express your new self-empowerment is a journey of self-discovery waiting to be taken, one that will expand and become more enjoyable the more you are on it. Your brain can do amazing things. If you want a positive, peak-performance life, your brain can "swish" to provide it.

Enhancing Your Brain's Natural Abilities

We've all heard stories that illustrate the amazing potential that lives within every one of us. Here are some of our current favorites. Years ago, a young student fell asleep in his advanced college mathematics class. Awakened by the class bell, he saw several complex problems on the board. He quickly copied them down for homework and went on to his next class. Over the weekend, he set his mind to them. He was surprised at how difficult they were. Come Monday, he had only been able to completely solve one of them and two others partially. He decided it was best to admit his classtime nap and get some assistance from the professor. Imagine his surprise when the professor told him that he had written the problems on the board as interesting problems in the field that had not yet been solved.

The classroom shades are pulled down, and beautiful baroque music is playing in the background. The language teacher speaks slowly and clearly, smiling and nodding at his students. Each has a name and identity in the language they are studying. When the teacher asks a question, he looks encouragingly at the student. "Of course, you know the answer, Paulo. You have lived here all your life. You've just momentarily forgotten. It's coming back, isn't it?" And more often than not, it does. Dr. Lozanov's "Suggestopedia" has gone on to create a worldwide revolution in language teaching and to question the most fundamental ideas about learning.

The doctors told her that with her disease, her chances of survival were very slim. There was a new drug on the market. It might help, but it was experimental. She could only receive it if she agreed to be part of an experimental study. She agreed. Many years later, completely recovered, she would discover that she had been in the "control" group and had received only an inactive sugar pill.

All three of these scenes are examples of the "placebo effect." Placebos are pills with no active ingredient in them—they are given in experimental trials of new medicines to provide a baseline against which the new drugs are measured. They often contain only sugar or flour.

When people are given a placebo, they take it with the understanding that it is something that will help them. Even though it contains nothing medicinal, a considerable percentage of people improve, and this is called the "placebo effect." They are prepared for a positive change, and their brains go ahead and make them better. In the instance of the young mathematics student, he believed that the problems on the board were homework any student in his class ought to be able to solve. Believing them solvable, his inner resources rose to the occasion. In the case of the foreign-language students, they believed they already knew the language. When a word or grammar point was forgotten, they assumed it would come back in an instant. In the classic sense of the placebo effect, the ill woman believed the new experimental drug would help her. And in a real sense it did. It helped her to access her own inner resources to combat her illness and reclaim her health.

NLP's codevelopers Richard Bandler and John Grinder decided to study the available data on the "placebo effect." They found that placebos were proven to be effective about 20 percent of the time. That meant that about 20 percent of the subjects in experimental drug tests actually got better, often from difficult or dangerous diseases, after taking a placebo—a pill with no medicinal value.

The current scientific medical research approach is to rule out the placebo effect, because physicians and scientists are searching for medications that will work regardless of what people believe about them. This is certainly the best course of action for developing truly effective new medicines, and it's an approach that has provided us with many of the "wonder drugs" of this century like penicillin and the polio vaccine.

Richard Bandler and John Grinder had a different goal in mind, so they looked at the same data differently. They saw the placebo effect as an untapped natural human ability. The placebo effect demonstrated the inherent ability of the brain to heal the body and to exceed expectations under certain circumstances. Belief can often overcome seemingly difficult or insoluble problems. The question became how to accomplish this.

At first, Bandler and Grinder joked among themselves that they could accomplish this by selling placebo pills directly. After all, since the pills would contain only inert ingredients, they wouldn't really be a drug or medicine. Each bottle of "Placebo" would include an instruction booklet telling the purchaser to imagine the health-promoting properties of the capsules and to take so many every few hours until the desired results were achieved. Placebo could honestly be advertised as effective about 20 percent of the time. Their imaginations began to run away with them as they envisioned the response of the FDA and an international effort to ban Placebo. In their flight of fancy, they saw themselves being called before a congressional committee to testify, and just before they did, they would release Placebo Plus—"now with even more inert ingredients."

Flights of fancy can be fun, and they can also lead our brains down unanticipated and very fruitful pathways, and cause us to ask different questions. When the math student began to work on the "homework" problems, what self-image did he have in his mind? Probably he saw himself solving the problems. When the language student thinks of himself as a native speaker of the new language he is learning and believes that he has only momentarily forgotten a word or phrase, he is able to access memories that would otherwise be unused. When the ill woman participated in the experimental study, she probably foresaw herself getting healthier and healthier as the drug successfully treated her illness. While we may never know exactly how a placebo works when it does, we do know it affects what we think about, how we think about it, and our beliefs about what's possible. The Swish Pattern provides a way to accomplish this quickly, easily, and much more dependably than a placebo does. After all, many people who receive a placebo continue to be pessimistic, seeing themselves failing, or stupid, or continuing to be ill.

In the next exercise, we want to use our NLP insights into the nature of placebos to create a technique that will accomplish the same thing: to affect what you think about, how you think about it, and your beliefs about what's possible.

EXERCISE 42: CREATING A PEAK-PERFORMANCE IMPRINT

This exercise uses Richard Bandler's Decision Destroyer again. In Exercise 36, you used it to give yourself a solid positive mental attitude throughout your life. This time, you'll use it to put a powerful peak performance into your past memories for you to draw on now. Before you begin, take a moment to recall the

Continued

positive attitude imprint you created in Chapter Eleven. After you have reexperienced it fully, then set it aside temporarily.

1. Peak-Performance Memory. Think back and find a positively exceptional time in your life, a time you experienced peak performance. It may have been a time when you had great creativity, or brilliant insight, or exceptional concentration or persistence. It may have happened in sports, at school, while working, or at home with family. What's important is that it's a time when you were "on"—giving an outstanding performance that you were very pleased with. When you find one, step back into it, and see what you saw, hear what you heard, and feel those exceptional feelings again. Reexperience it as if it's happening now.

2. Ordinary Memory. Now think of an ordinary memory that doesn't significantly affect your life one way or the other, such as a simple phone call or working in the yard.

3. Submodalities of the Peak-Performance Memory. Compare these two memories to find out what submodalities are different in the peak-performance memory that create this state in you. As you reexperience the sights, sounds, and feelings, imagine you are going to make a movie of this exceptional experience. Notice its cinematic qualities: its location, size, brightness, richness of visual and auditory details, etc. Make a quick inventory. This is your brain's special way of coding this time in your life when you performed so well.

4. Adding Positive Mental Attitude. Now we're going to supercharge your peak performance by adding in the positive attitude imprint you created in Exercise 38. When you created that new imprint, you gave it the qualities of a life experience that were-bigger, bolder, more real, and more important than the rest of your life. Begin to reexperience your peak performance again, and this time add these same visual and auditory imprint qualities to it. Watch as your peak-performance memory becomes bigger, bolder, more real, and more important. You're combining your positive attitude with an exceptional performance to create a "peak performance/positive attitude imprint."

5. Future Planning. You can use this combination to do some amazing things. What if you experienced this state the next time you gave a presentation? Or what if this moment were to come to mind fully whenever someone else needed your best? And what about those special moments with family or friends?

6. *Traveling Through Time*. Now you can use this new state to transform your past memories into a supercharged resource for your present and future. As you hold this peak performance/ positive attitude imprint in your mind and your body, imagine floating out of your body with that imprint and going back above your timeline into your past. Where in your past would this tremendous resource have made a dramatic difference in years gone by? Find one, and when you do, reenter into your timeline *before* you needed this resource. Now, quickly travel forward through time, noticing how this incredible resource transforms your past memories into exceptionally resourceful ones. When you reach the present, watch yourself with this resource traveling on into your future.

Many people gain even more value by repeating this process, either with the same past memory or with different past memories. With this process, you can literally reprogram your past and your future in minutes. Use it any time you want to add an attitude, a feeling, or a state of excellence to your whole life. We recommend taking time to do both. With peak performance present, you will live much more of your life.

When we know that peak performance is not just a dream, but a real possibility, we can then ask the question, What's beyond the peak? It seems to be human nature to sometimes strive after something with such focus and ferocious determination that we forget why it's so important in the first place. With the constant exhortations around us to be our best, to do our best, and to be all we can be, it's not surprising that some people have become convinced that the peak, whether it's in sports, business, politics, or entertainment, is the *only* worthwhile place to be. Since all their energy is focused on getting to the highest peak, when they fail to reach it, even by a step, it's often seen as an extreme personal failure. When they do succeed, the next question on every television commentator's lips is, How long will they last there?

Returning to our comparison of mountain peaks and peak performance, you can realize that it takes a lot of effort to reach a mountain peak, just as it takes a lot of effort to reach a career peak. When you attain it, there's a feeling of exhilaration, of accomplishment and satisfaction that is well deserved. And then what? You look around in every direction. You take in the sights. If you are with friends, you share the view and the excitement. You might even shout your triumph into the air. If you brought a camera, you record the event. After enjoying it, you realize that there are many very different peaks and that you often have to first go down before going up to the next peak. You can also realize that a peak is a place to visit, not to live. The very notion of a peak, whether it's made of rock or of human achievements, is that it's a different place than the base or the middle or even two thirds of the way up. A peak is created by contrast with what is not the peak, and proportionally, there is a lot more "not peak" to any given mountain than there is peak.

Yet some people continue to build their careers and their happiness around the idea of a permanent peak of perfection. This idealization of the peak leads them to think that in order to be happy, they need to have everything in their life in perfect order. Everything would be wonderful *if only* they had the perfect house, the correct car, the totally satisfying relationship, the fulfilling career, the challenging project, the efficient administrative assistant, the hand-tailored suit, the incredibly productive morning meeting, and the perfect cup of cappuccino. When they get this all lined up perfectly, then they will be at the peak, and then they get to be truly, deeply, and completely happy.

By celebrating only the peak, they may make the rest of their lives into long drawn-out drudgery just leading up to it. In addition, their "true happiness" will only last those few moments before something goes wrong; when the copy machine breaks down, or the computer crashes, or day care calls, or there's an argument, or the cappuccino machine isn't working, or whatever imperfection intrudes on their vision of the peak of perfection. So maybe they get to enjoy twenty minutes of pure happiness. And then, they have to go back to spending all their time working, building, and rearranging everything so that it's the way they think it ought to be. Once again, they must begin their climb up their mountain of an imperfect life. All so that someday in the next three or four years, they will once again attain that peak of perfection and get to feel truly happy for another twenty minutes.

How many people do you know that are living some version of this? They tell you they will be happy as soon as they lose some weight, or change jobs, or find a new lover, or own that new . . . whatever it is. Each of these is a variation on, "I'm not close enough to the peak to feel it's all right to really begin enjoying my life." Of course, it's possible that if they lose the weight, change the job or the lover, or buy the new car, they may actually get to feel happy. That is, until the weight comes back, or the new boss turns out to be a tyrant, or the lover starts to nag, or the car gets a scratch. Then it's a landslide back down the hill to unhappiness.

Then again, maybe there's an alternative route up that mountain. Maybe it's possible to be happy no matter what happens in the world. Maybe it's possible that happiness doesn't depend on what others do or don't do, or what one has or doesn't have. Maybe it's possible to be a happy person, whatever the situation. Then, if you managed to get the perfect house, since you're already happy, you could be even happier. Then, if you developed a satisfying relationship, you could be even happier still. Instead of struggling to be happy for a few fleeting moments, you could be continually adding to the fulfillment of your life.

Is this really possible? It is if you want it. It means learning to manage your experiences, instead of just letting life happen to you. It means deliberately changing the way you evaluate what happens to you, so you can see events in more positive and meaningful ways. It doesn't mean you won't have "bad days." It just means the day will be "bad," not you. It doesn't mean you'll have to become blindly optimistic. It does mean you'll take on the responsibility for creating your own inner environment; a world where achievement, peak performance, and happiness can coexist and even thrive.

If you desire to do this, you need to know there are no breakthrough instant techniques. You can begin by noticing what you like about the simple, everyday, and ordinary events of your life. What do you want to keep and remember about them? What do you appreciate in the smell of coffee, the feeling of silk, the smile of a waiter, or the patience of a reservations clerk? Look at your experience as you would a picture drawn for you by a small child. Find the gift in it. Find what's worth appreciating.

After you have practiced this awhile, move your attention to a more competitive part of your life. Whether you win or lose, practice paying attention to what you did exquisitely. Find what's worthy of compliment in your competitor. When you can do this, you will have attained the mental state of taking life lightly enough to play it seriously. Since you have been encouraging to yourself and complimentary to others, your senses have been open and relaxed. You will have undoubtedly found yourself acquiring the skills of others without directly concentrating on them. You're most likely to win much more often, and to know that it isn't central to your experience any longer. This is an answer to the question, What's beyond the peak?

Envisioning Your Future

You have experienced peak performance as an active, participative process. When you raise your overall performance, that becomes your new baseline. Remember the self-to-self comparisons great athletes make? Appreciate how far you've come from the beginning of this book. If you have done all the NLP exercises up to this point, you have taken charge of your motivation, clarified and developed your mission, programmed your future, developed better relationships with yourself and others, cleared up past difficulties, increased your self-confidence and self-esteem, created a positive mental attitude, and learned to access more of your peak performance, and that's a lot.

Let's take this one step further. Let's move into what University of Chicago psychologist Mihalyi Csikszentmihalyi calls the "Experience of Flow"[3]—when everything becomes effortless and time extends. "Flow" is what sports figures call being "in the zone." It's when the ball looks huge and slow as it comes toward them and they feel they can run all day without tiring. It's what Arnold Palmer compared to the feeling of a musician in the middle of a great performance. It's what jazz musicians call "being in the groove." The fact that so many different people in so many different fields have described this experience attests to its existence. Keith Jarrett, the great jazz pianist, knows this state of mind so well that he won't play a concert until he experiences it.

With the skills of NLP, we've been exploring the experience of flow. We've found that flow comes when people have focused all their attention on the task at hand. In their more usual states of consciousness, people either hold back or they're simply distracted by things around them. In flow, all attention is given over to the task. The "self" disappears into the doing. The golf club and the golfer become one. The musician experiences the music playing him as much as he plays the music.

We have found the state of flow to be free from concern, a virtual freedom to do anything. When people are in a flow state they have seen the "big picture" and from it developed a liberating perspective. Their minds are free, and they can let their creativity and talent go where it is needed. And because of this attitude, they have great success. They are also in peak performance, from where all great achievers act. The next NLP exercise is designed to give you much the same perspective.

**EXERCISE 43: LIBERATING YOUR PERSPECTIVE
FOR UNLIMITED ACHIEVEMENT**

PART 1: THE BIG PICTURE—SPACE

1. Notice Your Awareness of Your Self. Find a comfortable time and place and begin by becoming fully present in the here and now. Notice your body, the feeling of your skin and the parts of you touching your chair, table, even this book. Now notice where your awareness of *yourself* normally resides within your body. For example, do you sense yourself more in your head, or in your chest, or in your belly? Experiment by letting your awareness move around. Notice any changes.

Continued

2. Float Out of Your Body. Sense your awareness beginning to move up and out of your body. Soon you can sense yourself floating easily above your body. Imagine that you can see yourself and the room below in great detail.

3. Rise. Now let yourself float even higher until you are near the ceiling. Then move up to the next floor or through the roof until you have a view of the building and the surrounding area from the air. Next, let your motion accelerate as you move away from the ground and see your entire city below as well as any rivers or other natural landmarks. Continue to feel yourself moving out farther, through the clouds up so high that you begin to make out the shape of the continents. Soon you can see both oceans and the whole glorious earth as it floats in the darkness of space. See the sun and the diamond bright stars that surround it. Watch the earth's surface as clouds move above it. This is your home. Take in this view. See that world without borders. See that it really is one world. Some day you might see this view from a space-station window.

4. Use This Perspective. From this perspective, you cannot even see your body, which is so tiny, down on the surface of the big blue planet before you. Now think of some problem that that person has, and consider it from this perspective. What insights or possibilities does this position offer that person in his or her search for a resolution? Explore the usefulness of this perspective as long as you wish, and be sure to retain what you learn so that you can later offer it to that person on the planet's surface.

5. Descend. Now begin to descend, moving closer and closer to the earth. First, you will be able to see the shape of the continents, then the land where you are, eventually your area and neighborhood. Finally, you approach your building. Move down through the roof and then come to rest just above yourself.

PART 2: THE BIG PICTURE—TIME

6. See Your Timeline. Blinking your eyes a couple of times, you can begin to see your own timeline just below you. Notice your past and the direction it takes going out from your seated body. Then notice your future and the direction it is going.

7. Travel into the Future. Start to travel above your timeline into your future. As you travel, you might come across some of the goals you put on your timeline in earlier exercises. Now, as you travel on, you can see how having attained this goal is improving your future. See your sense of achievement and satisfaction. Now look even further into your future and see how having accomplished this goal makes other accomplishments possible. Look at these new opportunities for a better life.

You may wish to dip into a future experience, and as you enter it and touch it, some of those great future feelings will come into you. These feelings can serve to remind you that your dreams will be fulfilled one day. With an increasing sense of satisfaction that your dreams will be fulfilled, you can begin to move further and faster into your future above your timeline.

8. Explore the End. If your timeline ends earlier than you'd like, you can take hold of it and extend your future out longer than a hundred years of health and happiness. You can see a productive and fulfilling life right up to the end of your timeline. Now stop just before the end. What you'll see at the end of your timeline is unknown to any of us. Some say it's a door, others a wall of fire, and still others, a shimmering, ineffable presence or light. Whatever you find represented, acknowledge it and find out what you can learn about it.

9. See Your Wisdom in Old Age. It is said that after the age of thirty, the lines on our faces begin to trace the path of our lives. Turn to look at the end of your timeline and see the wise person you are going to become. Look deeply into that wise face and see the richness of experience you have planned for yourself, and observe and listen carefully as that oldest and wisest embodiment of yourself may want to deliver some special message or sign to you. Even if you don't understand it fully, be most respectful of the answer, and thank this old wise self for the message and the meeting.

10. Review Your Life. Now look back along your timeline into all the years of your history and review your experiences. Allow yourself to review your life fully. Consider with your heart as well as your head whether this is the life you truly wanted to live. Few people ever take the time to find out if the life they've been un-

Continued

consciously planning to live will be satisfying and worthwhile, particularly in retrospect. Take all the time you need to complete this.

11. Make Any Desired Changes. If you feel you need or want to make changes in your timeline, let your unconscious mind help you. Allow a mist or fog to roll across your future history. In this fog, allow your conscious wishes and desires to combine with the wisdom of your unconscious mind. If you see lightning flashes or different colors glowing off your timeline in the mist, you can sense that profound changes are being made. You'll be surprised how soon this process completes itself. And you'll be delighted as your new timeline, as your new life is revealed to you.

12. Return to the Present. Now, begin to travel back above your timeline toward the present. As you do this, you may wish to review your new future. As you do, take in and experience more new choices all the way back to the present.

13. Look into Your Past. Once you are at the present moment, take a moment or two to look into your past. See a younger you who at one time anticipated your existence. And then look into the future and see the future ''you'' that you are looking forward to becoming. Remember, that future ''you'' is looking to you to make it real. Now, reenter into your body in the present. Bring with you all your new learnings. Breathe deeply. Feel your fingertips and your feet and open your eyes.

Higher Peaks to Climb

Each year, NLP codeveloper John Grinder takes time to learn what he calls ''a new game.'' One year it was flying acrobatic aircraft; once it was stalking and tracking animals in the wild. And one year it was technical rock climbing. Typical of John, he sought the best instructor he could find. Someone who was among the highest achievers in his field—a model of excellence. This world-class climber gave classes and lessons to a small number of students. For several weeks, they studied the technical and safety aspects of the sport and conducted several climbs. As the class came to an end, the instructor informed his students that there were more advanced classes, but that to get into the class they would have to do one last climb in which their performance would be evaluated.

On the day set for the climb, the students arrived at the appointed place. They were met by people who said the instructor was delayed and that they should begin the climb without him. The route was a long and difficult one, and required all the skills they had learned during the class.

After several hours of exhausting climbing, each student reached what appeared from below to be the last face at the end of the climb. As each one pulled himself up over the top of this face, they saw that the mountain continued to rise up before them. The instructor, who was hidden from the students, watched the face of each student carefully as they realized that the climb was not over. Many of them sighed with disappointment that they had yet more to do. However, a few looked up with eagerness and anticipation that there were new heights to reach, and these were the ones the instructor accepted into the advanced class. He wanted to climb with people who were attracted to higher and higher peaks in the world—and in themselves.

Reviewing What You've Learned

In this chapter, you've been given some of the techniques you can use to achieve your peak performance and to inspire a peak performance in others.

Specifically, in this chapter you've learned how to:

- Gain, or regain, feelings of empowerment through the Swish Pattern
- Put peak performance into your memories using the Decision Destroyer
- Build a basis for happiness, success, and self-appreciation
- Liberate your perspective to access more of your peak-performance state
- See the limits and opportunities in thinking in terms of peaks to climb

The fact is, throughout this book you've been given techniques to systematically build those qualities that will improve your performance in all areas. The first two chapters primed your mind for the new thinking processes of NLP. Chapters Three and Four created a compelling future. The fifth and sixth chapters connected that compelling future to relationship skills. Chapters Seven, Eight, and Nine cleared up problems caused by past memories and set the stage for creating confidence and positive self-esteem. Finally, these last chapters have taught how to build pervasive attitudes and to create new possibilities for yourself.

Now, near the end of this book, we want to take a moment and acknowledge you, our reader and fellow traveler, for having joined us on this journey. We have not met you in person, yet we feel like we know you—you are a kindred spirit. We feel this for several reasons. We know we have asked a lot of you on this journey. From the very beginning we asked you for your active participation. We have probably often challenged some of your long-held beliefs, and yet you stayed with us. We offered you new worlds of possibilities, and you took up the challenge to explore them. You probably set out on this adventure with very different expectations about what it would be like than what you have now experienced. We hope we have repaid your efforts and attention manyfold by offering you both a comprehensive introduction to NLP and the skills and distinctions we've found in the minds of great achievers.

At last, we are reminded of Carlos Castaneda's Don Juan, who never rushed things and who knew that a good leaving was as important as a good arriving. Don Juan reminds us that whatever, and however powerful, the skills and techniques we may bring to our journey are, it is important to know if the path before us has a heart. As Don Juan says, "A path without a heart is never enjoyable. You have to work hard even to take it. On the other hand, a path with heart is easy, it does not make you work at liking it. . . . Before you embark on it you ask the question: Does this path have a heart?" We at NLP Comprehensive have found NLP to be a path with great heart. We hope our time with you has enriched yours, and that if it is your wish, our paths will cross in the future.

The NLP 21-Day Unlimited Achievement Program

This chapter is intended to be read after you have completed the rest of this book. It assumes a working knowledge of the NLP ideas and techniques found throughout the book and applies them in new ways.

In NLP we have a saying: If you only have one way to do something, you're a robot. If you have only two ways to do something, you're in a dilemma. You need at least three ways to do something before you have the beginning of some real flexibility. To really have choice, you need at least three ways to do anything. You have just completed this book and it has offered you a tremendous variety of new choices in various areas of your life. This 21-day program follows a different outline than the book you have just completed, providing you with yet another way to learn and apply this breakthrough technology. And what about the third way? That will be your own way, with your own innovations and discoveries as you apply this material in your own life.

Also, there's no rule that says you can't do more than one exercise a day, as long as each exercise gets the full attention it deserves. Once you have completed this program, you may want to return to the days that you found most useful or appreciated the most, and repeat them for greater benefit. Or you may want to return to days that appeared to offer you little; this might be where you still have much more to gain by repeating them. You can also simply repeat the entire program from the beginning. Do any of these as often as you like or until all of your goals are reached or you have learned everything this program has to offer, whichever comes first.

Week 1—Going for Your Goals

Day 1: Finding Your Current Coordinates

To serve as a baseline and a guideline for the rest of this program, we ask you to take an inventory of your life. In order to achieve anything, you need to know where you want to go. However, it is just as important to know where you are now. Then you can plot a course from where you are to where you want to be: from here to the fulfillment of your dreams.

Almost every one of us, probably without ever really thinking about it, has divided our lives into what we like and what we don't like. NLP cofounder Richard Bandler has remarked that while we're clear about what we like and don't like, we probably haven't noticed we can further subdivide our likes and dislikes into the things we like or want, but don't have—for example, a new car, a vacation, or a promotion—and the things we don't like or don't want and we have—for example, too many pounds, a quick temper, or ill-mannered kids.

To begin, what do you really like about your life? These can be the epic achievements, like the home run, winning that prize, or the promotion, and they can also be the simplest of moments; watching a child sleep, the sound of waves, the taste of chocolate ice cream. Make your list as long and full as your time allows you to do it. Title this list: **Want & Have.** Copy the columns we've provided to write these down.

Now to the more expected question: What do you have and don't want in your life? Some people spend much of their lives on this question in one form or another. As you spend a few minutes, you can include those extra pounds or troublesome habits, being stuck in traffic, days your boss is grouchy, or whatever it is that "rains on your parade." Make this list as long and as full as your time allows. Title this list: **Don't Want & Have.** Use the column on the next page to write these down.

Now to the NLP question: What do you want in your life that you don't have? This is the time to write down your "wish list." Begin anywhere—with your work, home, love life, finances, or whatever. Include your important dreams and also remember to write down at least a few of the everyday dreams, too, for example, sunny skies, clean sheets, or fresh-brewed coffee. Take time with this list as well. Title it: **Want & Don't Have.** Use the column on the next page to write these down.

The final column is a less-thought-of category: what you don't want in your life and you don't have. If you are like most people, you haven't spent much time mulling over this possibility, so take a few minutes now. There are more obvious things like a dreaded disease, crushing debt, a crippled child, poor health, the inability to work, etc. There are also many other things that you've never thought of wanting, and you don't want to try them—hang gliding, a prison sentence, a trip to a toxic waste site, etc. Include several of these on your list, too. Title this list: **Don't Want & Don't Have.** Use the column on the next page to write these down.

Make sure each item written down is real and specific. Be sure you have some for each column.

N   L   P

Want & Have	Want & Don't Have	Don't Want & Have	Don't Want & Don't Have

On completing this process, take a few minutes and notice:

- Which list is longest/shortest?
- Which list was easiest to create/most difficult to create?
- Which list felt most familiar/least familiar?
- As you look from list to list, are you comparing items of equal importance, or do you find you have ''mountains'' on one list and ''molehills'' on another?
- Right now, which list currently draws your attention more?

As you look over your answers, are you pleased with them? Do you like the items on your lists, or do you want to change some of them? As you go to sleep tonight, let your mind wander over how things are, and how you would like them to be.

Day 2: Discovering Your Motivation Direction and Priorities

Yesterday you discovered your current coordinates. Today you'll concentrate your attention on two of the lists you wrote down yesterday: what you **Want & Don't Have** and what you **Don't Want & Have**. Which list currently occupies more of your attention? Remember Motivation Direction? The **Want & Don't Have** list is another way of describing a *toward* motivation, while **Don't Want & Have** is another way of describing an *away from* motivation. Notice which list is more important to you now. Begin with that list first and go through the items you have written down and prioritize them. Which do you want to change most? And next, after that, and so on? Use any scale you like: A, B, C; 1, 2, 3; most, middle, least. After you complete prioritizing your first list, do the same with the second list.

When you have prioritized both lists, allow us to offer an additional way to think about priorities. Consider what change, if you were to get it, would make the *most* difference in your life? It might already be a top item, and then again, it might seem at first to be a minor one. For example, how much difference would it make to everything else in your life if you began each day in a good mood? What small, but significant change could you make in your day now that would encourage this—a good breakfast, nice china, good music, a conversation, a nice tie or accessory? Look through your priorities again for those items that will be most likely to produce the most change when they change and star them.

Day 3: Making Your Dreads into Dreams

Look again at your prioritized list for what you **Don't Want & Have.** If this is one of your longer lists, this exercise will be even more important for you. When someone has a well-developed *away from* Motivation Direction, they will naturally pay a lot more attention to what they *don't* like and *don't* want. While this can be motivating, they ultimately won't experience much satisfaction. As they get farther away from what they don't like, they get relief and less stress, but not excitement or satisfaction. What is needed for fulfillment is a reorientation of attention. This can be accomplished by redirecting attention from what is unwanted to what is wanted. This exercise will redirect your attention from what you don't want to what you do want, using the items you listed.

Copy your newly prioritized **Don't Want & Have** list onto the next page. Then take each item you **Don't Want & Have** and think of a positive phrase that means the same thing to you, but is something you **Don't Have & Want.** For example: If you **Don't Want & Have** a few extra pounds, what you probably **Don't Have & Want** is a slimmer, more muscular body. If you **Don't Want & Have** a dead-end job, then you **Don't Have & Want** work with more opportunities. Create a transformation for every **Don't Want & Have** into a new **Don't Have & Want** that is satisfying for you. Write down each transformation for future reference.

Don't Want & Have   into a new   **Don't Have & Want**

Day 4: Turning Your Dreams and Desires into Achievable Goals

Take a look at your original wish list of **Don't Have & Want** and your new list of **Don't Have & Want** from yesterday at the same time. Merge them according to your current priorities. You may want to copy them in their new order. Feel free to add more items to this list as they come to you.

Now, pick one of your top-priority goals, and take it all the way through the Well-Formed Goal Conditions for goal achievement. You may want to review Chapter Four. Use the Outcome Questions to assist you in making each item on your **Don't Have & Want** list from a desire or dream into an achievable goal. Do this completely with each item. To do your entire list would probably take you more than one day, so choose the five or ten most important items today and then do one each day for the next few days in addition to that day's program.

Outcome Questions	Well-Formed Goal Conditions
What do you want?	1. Goal stated in the positive.
	2. Goal is initiated and maintained by you.
How will you know when you've achieved it?	3. Evidence for your goal achievement.
What will you see, hear, and feel on achievement?	
What evidence will you have for goal fulfillment?	
When, where, and with whom?	4. Desired situation of your goal.
What effect will this (change) have on the rest of your life/ work/family?	5. Goal is worthwhile and ecological in your life.

Day 5: Making Your Goals Irresistible

We are drawn toward what we find attractive. It fills our attention and directs our actions. Now that you have made your dreams and desires into achievable goals, you can make them so compelling that you will be naturally drawn toward them. Remember to use the following *only* on goals you have fully taken through the outcome conditions for goal achievement. It is possible to make unwise or impossible goals compelling. Unrequited love and quixotic dreams are two examples. There are better uses for this technology. Use it carefully.

Take one high-priority goal from your list and begin by imagining the goal in your mind's eye and seeing yourself having already achieved it. If the goal isn't already a movie, have it take the form of a movie now. Increase the size and brightness of these images, adding vivid colors and dimension. Notice how this increases how attracted you feel toward the goal. Continue to increase the size, brightness, and color as long as the feelings increase, then hold them there. Add rich exciting upbeat music to your movie goal. Have the music in stereo coming from all directions. Hear strong, supportive, encouraging voices cheering you on to your future. Enjoy it. Then proceed to do the same things with your next goal, until you have taken all your goals through this procedure.

Day 6: Creating Inevitable Success

Creating inevitable success means setting your brain on the path toward achieving your goal so that it's working on it all day long, whether you are conscious of it or not. When you have vividly imagined that you have already achieved your goal and foreseen a possible path to get there, traveling the actual path becomes much easier. This is the process of chunking down a journey into the actual steps you need to take to get there. To accomplish this, you'll need to imagine going into the future to become the you that has already achieved your goal. When you momentarily become that future "you" who has already achieved your goal, you can look back and see the steps and actions that inevitably led to this achievement. Keeping this path in mind, you return to the present to plan for your future and take the necessary actions in the present.

Use the more detailed instructions to Exercise 19: Developing a Plan found in Chapter Five. Do this exercise fully with each of your well-formed goals.

Day 7: Appreciating the Rest of Your Life

Every world religion and spiritual discipline has times of rest. Whether this time is set aside to praise the Creator, or refocus the disciple's mind and spirit, or even to allow the body to rest, it has within it an appreciation of the gift of life and the gift of a self to appreciate this life. In recent years, with the ever-increasing demands of modern life, many of us have pushed aside our day of rest in favor of getting the rest of the things done we didn't have time to accomplish during the week. We may think that we've only pushed aside an arcane tradition and we're being more modern and efficient, but if we do, then when do we have time off the treadmill? When will we have time for ourselves? When will we have time to appreciate this life we have been given? When will we have time to notice this creation and in our own way or our own tradition, appreciate our Creator?

Today's exercise is as important as each of the rest of the days in this program. It builds a foundation for positive action and positive appreciation. Looking back to Day 1, you will see a list entitled "**Have & Want.**" These are the things that you want in your life and you already have. In your rush to attain, gain, and achieve more, it is easy to forget how far you have come. Take time today to review this list in detail. Linger over any items that enchant you. Savor them. Notice what you like about your life. If this prompts you to call someone, send a thank-you note, take a moment in meditation or prayer, or do something so that these items appear more often in your future—let your heart be your guide. Feel free to add to this list at any time.

When you have completely reviewed your **Have & Want** list, look over the previous week or month in your mind's eye and notice what you have done with this book and program to improve the quality of your life and yourself. Notice the exercises you have completed and the results you have obtained. While it is likely that some thoughts about how you haven't done them perfectly, or could have done more, or someone else has done better, might flit through your mind, let these thoughts do just that. Let them flit *through* your mind so that you can return your attention to what you have accomplished. Appreciate yourself for having taken the time with yourself to do what you have done, including this exercise. Consider what you could do for yourself to appreciate this progress. Many of life's pleasures are simply waiting to be enjoyed. A walk in a park, an old-fashioned malt, a visit with a friend, a good book, a picnic, or a game. Begin now.

Week 2—Persuasive Communication

Day 8: Finding and Transmitting Your Mission

To communicate your life mission is to speak what is in your heart. Men and women who live out their life missions are naturally charismatic. They have an eloquence born of their vision. All communication techniques pale in the face of simple words said by someone who truly believes them.

Before you do today's exercise, you need to have taken at least five of your priority goals completely through the process of Well-Formed Goal Conditions. You also need to have made them into compelling futures by enriching them in your mind's eye and ear. If you haven't done this yet, make it today's exercise.

Having done this, get each of these important goals in mind simultaneously and ask yourself, "What do they have in common? What themes or elements appear in all or most of them? How do they express your life's passion? How do they express your deepest values and principles?" Write down, draw, doodle, even dance or act out your answers. You are in search of your life mission. This is not something you decide; it is something that emerges from within you. Take time to explore what deeply motivates what is most important to you. For more detailed instructions, review the Mission and Vision exercises in Chapter Three. This could easily take more than today to complete. Begin it now and find out what ''bubbles up'' for you—today and in the days and weeks to come. Visions emerge from dreams, daydreams, and spontaneous thoughts. Be curious about how you'll discover yours.

When you have a sense of your mission, share it with someone. Expressing it will help refine its expression in words and will also serve as an invitation to others. Who might want to participate in your mission, or at least cheer you on, if he or she only knew about it? Let them know. Take time with them and you will be repaid manyfold. Letting others know your mission, and what truly motivates you, is half the secret of great communication.

Day 9: Listening with Rapport

Listening is the other half of great communication. But what kind of listening is meant? There is listening that is only waiting for the other to stop, so one can continue. There is listening to the words only to find a logical flow in order to most effectively rebut their argument. But there is also listening for understanding the heart and mind of another person. The magic of rapport is in this last kind of listening—listening for how another sees, hears, feels, and thinks.

This deep listening begins with hearing how another person makes sense of his or her world: what is seen, what is heard, and what is felt. To deepen your listening and increase the magic of your rapport-building skills, begin by simplifying your learning environment. When someone is face-to-face with you, there is an incredible amount of information being communicated: the words, gestures, emotions, and unconscious cues. Instead, you might begin by practicing rapport auditorily on the telephone. While listening to their words, practice speaking at the same rhythm or tempo as the person who is talking to you. Practice using their intonation patterns. Use your voice in a manner similar to the person speaking to you. If their voice is flat, practice flattening your own voice. If they are expressive, practice speaking more expressively. Place the following list of "process" words near your office phone and begin to "feed back" to your callers the same kinds of words they use. For more detailed rapport practice, refer back to Chapter Five.

Generic (Unspecified)	Visual	Auditory	Kinesthetic
know	see	hear	feel
understand	look	listen	touch
believe	appear	tell	grasp
sense	imagine	ask	catch on
discover	perspective	sounds	contact
communicate	reveal	in tune	push
	Words That Imply Visualization	Words That Imply Sounds	Words That Imply Feelings and Sensations
	color	dissonance	weigh in
	sparkle	crackle	curious
	clear	silence	warm
	flash	orchestrate	soft

Day 10: The Magic of Physical Alignment

It's an often-repeated statement that 93 percent of face-to-face communication is nonverbal, or to put it the other way, words are only 7 percent of a communication. Demonstrate this for yourself today. With every person you meet face-to-face, practice matching his or her body rhythms and postures. If they move slowly and deliberately, you do the same. If they move quickly or gesture a lot, then move more at their rate and add some gestures similar to theirs.

For the advanced practitioner, first mismatch the others' nonverbal behavior (moving fast when they move slow, gesturing a lot when they don't gesture at all) and then, after rapport has begun to drop off, reestablish it again by matching their rhythms and gestures.

Day 11: The Secret to Wonderful Feelings

Today make it your secret job to encourage whomever you meet to feel better. You might use a kind and sincere word, a gesture or a smile, an offer or an offering. Innovate and create according to your circumstances. Write down your results at the end of the day. Continue this experiment as long as you find it rewarding.

You can also apply this to yourself. What emotion, if you experienced it at least several times every day, would make all your life and work smoother and more wonderful? What are three things you could do to encourage this emotion in yourself? Start today.

Day 12: Understanding the Values of the Heart

In Stephen Covey's best-seller *The 7 Habits of Highly Effective People,*[1] Habit #5 is: "Seek first to understand, then to be understood." Today, practice your NLP listening skills for hearing and understanding the heartfelt values of others. Listen for their goals and values. Repeat what you hear about their goals and values aloud to give them an opportunity to confirm or clarify your understanding. Ask them what's important about achieving their goals and values? When you do this you are asking for their higher and deeper values, their heartfelt values. Listen as they tell you. There are many different heartfelt values, and all of them are uniquely important to the person who holds them. You may even want to begin a file of heartfelt values for those around you, for these are the values people work and live for. These are the ones they look for to be fulfilled before they commit themselves completely. One of the most empowering things you can do is assist the people around you in finding ways to express their heartfelt values. Where people express their hearts, they also release their talents.

NAME _____

GOALS _____

_____

VALUES _____

_____

HEARTFELT VALUES _____

Day 13: Finding Motivation and Giving Direction

An effective parent, president, or other person in authority gives those he or she is responsible for clear and positive goals with measurable evidence of achievement. Everyone involved needs to know what the goals are, and how to know when they have been achieved. Such a leader demonstrates how the goals and values of the enterprise are in alignment with the goals and heartfelt values of the individuals involved. An effective leader doesn't think of this as a necessary burden of the job or a management ploy, but rather the reason for being a leader in the first place. An effective leader is an individual who respects each member of the team individually. All men and women may have been created equal, but they do not respond equally to the same Motivation Direction.

Return to the previous day's list of goals, values, and heartfelt values. Return to these individuals and ask them what the fulfillment of their goals, the fulfillment of their values, and the fulfillment of their heartfelt values will do for them and then listen for the Motivation Directions expressed in their answers. Do they want to gain, attain, or achieve something, moving ever closer *toward* it, or do they want relief, release, and relaxation in getting *away from* it. Notice whether they are more interested in solving problems (*away from* motivation) or pursuing goals (*toward* motivation). Use this information whenever giving instructions or offering guidance by speaking to them in ways they will much more readily understand and appreciate. With NLP, these skills become a covenant for good communication. For more detailed practice, review Chapter Six.

Day 14: Appreciating the Love in the World for You

On this day of rest, take a few moments out of your busy schedule to reflect on the people in your life who love and care for you. You have obviously touched their lives. Take a few minutes with each one in turn, and in your mind's eye imagine what it would be like to be this person and appreciate most what he or she appreciates about you. First of all, you will most likely notice what you have done and been for this loved one, so far. You might have in mind what dramatic events you were involved in. Also take time to notice in what ways your presence—in silence, in jest, in seriousness, and in just being—has also touched this person. When you have given yourself an opportunity to appreciate this perspective, go on to the next person in your life, and then the next. When you have completed this, notice any patterns of appreciation. Are they different than what you expected before this exercise? Take a few more quiet moments and let yourself absorb as much of the love, acknowledgment, and appreciation you have just discovered as is humanly possible. If this prompts you to call someone, send a thank-you note, take a moment in meditation or prayer, or do something so this experience appears more often in your future—let your heart be your guide. For a refresher on how to access these loving states, refer back to Chapter Nine.

Week 3—The Peak Performance Program

Day 15: Stepping Out of Limitations and into Resources

When many people think of achieving peak performance, they often turn their attention to the obstacles they perceive blocking their way. Henry Ford is quoted as saying, "If you think you can or you think you can't, you're right." Achieving peak performance has much more to do with how we *think* about our experience than with our actual experience.

To demonstrate this for yourself, begin by noticing how you mentally "code" the positive and negative memories in your life. Are you associated (into the memories as if they are happening to you now) or are you dissociated (watching yourself on a TV or a movie screen) in your memories? Take enough time to sample at least ten memories. You may even want to list them. Very often, people find they have inadvertently coded many of their negative memories in the associated form and therefore reexperience them, and the negative feelings, strongly at inappropriate times. For example, they vividly recall a flubbed putt when they are on the putting green, or they mentally relive a social embarrassment as they are about to speak to a crowd, or they remember earlier rejections as they are about to explore a new relationship.

Now let's look at the other side. Check to discover if you are associated into your positive and resourceful memories. Too often people have accidentally coded these in the dissociated form and thereby made their own resources inaccessible to themselves. Both of these memory codes can be changed for the better.

Begin by thinking of a single negative memory that is specific and associated. As you begin to reexperience it, vividly imagine yourself stepping out of it and seeing that memory at some distance away from you, with a big, black frame around it and thick glass separating what is in the heavy picture frame from what is outside it. Examine the heavily framed picture to confirm that a younger you from that time is truly in that image and that you are outside it. Take your time and repeat this process with each associated negative memory that you wish to change. If there are quite a few, you might make a plan to change ten of them each day until you are completed.

On completing the stepping-out process with ten of your negative memories, turn your attention to your positive memories. If you find some of them are coded as dissociated experiences, begin by taking a single and specific positive memory and stepping into it and pulling it around you, so that you experience it as if it's happening to you right now in vivid color and big as life. Leave it in this associated form and repeat this same process with each dissociated positive memory you find. If there are quite a few, you might want to change ten of them each day until you have completed the transformation.

Practicing the process of stepping out of negative memories and stepping into positive ones every day begins to send a message to your brain about how you want all your memories coded. Continue this process and in a few weeks you'll awake one morning to find them all changed in these useful ways. For more details on changing memories, refer to Chapters Seven and Eight.

Day 16: Amplifying What Is Excellent

One way to achieve excellence is to remove the roadblocks and difficulties on the way to it. Another is to amplify the excellence so much that the roadblocks become little bumps in the road. Pick an area of your life where you're already excelling. Find a real and specific event, a memory of personal excellence you're pleased to remember and relive it. As you begin to reexperience it, also begin to amplify it. Make it bigger and brighter and more colorful and compelling. As you enjoy this excellence thoroughly, where would you like to experience it in your near future? Vividly imagine that happening now. And where would you like to experience this resource in your further future? Take it there and notice how real that excellent future moment feels now. Continue to place this amplified excellence in your future moments wherever you want or need them. When you have "spread it around" to your satisfaction, let it go and recall another memory of personal excellence and repeat the process. By amplifying more and more moments of personal excellence and placing them in your future, you will raise the overall quality of your life and the level of your performance, and you're making them a much more likely occurrence. For more details on using submodalities and anchoring, refer to Chapter Two.

Day 17: Accelerating Your Learning

You have to learn new skills in every endeavor. How efficiently and effectively you learn them can make a tremendous difference. Two areas of crucial importance are how to acquire good form from the beginning, and how to successfully reprogram poor form created by habitual errors.

Many people are aware of the studies in which college students were asked to shoot basketball free throws with varying degrees of mental rehearsal and actual practice. Not surprising, those that didn't practice at all showed no improvement. More surprising was that the students who divided their time between mental rehearsal and physical practice scored within a point of the students who got to practice full-time. It was some of the first hard evidence that visualization made a difference. With NLP, we understand how this is possible. Mental rehearsal stimulates and reinforces the same neural pathways and micromuscle movements as the actual activity. The mind and body are learning, remembering, and developing habits both ways.

Whether your activity is a putt, a performance review, or a presentation to the board, you can use this for yourself. When your performance is extraordinary, you can increase the likelihood of a repeat performance by taking a moment to mentally rehearse your excellence. Since you just performed it, the patterns are fresh in your mind and body. Mental rehearsal will reaccess these pathways again each time you relive the experience—that day, the next day, and in the weeks to come. Replaying your excellence makes it more and more your regular and usual performance pattern.

On the other side, if you've developed a habit that no longer serves you, whether it's an athletic misalignment like a slice, or a useless behavior pattern like performance anxiety, you can eliminate it by ''writing over it.''

You can do this by first reviewing your undesirable experience from a dissociated position. See yourself with your undesired habit in the movie. Keeping the beginning of the movie the same, consider how would you like it to turn out differently? Watch the movie again starting from the beginning, only this time, watch yourself with a more useful response. Try several alternatives and pick the one that you like best. Now step into this new revised movie as a real and associated experience. Begin it at its beginning and vividly experience this new movie as if it's happening to you right now all the way through to its new ending. When you have completed this, you have set yourself on a new track with a new natural response. For further details review how to apply the NLP Frustration into Flexibility technique in Chapter Nine.

Day 18: Making the Peak a Regular Part of Your Life

Another way to encourage peak performance is to let your brain know you want to go there. You already know you can change a habit by showing your brain a picture of yourself having already overcome the habit even though you don't know how you did it. We have a saying in NLP that goes, "You don't have to be bad to get better." You can use the Swish Pattern to take yourself to ever higher levels of performance.

Recall to mind a specific moment when your performance faltered or you felt yourself on a familiar plateau. Bring this particular example vividly to your mind's eye, and in the center of it see a dot. In the dot there is an image of you having already exceeded your current level of success. You don't know how you did it. You just know you did. When the image moves closer, you'll see your satisfied smile and a gleam in your eyes, that will let you know you did it within the rules of your game and you also enhanced your health. Watch as the performance-plateau experience rushes away from you, getting smaller and darker and farther away until it loses all significance. While at the same time, that dot blossoms toward you, getting bigger and brighter and more real, until you are face-to-face with your exceptional self. Blank your internal screen and repeat this process from the beginning at least half a dozen times. Then discover if the performance plateau image naturally fades away and/or the "exceptional self-image" automatically comes in. Repeat this Swish Pattern process until this happens without conscious effort. Repeat this with other performance plateaus to maximize the effect. For further details on how to do the Swish Pattern, see Chapters Ten or Twelve.

Day 19: Creating a Breakthrough Mind

When the British runner Roger Bannister broke the four-minute mile and the Russian weight lifters broke five hundred pounds, they all didn't know they had done it. In both cases, their coaches had conspired to keep them from knowing they were even attempting it. In later interviews, their coaches were quite clear about their reasons for doing this and were even consistent with each other, even though the interviews were given generations apart. They reasoned that their athletes were promising enough to do what hadn't been done, something that no athlete had ever done before. They noted that the numerical difference between four minutes and less than four minutes was a hundredth of a second, and the difference between five hundred pounds and more than five hundred pounds was less than an ounce. Therefore, they concluded, the limitations were not in their athletes, but in the meaning the numbers held in their minds. This proved true in both cases, for within months of each athlete's breakthrough, several others repeated the achievement, which had previously been thought impossible.

To create an athletic or personal performance breakthrough, it isn't necessary to find a coach to deceive you, but rather to change your own mental limitations. With the NLP Decision Destroyer technique from Chapter Eleven, this is easy to accomplish.

Begin by thinking of something that you decided years ago wasn't possible for you. You may have had a personal experience that led you to conclude it's not possible, or you may believe it's not possible because others told you so. It might be making a tremendous amount of money, or achieving a level of success in an extremely short time, or it may be a matter of health, or even your ability to master something complex quickly and effortlessly. With this limitation in mind, what experience—if you had it *before* you acquired this belief or made this decision—would have transformed it from an "impossibility" to a high probability? Take a moment to create this enabling experience in your mind. It may be similar to something that happened to you later in life, or it may never have happened to you. This doesn't matter. Just create it vividly in the submodalities of your positive Peak Performance Imprint experience from Chapter Twelve. For many people, their imprint experiences are panoramic, bigger than life, in vivid colors and sharply focused. Make the submodalities qualities of your enabling experience into your imprint submodalities and then take it back with you on your timeline to just before your limiting memory. Now move down into your timeline with this new memory and travel forward, transforming that limiting memory as you pass through it, changing all of its limiting effects into positive ones all the way up through your present as you relive your personal history with this new empowering imprint. Check to sense if your limitation is completely gone. Repeat the process to strengthen your new imprint if you desire or feel it's appropriate. This new imprint will not guarantee success, but it does guarantee that the limitations will be in the world, not in your mind. In NLP, we believe that anyone can do anything. If it's not possible, the world of experience will let us know. We'll find out by doing, not by thinking that we can't.

Day 20: The Practice of Loving What You Do

Even as you transform your negatives, increase your positives, orient yourself to your excellence, and raise new expectations, there is still the need to practice. In fact, George Leonard, author of the acclaimed book *Mastery*,[2] has noted that a crucial difference between an achiever and a master is that the achiever aims for a goal and his practice is something he *does* to get him there, while the master aims for excellence and his practice is something that he *has* and *is*. "Ultimately," Leonard writes, "practice *is* the path of mastery."

It is a truism of almost every endeavor that those that truly excel, the masters of the game, love to practice. Basketball great Magic Johnson has his own full-size basketball court. Larry Bird would find a court wherever he went, spending hours a day there, all through his "off seasons." Rock-and-roll greats Eric Clapton and Bruce Springsteen play their guitars as much when they are off the road as when they are on. Chess masters the world over study and replay famous games. The great American architect Frank Lloyd Wright used to rebuild his own studio almost annually just to try out new ideas. These greats, and others like them, are attracted to practice. They want to find out what they have missed. They want to find out what they might do this time that they have never done before.

You can increase the attractiveness of practice in the important areas of your life with a simple NLP technique. Once you have decided to do something worthwhile, you might as well enjoy doing it. Most people do things for the results, yet everyone has a few things they do simply because they enjoy doing them. Find an example of a time when you wanted the results, but getting them proved to be drudgery. Figuring out your taxes has this quality for most people. Now think of an activity that you do simply because you enjoy it and the end result doesn't really matter. For many people, games and puzzles have this quality. Now step into these experiences, and play the movie director role to discover the visual and auditory submodality distinctions of these experiences. Go back and forth until you have found the visual and auditory submodalities that make the difference between the two experiences. Use the lists below to write down these differences. Find a number of differences. Associate into the wanting results experience and, holding the content of its images constant, transform its submodalities into the ones you found in the experience of enjoying the doing. Notice the effect this has on your experience. Now associate into the practice of a skill you would very much like to improve and transform its submodalities in the ones of enjoying the doing. Do this with as much of your practice as you would like to enjoy.

Want the Results   **Enjoy the Doing**

Day 21: It's a Wonderful Life—If You Notice

On this day of rest, you might begin by congratulating yourself on having followed this course of instruction all the way to its conclusion. Each of us has made a difference, in fact, many differences, with our own lives and in the lives of others. Frank Capra's classic movie *It's a Wonderful Life* reminds us all that our lives are deeply interconnected. Yet even with the movie shown dozens of times a year, few of us take the time to notice the weave of interconnections that form the tapestry of our life.

So take a few moments now, in your mind's eye, to go into your past and find small as well as significant ways you have affected the world around you in positive ways. Perhaps you helped your siblings with their homework, or won a game with a future athlete, or gave guidance to a friend at a crucial juncture, or helped a homeless person, or gave an opinion that stopped a poorly conceived project, or gave to a charity. Seek out the times you have touched others' lives with your words or your deeds. Make a list of them and their effects, even if their effects weren't obvious until years later. Sometimes our actions most valued by others aren't the ones we value. Expand your measuring stick to include how important you have been to others as well as what is important to you. A nudge at "the right time" can make all the difference. With these experiences as proof of the importance of even your everyday actions, take a few moments to write down actions you would like to take in the future, actions that will add to the lives of others and the world. As you write them down, rehearse where you will take these actions and enjoy your participation in the world.

Words or Actions Taken	Positive Effect on Others' Lives	Actions I'll Take in the Future

You are part of the experience the universe is having, right now, even as you read this. Notice how your individual actions have been important in moving this universe forward to where it is now. Consider what you have learned from this book, and how much more you could participate and be an active participant in your world in the weeks, months, and years to come. Begin to wish, desire, and dream. If you like, you can begin a new cycle tomorrow. Today, do something for yourself that really delights you. Smell the flowers, watch the sunset, feel the rain, dance to the music, and touch another heart. Thank yourself and thank your Creator. Live this miracle called life. You deserve it.

NLP Glossary

Accessing Cues—Unconscious behaviors, including breathing, gestures, head movements, and eye movements, that indicate specific sensory modalities are being used for thinking/the internal processing of information.

Alignment—To match another person's behavior or experience by getting into the same line of sight and/or thought as them.

Anchor—A specific stimulus; sight, sound, word, or touch that automatically brings up a particular memory and state of body and mind. Example: "our song."

"As If" Frame—To pretend that something is possible or completed and begin thinking with that in mind.

Associated—Seeing the world out of your own eyes. Experiencing life in your body. See also **First Position**. Contrast with **Dissociated** and **Third Position**.

Auditory—The hearing/speaking sensory modality, including sounds and words. See *Representational Systems*.

Behavior—Any activation of muscles, including micromuscle movements like **Accessing Cues**.

Behavioral Flexibility—The ability to vary one's actions in order to elicit a desired response in another person.

Beliefs—Generalizations about yourself and/or the world.

Break State—Any abrupt interruption of a current state. Usually used to interrupt so-called negative or unresourceful states.

Chunk Size—The amount of information or level of specificity considered at one time. People who are detail-oriented are "small chunkers." People who think in general terms are "large chunkers"—they see the big picture. George Miller established that human beings could typically handle 7 ± 2 chunks of information at one time; thus, the length of telephone numbers.

Congruence—When goals, thoughts, and behaviors are all in agreement.

Content—The who and what of a situation. Contrast with **Process.**

Context—The when and where of a situation.

Criteria (Value)—The standard by which something is evaluated. Obtained by asking, "What's important to you?"

Critical Submodalities—The submodalities that, when they are changed, the rest of the submodalities will change automatically. See **Swish Pattern.**

Dissociated—Viewing/experiencing an event from outside of one's body. See also **Observer** and **Third Position.** Example: Seeing yourself on a movie screen. Seeing oneself floating above an event. Contrast with **Associated.**

Ecology—From the biological sciences. Concern for the whole person/organization as a balanced, interacting system. When a change is ecological, the whole person and organization (or family) benefits.

Elicitation—NLP information-gathering techniques.

External Behavior—Behavior that anyone can see.

Eye-Accessing Cues—Unconscious movements of the eyes that indicate internal information processing and let us know if someone is seeing internal images, hearing internal sounds, or experiencing feelings. See **Accessing Cues, Representational Systems,** and **Sensory Modalities.**

Feedback—The visual, auditory, and kinesthetic information that comes back to you as responses to your behavior. **Positive Feedback** encourages continuing with the same behaviors. **Negative Feedback** is news of difference and encourages changing behaviors.

First Position—Viewing/experiencing the world through one's own eyes and with one's body. See **Associated.**

Flexibility—Having behavioral choice in a situation. Requires, minimally, three possible alternatives. If you have only one choice, you are a robot. If you have only two choices, you are in a dilemma.

Future Pace—A process for connecting **Resource States** to specific cues in one's future so that the resources will automatically reoccur. See also **Anchoring, Resource States.**

Gustatory—The **Sensory Modality** of taste.

Incongruence—When goals, thoughts, and behaviors are experienced as being in conflict. Example: A person may say one thing and do another.

Intention—The underlying desire or goal of a behavior, assumed to be positive.

Kinesthetic—The **Sensory Modalities** of touch, muscle tension (sensations), and emotions (feelings).

Meta-Model—A set of linguistic distinctions and questions for determining from a person's language their **Model of the World.**

Meta-Program—A mental program that operates across many different contexts of a person's life.

Meta-Outcome—The higher-level value fulfilled by a specific behavior (the value above a value).

Mirroring—Putting oneself in the same posture as another person in order to gain rapport. A naturally occurring communication process.

Model—A description of the essential distinctions of an experience or ability.

Model of the World—A description of a person's mental map of experience.

Modeling—The NLP process of studying living examples of human excellence in order to find the essential distinctions one needs to make in order to obtain the same results.

Motivation Direction (Meta-Program)—A mental program that determines whether a person moves *toward* or *away from* experiences.

Negative Command—Telling someone what not to do, which leads him or her to think it. Example: "Don't worry." "Don't relax completely until you're seated comfortably."

Neuro-Linguistic Programming (NLP)—The process of creating models of human excellence in which the usefulness, not the truthfulness, is the most important criterion for success. The study of the structure of subjective experience.

Olfactory—The **Sensory Modality** of smell.

Outcome—A goal, desire, or dream that has met the five **Well-formedness Conditions** for goal achievement.

Pacing—Matching another's behavior, posture, language/predicates, in order to build rapport.

Parts—A term for the sense that there are different behaviors, goals, and intentions within oneself organized around specific values like security, creativity, "going for it," etc. Example: "A part of me wants security, while another part just wants to go for it."

Predicates—The words that indicate which representational system is being used in consciousness. Examples: "As I see it." "I asked him to listen." "They felt they weren't in touch."

Preferred Representational System—The most developed and used **Sensory Modality** of an individual.

Process—The how of a situation.

Rapport—The natural process of matching and being in alignment with another person.

Reframing—To change the frame or meaning of an event.

Representational Systems—The Sensory Modalities: **Visual, Auditory, Kinesthetic, Olfactory,** and **Gustatory.** Called representational because it is the way memories and ideas are represented by human brains.

Requisite Variety—The systems-theory postulate that the element of a system with the most flexibility of behavior will be the controlling element in the system.

Resource State—While any experience can be a resource state, typically a positive, action-oriented, potential-fulfilled experience in a person's life.

Second Position—Viewing/experiencing an event from the perspective and experience of the person you are interacting with.

Sensory Acuity—Developing a more and more refined ability to detect slight differences in what is seen, heard, and felt.

Sensory Modalities—The five senses through which we take in experience: sight, hearing, touch, taste, and smell. See *Representational Systems.*

Sensory-Based Description—To describe an event in terms of what can be seen, heard, and touched.

State—The physiology and neurology of a particular mind-set or skill, positive or negative.

Strategy—A prepared mental program that is designed to produce a specific result. Example: Responding Comfortably to Criticism.

Submodalities—The components that make up a sensory modality. Example: In the visual modality, the **Submodalities** will include color, brightness, focus, dimensionality, etc.

Swish Pattern—A generative submodalities technique in which the cue for the difficulty becomes the trigger to overcome the difficulty. Useful for changing habits and emotional responses.

Timeline—The unconscious arrangement of a person's past memories and future expectations. Typically seen as a ''line'' of images.

Third Position—Viewing/experiencing an event as an observer from outside.

Triple Description—Considering something from the three basic perceptual positions: **First, Second,** and then **Third Position.**

Values—See **Criteria.**

Visual—The sensory modality of seeing.

Well-Formed Goal Conditions—The five conditions for Goal Achievement. The five conditions that must be met for a dream or desire to be a fulfillable goal. They are: (1) stated in the positive; (2) initiated and maintained by self; (3) sensory-based; (4) specified as to who, where, and when; (5) ecological for the rest of the individual and the system (family, business) he/she lives in.

Would You Like to Be Trained in NLP?

For more information about NLP,
NLP products, and
NLP training and certification contact:

NLP Comprehensive
4895 Riverbend Rd., Suite A
Boulder, Colorado 80301

1-800-233-1657
303-442-1102

Notes

Acknowledgments

1. NLP Comprehensive, *NLP: The New Technology of Achievement* (Chicago: Nightingale-Conant, 1991), audiocassettes.

Chapter Two: What Is NLP?

1. Edward T. Hall, *The Silent Language* (Greenwich, Conn.: Fawcett Publications, 1959).
2. Connirae Andreas and Steve Andreas, *Change Your Mind—and Keep the Change* (Moab, Utah: Real People Press, 1987). These brief NLP techniques, developed by NLP cofounder Richard Bandler, are adapted from the book.
3. "Richard Burton Dies at 58," *Chicago Tribune,* August 6, 1984.

Chapter Three: Getting Motivated

1. Richard Bandler, *Using Your Brain—for a Change* (Moab, Utah: Real People Press, 1985).

Chapter Four: Discovering Your Mission

1. "In Quest of the Universe," Discover Channel, August 15, 1993.
2. Russell Schweickart, interview by Kelly Patrick Gerling, July 1, 1983.
3. Hank Whittemore, CNN: The Inside Story (Boston: Little, Brown, 1990).
4. I, Michelangelo, Sculptor: An Autobiography Through Letters, ed. Irving Stone and Jean Stone and trans. Charles Speroni (New York: Doubleday & Company, 1962).
5. Studs Terkel, Working: People Talk About What They Do All Day and How They Feel About What They Do (New York: Pantheon Books, 1974), pp. xi, xii.
6. Ibid., p. xxiv.
7. Susan Butcher, interview by Kelly Patrick Gerling, October 22, 1990.
8. Ibid.
9. Ibid.
10. "I Dream for a Living," Time, July 15, 1985, pp. 58, 62.
11. Whittemore, 1990.
12. Ibid., p. 11.
13. Ralph Aguayo, Dr. Deming: The Man Who Taught the Japanese About Quality (New York: Simon & Schuster, 1990), pp. 98, 99.
14. Aguayo, pp. 98, 99.
15. John R. Wooden and Jack Tobia, They Call Me Coach (Waco, Tex.: Word, Inc., 1972), p. 60.
16. Whittemore, 1990.
17. Donald W. Robertson, Mind's Eye of Richard Buckminster Fuller (New York: St. Martin's Press, 1974), p. 45.
18. Hugh Kenner, Bucky: A Guided Tour of Buckminster Fuller (New York: William Morrow & Company, 1973).
19. Russell Schweickart, interview by Kelly Patrick Gerling, July 1, 1983.

20. Alden Hatch, *Buckminster Fuller: At Home in the Universe* (New York: Delta Book, 1974), p. 91.
21. "I Dream for a Living," p. 57.
22. Ibid, p. 57.
23. Irving & Jean Stone, eds., 1962.

Chapter Five: Achieving Your Goals

1. Ralph Aguayo, *Dr. Deming: The Man Who Taught the Japanese About Quality* (New York: Simon & Schuster, 1990). pp. 98–100.
2. Joseph R. Dominguez and Vicki Robin, *Your Money or Your Life: Transforming Your Relationship with Money and Achieving Financial Independence* (New York: Penguin Books, 1992).
3. Ewing Kauffman, interview by Kelly Patrick Gerling, June 4, 1991.
4. Kelly Patrick Gerling and Charles Sheppard, *Values-Based Leadership* (Shawnee Mission, Kans.: The Leadership Project, 1993).
5. Susan Butcher, interview by Kelly Patrick Gerling, October 22, 1990.
6. Carol S. Pearson, *Awakening the Heroes Within: Twelve Archetypes to Help Us Find Ourselves and Transform Our World* (San Francisco: Harper, 1991).
7. Morris Berman, *Coming to Our Senses* (New York: Simon & Schuster, 1989).

Chapter Six: Creating Rapport and Strong Relationships

1. Richard Bandler and John Grinder, *Frogs into Princes* (Moab, Utah: Real People Press, 1979).

Chapter Seven: Powerful Persuasion Strategies

1. Connirae Andreas, *Aligning Perceptual Positions* (Boulder, Colo.: NLP Comprehensive, 1991), videocassette.
2. Connirae Andreas with Tamara Andreas, *Core Transformation: Reaching the Wellspring Within* (Moab, Utah: Real People Press, 1979).

Chapter Eight: Eliminating Your Fears and Phobias

1. Gerald Rosen, *Don't Be Afraid: A Program for Overcoming Your Fears and Phobias* (Englewood Cliffs, N.J.: Spectrum Books/Prentice-Hall, 1976).
2. Connirae Andreas and Steven Andreas. *Heart of the Mind: Engaging Your Inner Power to Change with Neuro-Linguistic Programming* (Moab, Utah: Real People Press, 1989).
3. Richard Bandler, *Using Your Brain—for a Change* (Moab, Utah: Real People Press, 1985).
4. Richard Bandler and John Grinder, *Frogs into Princes* (Moab, Utah: Real People Press, 1979).

Chapter Nine: Building Self-Confidence

1. Richard Bandler and John Grinder, *Frogs into Princes* (Moab, Utah: Real People Press, 1979).

Chapter Ten: Creating Self-Appreciation and Self-Esteem

1. John Bradshaw, *Healing the Shame That Binds You* (Deerfield Beach, Fla.: Health Communications, Inc., 1988).

2. Leslie Cameron-Bandler, *Solutions* (San Rafael, Calif.: Future-Pace, Inc., 1985).
3. Richard Bandler, *Using Your Brain—for a Change* (Moab, Utah: Real People Press, 1985).
4. Connirae Andreas and Steve Andreas, *Change Your Mind—and Keep the Change* and *Heart of the Mind: Engaging Your Inner Power to Change with Neuro-Linguistic Programming* (Moab, Utah: Real People Press, 1987 and 1989).

Chapter Eleven:
Securing a Positive Mental Attitude

1. Gary J. Faris, "The Power of Positive Thinking: The Psychological Profile of the Successful Athletic Rehabilitation Patient," *Clinical Management Magazine,* Vol. 9, No. 6, (1989).
2. Jack D. Schwager, *The New Market Wizards: Conversations with America's Top Traders* (New York: HarperBusiness, 1992).
3. Connirae Andreas and Steve Andreas, *Heart of the Mind: Engaging Your Inner Power to Change with Neuro-Linguistic Programming* and *Change Your Mind and Keep the Change* (Moab, Utah: Real People Press, 1989 and 1987).
4. Steve Andreas, *The Decision Destroyer* (Boulder: NLP Comprehensive, 1990), audiotape.

Chapter Twelve: Achieving Peak Performance

1. Charles Garfield, *Peak Performers: The New Heroes of American Business* (New York: Avon, 1987).
2. Michael Lerner, *Surplus Powerlessness* (Oakland: Institute of Labor and Mental Health, 1986).
3. Mihaly Csikszentmihalyi, *Flow: The Psychology of Optimal Experience* (New York: Harper & Row, 1990).

The NLP 21-Day Unlimited Achievement Program

1. Stephen R. Covey, *The 7 Habits of Highly Effective People* (New York: Simon & Schuster, 1989).
2. George Leonard, *Mastery* (New York: Dutton, 1991).

Bibliography

ANDREAS, CONNIRAE. *Aligning Perceptual Positions*. Boulder, Colo.: NLP Comprehensive, 1991. Videotape.

ANDREAS, STEVE. *The Decision Destroyer*. Boulder, Colo.: NLP Comprehensive, 1990. Audiotape.

ANDREAS, CONNIRAE, and STEVE ANDREAS. *Change Your Mind— and Keep the Change*. Moab, Utah: Real People Press, 1987.

ANDREAS, CONNIRAE, and STEVE ANDREAS. *Heart of the Mind: Engaging Your Inner Power to Change with Neuro-Linguistic Programming*. Moab, Utah: Real People Press, 1989.

ANDREAS, CONNIRAE, with TAMARA ANDREAS. *Core Transformation: Reaching the Wellspring Within*. Moab, Utah: Real People Press, 1994.

BANDLER, RICHARD. *Using Your Brain—for a Change*. Moab, Utah: Real People Press, 1985.

BANDLER, RICHARD, and JOHN GRINDER. *Frogs into Princes*. Moab, Utah: Real People Press, 1979.

BANDLER, RICHARD, and JOHN GRINDER. *Reframing: Neurolinguistic Programming and the Transformation of Meaning*. Moab, Utah: Real People Press, 1982.

BAGLEY III, DAN S. and EDWARD J. REESE. *Beyond Selling*. Cupertino, Calif.: Meta Publications, 1987.

CAMERON-BANDLER, LESLIE. *Solutions*. San Rafael, Calif.: Future-Pace, Inc., 1985.

DILTS, ROBERT, ET AL. *Beliefs: Pathways to Health and Well-Being*. Portland, Ore.: Metamorphous Press, 1990.

DILTS, ROBERT B., ET AL. *Tools for Dreamers*. Cupertino, Calif.: Meta Publications, 1991.

FAULKNER, CHARLES, and LUCY FREEDMAN for NLP Comprehensive. *NLP in Action*. Chicago: Nightingale-Conant, 1993. Videotape.

FAULKNER, CHARLES, and ROBERT MCDONALD for NLP Comprehensive. *Success Mastery with NLP*. Chicago: Nightingale-Conant, 1992. Audiocassette.

NLP COMPREHENSIVE. *NLP: The New Technology of Achievement*. Chicago: Nightingale-Conant, 1991. Audiocassette.

O'CONNOR, JOSEPH, and JOHN SEYMOUR. *Introducing Neuro-Linguistic Programming*. New York: Harper & Row, 1990.

Biographies

Steve Andreas, M.A.

Steve cofounded NLP Comprehensive with his wife and partner, Connirae Andreas, Ph.D., in 1979 in order to bring the highest quality NLP training to the world. They started by offering the first NLP practitioner certification training ever. Together, they've edited and published NLP books that have helped shape the field, including the best-seller *Frogs into Princes*. They are coauthors of *Heart of the Mind, The NLP Trainer Training Manual,* and the advanced book *Change Your Mind—and Keep the Change,* which features their discovery of timelines. Steve's book about Virginia Satir is an NLP study of the renowned family therapist. He and his family live in Boulder, Colorado.

Charles Faulkner

Charles is the architect and coauthor of the Nightingale-Conant audiocassette programs *NLP: The New Technology of Achievement, Success Mastery with NLP,* and the video *NLP in Action*. A certified NLP trainer, expert modeler, and international consultant, his modeling of outstanding futures traders is featured in best-selling books, including *The New Market Wizards*. With his *Metaphors of Identity* and *The Mythic Wheel of Life,* he established a new paradigm for change with applications to individuals and organizations. An active entrepreneur, he's cofounded E.P.I.C. Golf, Mental Edge Trading Associates, NLP Innovations Atlanta, and Influential Communications, Inc. of Chicago.

Kelly Patrick Gerling, Ph.D.

Kelly Gerling's mission is developing leaders. A change agent with fifteen years of experience in NLP, psychology, and consulting, he brings about revolutions of leadership in corporations and school systems. He cofounded the consulting firm The Leadership Project and cocreated Value-Based™ Leadership. This process brings values to life in corporations. He also cofounded the not-for-profit Enthusiasm for Learning Foundation (ELF). The ELF™ Model is an entirely new educational system for children, our future leaders. Kelly contributed the chapters entitled "Discovering Your Mission" and "Achieving Your Goals" to this book. He lives in the Kansas City area, in Shawnee Mission, Kansas.

Tim Hallbom, M.S.W.

Tim is cofounder of Western States Training Associates/ NLP of Utah. He is a coauthor of *NLP: The New Technology of Achievement,* the audiotape *How to Build Rapport,* and the book *Beliefs: Pathways to Health and Well-Being.* In partnership with the esteemed NLP innovator Robert Dilts and his colleague Suzi Smith, Tim pioneers new NLP applications to the field of health. He and his colleagues are creating the NLP World Health Community for the 21st Century, which is based in Salt Lake City, Utah, where he works and lives with his wife and children.

Robert McDonald, M.S.

Robert is an internationally known author, lecturer, and NLP trainer. He's a coauthor of *NLP: The New Technology of Achievement* and *Success Mastery with NLP.* Robert also pioneered the use of NLP in the fields of addiction, codependence, relationships, and spirituality. He's been creating highly effective communication seminars since 1970, facilitating deep personal transformation for individuals and groups. He also created many NLP tools, including: *The Belief Exchange, The Coupled Heart, The Heart's Reunion,* and *Self-Parenting.* In addition, his *Releasing Emotional Enmeshment Process* is featured in John Bradshaw's book *Homecoming.* He lives in Santa Cruz, California.

Gerry Schmidt, Ph.D.

Gerry has over twenty years' experience as a consultant, trainer, and teacher of communication technologies for personal and organizational change. As a psychotherapist, Gerry has worked with individuals, couples, and families, using the NLP models for over ten years. He is a coauthor of the Nightingale-Conant program *NLP: The New Technology of Achievement*. Gerry is currently the director of training for an international consulting firm that specializes in producing cultural transformation of organizations and works with NLP Comprehensive on training design. Gerry makes his home in the country outside Denver, Colorado, with his wife and two children.

Suzi Smith, M.S.

Suzi has been actively engaged in training NLP for the past decade as well as consulting with business and government organizations. She is a coauthor of the Nightingale-Conant audiocassette program *NLP: The New Technology of Achievement*, the book *Beliefs: Pathways to Health and Well-Being,* and several other audio and videotape programs. Suzi is cofounder of Western States Training Associates/NLP of Utah, which is based in Salt Lake City. Most recently, she has been working with Robert Dilts and Tim Hallbom to create the NLP World Health Community for the 21st Century. She divides her time between training and relaxing in Idaho.

Permissions

Aguayo, Ralph. *Dr. Deming: The Man Who Taught the Japanese About Quality.* New York: Simon & Schuster, 1990.

Andreas, Connirae. *Aligning Perceptual Positions,* videotape. Boulder, Colo.: NLP Comprehensive, 1991.

Andreas, Connirae, and Steve Andreas. *Change Your Mind—and Keep the Change.* Moab, Utah: Real People Press, 1987.

Andreas, Connirae, and Steve Andreas. *Heart of the Mind: Engaging Your Inner Power to Change with Neuro-Linguistic Programming.* Moab, Utah: Real People Press, 1989.

Andreas, Connirae, with Tamara Andreas. *Core Transformation: Reaching the Wellspring Within.* Moab, Utah: Real People Press, 1979.

Andreas, Steve. *The Decision Destroyer,* audiotape. Boulder, Colo.: NLP Comprehensive, 1990.

Bandler, Richard. *Using Your Brain—for a Change.* Moab, Utah: Real People Press, 1985.

Bandler, Richard, and John Grinder. *Frogs into Princes.* Moab, Utah: Real People Press, 1979.

Bandler, Richard, and John Grinder. *Reframing: Neurolinguistic Programming and the Transformation of Meaning.* Moab, Utah: Real People Press, 1982.

Berman, Morris. *Coming to Our Senses.* New York: Simon & Schuster, 1989.

Cameron-Bandler, Leslie. *Solutions.* San Rafael, Calif.: Future-Pace, Inc., 1985.

Gary J. Faris. "The Power of Positive Thinking: The Psychological Profile of the Successful Athletic Rehabilitation Patient." *Clinical Management Magazine,* Vol. 9, No. 6, 1989.

Gerling, Kelly Patrick. Personal interview with Susan Butcher, October 22, 1990.

Gerling, Kelly Patrick. Personal interview with Ewing Kauffman, June 4, 1991.

Gerling, Kelly Patrick. Personal interview with Russell Schweickart, July 1, 1983.

Gerling, Kelly Patrick, and Charles Sheppard. *Values-Based Leadership.* Shawnee, Kans.: The Leadership Project, 1993.

NLP Comprehensive. *NLP: The New Technology of Achievement,* audiocassette program. Chicago: Nightingale-Conant, 1991.

Robertson, Donald W. *Mind's Eye of Richard Buckminster Fuller.* New York: St. Martin's Press, 1974.

Stone, Irving, and Jean Stone, eds. *I, Michelangelo, Sculptor: An Autobiography Through Letters.* Trans. Charles Speroni. New York: Doubleday & Company, 1962.

Terkel, Studs. *Working: People Talk About What They Do All Day and How They Feel About What They Do.* New York: Pantheon Books, 1974.

Turner, Ted. "I Dream for a Living." *Time,* July 15, 1985.

Whittemore, Hank. *CNN: The Inside Story.* Boston: Little, Brown & Company, 1990.

Index